PSYCHOLOGY OF NONVIOLENCE AND AGGRESSION

Psychology of Nonviolence and Aggression

V.K. Kool

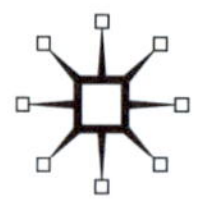

First published 2008 by
PALGRAVE MACMILLAN
Houndmills, Basingstoke, Hampshire RG21 6XS and
175 Fifth Avenue, New York, N.Y. 10010
Companies and representatives throughout the world

PALGRAVE MACMILLAN is the global academic imprint of the Palgrave Macmillan division of St. Martin's Press, LLC and of Palgrave Macmillan Ltd. Macmillan® is a registered trademark in the United States, United Kingdom and other countries. Palgrave is a registered trademark in the European Union and other countries.

ISBN-13: 978–0–230–54554–0 paperback
ISBN-10: 0–230–54554–8 paperback

This book is printed on paper suitable for recycling and made from fully managed and sustained forest sources. Logging, pulping and manufacturing processes are expected to conform to the environmental regulations of the country of origin.

A catalogue record for this book is available from the British Library.

A catalog record for this book is available from the Library of Congress.

10 9 8 7 6 5 4 3 2 1
17 16 15 14 13 12 11 10 09 08

Printed in China

Contents

List of Figures, Tables and Boxes

Figures

Tables

Boxes

Preface

A psychological study of nonviolence and peace involves two questions of fundamental significance:

1. Who initiates and constitutes such peace institutions?
2. What is the model for developing an institution of peace?

With regard to the first question, the answer is simple, that is, it is individuals who form the units of a peace institution. Obviously, psychology, as a science focusing on an individual's behavior, has a pivotal role to play in understanding not only the nonviolent behavior of individuals, but also in delineating its optimal level. Just as we cannot foster democracy in a country with members having autocratic beliefs, so also nonviolence will be elusive in a community with a Rambo cult. Unfortunately, the scientific knowledge of the psychology of nonviolence is meager because the unit of the peace institution, the individual, has not been sufficiently studied with reference to his/her nonviolent behavior. Topics such as the measurement of nonviolence, forgiveness, self-control, and others are very recent phenomena in modern psychology. Even the establishment of the Peace Division of the American Psychological Association and its official journal are not even two decades old. In writing this book, I have made an attempt to put together advances made in the field of the psychology of nonviolence, many among them emerging as an antithesis to the studies on violence.

With reference to the second question, concerning the adoption of a model for establishing peace institution(s), the reader can easily make out that this issue is broader, inviting psychologists to collaborate not only with the fellow scientists in other fields but also with the policy makers and community leaders. In this venture, the role of psychologists has been exceptionally limited (please see Chapter 7). I believe that this state is primarily due to our limited capacity to answer question 1. As the founding father of modern psychology, William James, wrote almost a century ago, war against war is not going to be a holiday party; we would need to glorify how those who provide service to the community, for example, those engaged in the helping professions, could foster nonviolent tendencies in a society. Even a scientifically developed theory offered by Skinner, a forerunner in psychology, suffered when tested by his followers in a new community. Psychologists cannot operate in a vacuum, for a community cannot be built without multiple perspectives, including cultural, political, historical, religious/spiritual and others. In various sections of this book I have attempted to show how the psychology of nonviolence would flourish in an interdisciplinary context.

The legitimacy of the psychology of nonviolence in its present form is well established (Mayton, 2001). Its core concepts, such as cognition, motivation, affective and emotional processes, and personality, have been researched on for quite some time offering insights into the internal states and behavior of individuals who choose to behave nonviolently when offered both violent and nonviolent options. Given this scenario, I have divided the theme of this book into seven chapters: the nature of nonviolence and its measurement, human aggression, cognition, motivation, the nonviolent personality, conflict resolution, and the future of nonviolence. I also believe that a book on this subject could be written in many other ways, but I opted to confine this volume to the mainstream psychological framework consisting of cognition and motivation.

Unlike most other books that focus on either aggression or nonviolence, in writing this book I have focused on both components of human nature. In the Letters to the Editor column of the *Time* magazine (October 9, 2006), Daren Kourajan, commenting on the 99 percent similarity of genomes of apes and humans and "How we became human", wrote, "Let's not forget that the slim 1% difference between humans and chimps that gave us Mozart, Einstein and Socrates is also responsible for social killers, totalitarian despots and greasy-palmed politicians."

For their survival, genes may be described as the most selfish of all things ever created by nature, for they know how to survive. In doing so, genes favor the survival of our own children, but increase the cost for those of others by depriving them of the necessary resources or through killing. Knowing that all such processes constitute the holistic functioning of the human being, it is worth examining two contrasting and important characteristics of human existence in this book: Nonviolence and aggression.

The tendencies of nonviolence and violence have coexisted in us, albeit in varying proportions, throughout the course of human history. However, there is at least one important difference between the two. Unlike war, peace as an institution is not an old enterprise (Schwebel, 2005). The contribution of psychology in the study of peace institution is no less significant than any other discipline.

I read somewhere on the Internet that when you are unable to judge whether a scholar is a scientist or a cleric, your best bet will be that he or she is a psychologist. When psychologists began to scientifically examine the nature of love, many scholars were skeptical and felt that we would not be able to obtain any tangible result. If there is not much to offer in terms of neurotransmitters and localized areas in the brain, the scientific base of a concept in psychology remains frail. A good example is positive psychology which has had to struggle to make its mark in the mainstream academic psychology. Whereas William James' concepts on primary and secondary memory and emotion got credence as psychology grew in its scientific form, his concept of nonviolence remained unattended to for several decades.

Fortunately, there are many studies on altruism, empathy, forgiving, wisdom, and self-control that enhance our understanding of nonviolence. Current research on oxytocin, a hormone that is associated with lactation and labor pain in females, illustrates how nonviolent tendencies, such as cooperative behavior, enhance with the increase in its flow. Additionally, through the time analysis of genetic transformation, it is being demonstrated that in the course of human evolution this hormone also became the property of males. Unfortunately, until the developments in paleoneurology are further established and substantiated to testify how such neurotransmitters and hormones survive and are passed on to the next generation in the course of evolution, I believe that it will be a long wait for the maturing of the psychology of nonviolence. Further, as Kosslyn and coworkers (2002) concluded, because the neurological correlates of behavior are not uniformly predictable, our dependence on a biological model will question the ripeness of a mere psychological inquiry of behavior.

I deeply appreciate the Senior Fulbright Research Award given to me by the International Institute of Education, Washington, the Fulbright Foundation in the USA and the United States Educational Foundation in India that afforded me the opportunity to write this book. I also express my gratitude to Dr Rita Agrawal who offered numerous suggestions during the preparation of this manuscript, especially her passionate engagement with the chapter on conflict resolution. I want to thank my students who read the first draft of this manuscript and offered valuable insights for improving the contents. I also commend the warm hospitality offered to me by the administrators and staff of NITIE, Mumbai and the Himachal Pradesh University, Shimla, India, where I wrote a few chapters of this book.

I express my gratitude to Ms Anna Van Boxel for managing the entire project very efficiently. Despite her busy schedule and marriage, she managed to find time to respond promptly to my communication. Her colleague, Ms Neha Sharma, took charge during the production schedule of the book and I thank her for steering this project to the final stage.

I also appreciate the support and services of the Integra Software in the preparation of a final copy of this book.

V. K. Kool

Understanding and Measuring Nonviolence

OUTLINE

On the implications of studying nonviolence and violence together
Nonviolence and violence as passions
Nonviolence in academic psychology
Nonviolence: Its nature and definition
Nonviolence: A psychological perspective
Nonviolence and prospect theory
Measurement of nonviolence
Summary
Suggested readings
Appendix: The noviolence test (NVT)
The NVT code sheet

Let's think of what you had been doing in the past one hour, 24 hours, one week or one year. Now, figure out the total minutes or hours that you had been aggressive or violent. If your answer is "many days" or "months", it is better to seek some therapeutic help because, as the mental health expert would say, you are heading for a major crisis in your life. The bright side of our lives is that most people would answer the question by saying that they had been aggressive or violent only on rare occasions and that they had been quick to control themselves without causing any significant harm. Misperceptions, misjudgments and misunderstandings are common features in our interpersonal relationships, but if they prolong unduly and frequently lead to intentional harm to another individual, the peace and tranquility of our orderly living is disturbed and in extreme cases, even annihilated. The violent behavior of school children of Columbine High School that led to the killing of many children and personnel, the Oklahoma City federal building bombing that led to the death of hundreds of innocent civilians caused by the US military personnel, and frequent outbursts of lethal violence at workplaces all over the world are generally committed by ordinary people with no marked pathological disorder. Why did such people prefer the violent route and did not opt for alternate methods to seek a solution?

Most books written so far treat subjects of violence and nonviolence separately. This book is about both nonviolence and aggression, but primarily about nonviolence. Most of us live peaceful, orderly lives. In general, we strive to minimize tension caused by a conflict unless we are pushed to a level where our passivity is perceived as our weakness. Thus, the desire for seeking peace within ourselves is of paramount significance to us even when we are facing uphill competition for our survival. Elise Boulding (2000) contended that human beings not only spend most of their time in peaceful activities but also in dreaming about an enriched life. Quoting from the work of Bernhard Grun's *Time Table of History*, she noted that there was only one column for war in his work, but the rest was about human endeavors involving literature, music, science and technology, and religion. The total picture of human history outweighs common conceptions that exaggerate our concern for violence and war.

The paradoxes of the human mind have been studied by psychologists for a long time, for example, introverts behaving on occasions like extroverts, those scoring high on neuroticism overcoming their anxiety in a critical situation, and the most humble-appearing employee in front of her boss changing into a bully when interacting with her subordinates. In his research on prisoners, Toch (1969, 1975) found that many prisoners who had no history of any violence in their life, the overcontrolled type, were the ones that were sentenced for the most heinous crimes.

On the implications of studying nonviolence and violence together

From the evolutionary perspective of adaptation, we know that both nonviolent and violent behaviors have contributed to our survival. However, violence on our part certainly does not make us look good if several alternate peaceful means for solving the problem are readily available. If a boss is nasty at work, killing or assaulting him is not the only option. And yet, an insult to our honor or dignity leads to the usage of deadly weapons in schools, at the workplace, and in community forums with or without the support of socio-cultural beliefs. On 7 September 2005, the CNN presented a story of a Palestinian family that approved the killing of a virgin girl at the hands of her brother. She was involved in a relationship with a man not approved by the family. Ironically, this family had no prior history of violence and by all the sources of information that were available to the CNN reporter, the brother loved his sister immensely. For this family, the life of its member was less important than preserving the honor of the family. This type of violent behavior is guided by the mainstream beliefs characterizing a culture (Huesmann & Guerra, 1997) or as described by Bandura (1997), by the internal standards that we set for ourselves and how we regulate them.

Second, the social orientation of human beings demands that we coexist and restrict violence to the level that its use is warranted only when our own survival is threatened. Thus, our desire to remain nonviolent is ingrained within us. The family nurtures its children for positive values that promote survival and subsequently, we learn from the community at large to respect the sanctity of life. Consider the following example. When a mother is dusting a doll, the young baby begins protesting by saying, "Don't hit the doll. It will be hurting". This child would sound more compassionate than Mother Teresa or Gandhi, albeit owing to her being in the Piagetian egocentric stage in which her perceptions and motives are dominated by her own attachment to the doll and there is a lack of differentiation between animate and inanimate objects.

Is it possible to evaluate nonviolence from an evolutionary point of view? One easy way to do so is to examine the opposite side of behavior, that is, violence. According to Duntley and Buss (2004), an evolutionary perspective would need answers to the following questions:

a. Are there adaptations that lead to violence?
b. Do human beings show defenses against violence?
c. Is harm inflicted to a family member or a close relative be perceived as more evil than the harm inflicted to a stranger?

Although the basic idea of evolution is that adaptations enhance fitness, it is "value-free" (ibid., p. 103). Adaptation does not guarantee violent or nonviolent behavior. The form of behavior—violent or nonviolent—that contributes to the successful survival has greater chance of transmission to the next generation.

In response to the above-mentioned three questions, the answers to the first two questions are not difficult in the understanding of nonviolent behavior. Nonviolent forms of behavior are known for enhancing survival. Parents tolerate their own children and pacify them, but they behave differently with children outside their family. If indeed they treat them similarly to those outside, the cost for such an act would be too high for them because of the lack of bonds that normally facilitate smooth interaction. In a given scenario involving nonviolence, the nonviolent actor shows willingness to absorb higher cost to maximize fitness leading to the survival of all individuals under adverse conditions. This is in sharp contrast to violence that inflicts higher cost to the victim to manage his/her survival. Thus, hurting someone within the family is perceived as a greater evil than hurting an unknown adversary for the same reason (Baumeister & Vohs, 2004). By demonstrating similar treatments, the nonviolent individuals mitigate the boundaries between us and them. For further discussion, the reader is referred to the section on altruism and empathy in Chapter 4. In addition, in Chapter 3 I have also described how people in many cultures live peacefully and respect their environment.

The roots of nonviolence are so strong that they could be traced very soon after birth. Several babies in a pediatric clinic begin to cry with the moaning of one baby, an empathetic reaction that is triggered by discomfort to others. In contrast, it's too bad that we switch off our television set or change the channel when we see a program on hungry children in Africa. Our empathetic reaction tends to transform into an avoidance behavior as we get accustomed to frequent exposure to such programs. In short, in addition to the popular social science explanations, we will also examine the significance of nonviolent behavior in an evolutionary context and show how positive behavior, like empathy, tends to promote our survival. Recent research involving genetics and paleoneurology suggest that oxytocin, a hormone normally associated with labor pain and lactation in women, is correlated with many important psychological functions such as trust and cooperative behavior. Such behaviors lead to coexistence and common good. The genome experts argue that over a period of time, oxytocin became the property of the brain of both males and females.

Third, preference for nonviolence or violence is a matter of one's choice. In our lives, we come across many scenarios in which we are placed in a dilemma: to remain nonviolent or to be violent. In matters of dispute or disagreement, we generally seek a solution through dialogues, mutual understanding and trust, mediation or other peaceful means. In some cases, we take a violent route. In still others, we show displacement by throwing objects or poking fun. While driving on Interstate 90 in New York, I saw a bumper sticker on a car that read: "My boss is like a diaper. No matter how hard I work, it would stink again." I just hoped that his boss would never see this sticker.

The controversy that behavior is innately determined or influenced by environment is an old one for the science of psychology. The classic Behaviorists and Gestaltists had debated it for decades, the former supporting the influence of environment. Irrespective of whether preference for nonviolence or violence is biologically triggered or conditioned by environmental forces, we need to focus on the behavior that is the product of an individual's decision. For this purpose, we will examine the relevance of available psychological theories in explaining nonviolent behavior and subsequently focus on the application of prospect theory proposed by Kahneman to explain our preference for nonviolence or aggression (Kahneman, 2003; Kahneman & Tversky, 2000).

Goldstein (1986) stated that given the option between aggression and nonaggression, individuals tend to make a rational choice based on situational and normative forces. He further contended that such factors are weighed in terms of short- and long-term consequences of behavior. In a 2 × 2 matrix (Table 1.1), he presented a very clear analysis of aggression and nonaggression. The long-term factors are norm-based, referring to the beliefs of an individual and how they are reinforced by the society. A typical example of this category is war. However, if the same individual learns not to aggress in a church, it will be an example of long-term factor in nonaggression.

Table 1.1 Long- and short-term factors in aggression and nonaggression

	Long-term factors	**Short-term factors**
Aggression	Norm-based (war)	Decreased inhibition (alcohol)
Nonaggression	Norm-based (belief/religion)	Increased inhibition (pressure of police)

Source: Goldstein (1986).

The situational factors associated with aggression and nonaggression are defined in terms of the impact of a situation. In the presence of a police officer, nonaggressive behavior is the common choice but at a pub, a fight easily breaks out (Table 1.1).

Social scientists know that employing a powerful dependent variable, that is, a measure of response, is critical in any research. One potential advantage in Goldsein's model is that it provides concrete opportunities for measuring the decision time, that is, the dependent variable, consumed in shaping an aggressor or nonaggressor's response.

If you are asked, "What would you do if someone at a party, without any provocation, begins to abuse you in front of many guests: choice #1: ignore for some time and deal with the individual later OR choice #2: give him back in his own language and terms (forced-choice item, that is, you are required to endorse option 1 or 2)?" I asked this question semester after semester in my aggression and nonviolence course and each time the answer was more or less the same: very few students responded in favor of choice "1" quickly and a few in this group took somewhat longer time, but the majority endorsed choice "2" very quickly, that is, retaliation was considered an immediate and swift solution of the problem. Usually, the choice of violent behavior is instant, poorly processed (or irrational), and mediated by anger or provocation. On the other hand, a restraint against forces of aggression requires self-control, rational judgment, higher levels of processing and forgiving.

Another advantage of Goldstein's model is the ease with which the inclination toward violence or nonviolence can be delineated. For example, compared to the West, the students in India have deeper respect for their teachers, popularly known as the Guru tradition (the Sanskrit word "Guru" is now a common word in the English language). Any sexual transgression on the part of teachers is considered more offensive than in any other profession. In a study, when Indian students were asked if they would punish their teacher for sexual misconduct more than anyone else in another profession, they affirmatively endorsed stronger punishment for their teacher (Kool, 1990). Comparative US and Polish samples showed greater tolerance for this offence than their Indian counterparts.

Fourth, most books and research articles often do not deal with violence and nonviolence together. Is our preference for violence and nonviolence not an example of a decision that involves movement toward or away from these two opposite choices in determining the level of our behavior? If behavior oscillates in deciding whether to aggress or not, it is representative of one's choice, not simply of one's ambivalence. If the President of the USA does not sway before ordering atomic bombing, like the one in Hiroshima, he would be no different from the worst mercenary known in human history.

Further, in writing a book on nonviolence, the reader simply gets one perspective—nonviolence *per se*. Over the years, the analysis, interpretation and implementation of the subject of nonviolence have been associated with saints and sages. The kings or the heads of clan in the past were known to consult their spiritual and moral leaders for guidance on the ethics of war and treatment of prisoners. In short, preference for nonviolence, whether by the heads of state or by the ordinary citizens, is perceived as an extraordinary step that is guided by a special category of virtuous and moralistic leaders, for example, the local clergy or a spiritual guru. Such behavior is generally perceived as uncommon and beyond the normal domain of thinking by an average human being. In other words, in our normative everyday life, nonviolence is not salient unless we put an effort to make it appear salient. Ironically, violence automatically becomes salient in society, but to make nonviolence salient, we have to make exceptional efforts by raising it significantly above the baseline of existing standards.

Nonviolence and violence as passions

The existence of our civilization is a clear proof of our positive values that have led to our coexistence. However, genes are selfish by nature and their survival depends upon adaptation to the changing conditions in the environment. In the course of evolution both nonviolent and violent forms of behavior have been useful tools for promoting the interests of an individual or that of the community or both. Sterile bees sacrifice their lives in protecting the fertile ones and buffalos form a ring to save their young ones from predators. In doing so, they sacrifice their own lives. With their ability to make complex decisions, human beings carry such altruism further by tolerating humiliation and physical assaults from their adversary until their tyrants sense moral shaming and mend their behavior. A dedicated spouse at home or a nonviolent leader in a community is known to have tested the limits of nonviolence. In doing so, they also create hardships for themselves, for their family members, or for the community at large. The extreme form of nonviolence has its price and is not the norm of most communities as it mandates deferment of self-interest, if any, to an uncertain future. A good example is that of Nelson Mandela who finally gave up on his nonviolent method and endorsed violence to secure the rights of the oppressed black community in South Africa (Presbey, 2006).

Let's now think of the other side of nonviolence, say war, an extreme case of violence. Even during war, there are restraining forces that work. Referring to the "just war" tradition in the military of the USA, Roblyer (2005) argued that neither the pacifist position nor the extreme violence is acceptable; somewhere a middle-of-the-road position is normally adopted with minimum damage to collateral civilian property. According to Roblyer, "The Just War tradition can be functionally divided into two parts: guidance for determining the justice of going to war (*jus ad bellum*) and principles for fighting justly within a war (*jus in bello*). It is this latter portion that is more directly applicable to the matter of collateral casualties and damage . . . ." (p. 20). In this sense, one may argue that reifying violence and nonviolence is unfair because if there is a dark side in us, there is also a bright side in each one of us. And yet book after book tends to focus on one dimension only. In Kevin Murphy's (1992) book, *Honesty in the Workplace*, I did not read anything about honesty in the first five chapters, that is 141 pages out of a total of 221 pages, but only about dishonesty. The subsequent part of the book, that is, the remaining three chapters, then focused on honesty.

What message do we get from such publications? Among many possible explanations, the nature of the concept itself appears to be the most plausible one. Because we generally believe in a just world in which most of the things would not easily go wrong, as contended by Lerner (1970), honesty is taken for granted and hence there is an increased focus on dishonesty. The message we get is that sometimes it is more meaningful to analyze both sides of behavior—honesty or dishonesty, nonviolence or violence—in order to better understand human behavior. Not surprisingly, in spite of four decades of serious research on human aggression, even today we have a very limited understanding of the range and etiology of human aggression (Bushman & Anderson, 1998). The landmark studies of several scholars gave a jump-start to a hitherto unexplored concept of aggression in the early sixties, but its variety and infusion with other forms of behavior, especially in a social context, makes a psychological analysis ambiguous and ineffective (Groebel & Hinde, 1989). It is time for psychologists to look for other options to the study of human aggression. The approach suggested in this book is to study violence and nonviolence together.

Nonviolence in academic psychology

Several years ago I was invited to organize a symposium on nonviolence at a famous university in Europe. I suggested the title, *Psychology of Nonviolence*, along with a slate of presenters. In response to my proposal, the organizer wrote to me that I would be better off changing the title of the symposium by presenting it as *Psychology of (Non)violence.* Upon my inquiry, the organizer told me that the members of the executive committee of the conference felt that the title was less meaningful to many and it conveyed no meaning at all to some. Seventeen years later, my visit to Europe (2005) reconfirmed the same experience when a number of peace psychologists communicated to me that they did not represent the mainstream of research in psychology in Europe. Is it any different in the USA and other parts of the world? I believe that the story is very much the same everywhere but not as pessimistic as it was in the previous century.

Funding for the understanding and control of violence is a priority for public policy makers. Such attraction for the money and prestige associated with guiding research draws a significant number of academic scholars for participation in research. As a result, both public policy makers and scholars invest more time and resources for the study of violence with the hope of getting insight into all that violence does to derail the tranquility of our lives. Again, nonviolence becomes less salient and attractive to the majority of public policy makers and researchers, a domain with poor funding and recognition.

Given the books available on modern psychology, we learn that human behavior is best understood when it is tested in specific, narrow conditions, called the controlled conditions of experimentation. It is well known that the scientific creed requires a focus on the classification of objects to sharpen the level of understanding of a phenomenon. In this sense, violence and nonviolence are best understood if these two concepts are treated separately. On the other hand, if behavior fluctuates toward or away from violence or nonviolence, especially when critical decisions are to be made, such behaviors should also be subjected to a scientific scrutiny. An overview of literature on human aggression reveals that genuine experimental work focusing on the etiology of aggression began with the publication of classic work on the frustration-aggression hypothesis by Dollard, Doob, Miller, Mowrer, and Sears (1939). After a brief pause, two major books appeared in the early 1960s (Berkowitz, 1962; Buss, 1961). Since then and four decades later, the topic of human aggression has been receiving enormous scrutiny and funding for research.

Now let us look at the other side, that is, nonviolence. Although Psychologists for Social Responsibility handled issues of peace and nonviolence along with other social issues, it was not until 1990 that the apex body of psychologists in the world, the American Psychological Association, founded its division of Peace Psychology. Its first official journal was established in 1994. In sharp contrast, the division of Military Psychology was in existence for several decades prior to the Peace Psychology division. Summarizing the status of research and publication in the area of peace psychology, Daniel Mayton (2001) wrote:

> Nonviolence, as an active behavior, falls clearly within the domain of psychology; however, to date only a handful of psychologists have written about nonviolence (e.g. Kool, 1990, 1993; Pelton, 1974) or researched nonviolence . . . . (pp. 143–144)

The reader need not look into the annals of the history of psychology to find out the extent to which the field of psychology of nonviolence has been neglected. Simply open a popular textbook of social psychology and you will find a chapter on aggression, but nothing mentioned on nonviolence. At the best, you will find a few pictures of Dr King or Gandhi at the end of the chapter or some reference to conflict resolution or control of aggression. According to Nelson and Christie (1995), the topic of peace did not figure in many textbooks of social psychology with the exception a few authors. Since the publication of their article, the recent edition of Myers (1999, 2004) and only a few more books in the introductory level courses have added topics such as conflict resolution.

It seems that the above-mentioned neglect of the psychology of nonviolence was not enough. The highly significant and powerful work on nonviolence by the father of modern psychology in America, William James, is missing from the modern textbooks on psychology, albeit his work on emotions and primary and secondary memory is well documented (Kool, 1993). According to Lynd (1966), of Yale University, James' contribution to nonviolence was second only to that of Henry David Thoreau. It is embarrassing to point out that psychologists have not benefited from the contributions of their forerunners in their discipline. The fate of other pioneers in psychology, such as Tolman (1942), is well known. When Tolman began to take interest in nonviolence, he suffered a professional setback in his career. In her book, *American Psychology in the Quest for Nuclear Peace*, Marilyn Jacobs (1989), reported that psychologists were looked upon with suspicion in the early 1950s, presumably linked to the leftists, when they argued for international peace. She further stated that peace psychologists were considered to be working in "politically and legally dangerous" ideology. Gordon Allport, Hadley Cantril, Otto Klineberg, Gardner Murphy and others contributed immensely to the peace psychology movement, but it did not prosper owing to the hostile cultural and political climate that was pervasive during that era. For details, the reader is referred to Jacob's book (1989).

Among the many psychologists adhering to activism I would particularly mention Ralph White, a PhD from Stanford University and member of Lewin's team, who produced the famous study on leadership—Lewin, Lippitt, and White (1939). He served as a faculty member at leading universities and worked also at the US Information Agency (USIA). Some of his writings on war were not approved or were held back when he worked for this government agency. Feeling uncomfortable in this unsavory situation, he quit his job to accept a teaching position at the George Washington University. Although not fired from his job, but having the wrath of a US Senator pressuring the Congress for an investigation against him, his move from a government job to George Washington University was considered as sequelae (Kelman, 2004). The American Psychological Association's Peace Psychology Division journal, *Peace and Conflict: Journal of Peace Psychology*, devoted its entire volume 4 (2004) in honor of White, with articles from well-known scholars such as Kelman (Harvard University), Smith (University of California, Santa Cruz), and others.

Nonviolence: Its nature and definition

In the above section I pointed out that most social psychology textbooks have a chapter on aggression. At the end of the chapter, you are most likely to come across some description on control of aggression and a few pictures of nonviolent leaders, giving you an impression that control of aggression is synonymous to nonviolence. It appears to be one easy way of defining nonviolence.

The problem with such an oversimplified definition is the connotation of the prefix "non" that precedes violence. You may recall my experience that I described earlier regarding the problem with the European conference. The first question that we need to address is: Can a prefix or suffix reverse the meaning entirely? Probably it does not. A cognitive representation of a word is often coded in a specific context and its negation or reversal may not lead to generation of a proportionately opposite meaning. The reverse of hazardous material is nonhazardous material, but the latter does not imply that it is safe to use it.

According to Joan Bondurant (1965), the word "himsa" in India means harm or injury and by adding the prefix "a", the word "ahimsa" reverses in meaning. It is usually translated as "nonviolence". However, Bondurant emphasized that "ahimsa" should never be construed as simply abstaining from negative action as it sounds after adding the prefix "a" to "himsa". Actually "ahimsa" also implies efforts to create understanding and love. In the English language, she argues, it approximates agape. Quoting Gandhi, she extended the concept of "ahimsa" to resisting the wrongdoer and even hurting him/her in the process, if necessary.

Let us analyze the above issue in our conceptualization of nonviolence and violence. In a study in which subjects were required to classify an "act of violence", like war, and "violent acts", like kicking a chair, they reported no difficulty in classifying such acts, but the same subjects had problems in identifying "act of nonviolence", such as sit-ins, or "nonviolent acts" like helping the elderly (Kool, 1993). An act of violence, like war, is a highly categorized act owing to its salience, but conversely, the acts of nonviolence do not necessarily convey the mirror image and reversal of meaning. For many people, sit-ins are nothing but a nuisance.

BOX 1.1 (NON)VIOLENCE

At an interview for a faculty position, I was asked about my favorite area of research work. The following dialogue will give you an idea of what happens with the use of prefix or suffix.

Interviewer:	Will you please tell me your favorite field of research?
Candidate:	Psychology of nonviolence.
Interviewer:	I never heard of this field. Is there something called nonindustrial psychology or nonhealth psychology?
Candidate:	Are you a vegetarian?
Interviewer:	No, I am a nonvegetarian.
Candidate:	Does it mean that you can eat the meat of pets like dogs and cats?
Interviewer:	No. I can't. They are pets—like family members.
Candidate:	But in some Asian countries, they do eat such meat. By the same token, violence and nonviolence are two ways of coping in a conflict, and understanding one form may not necessarily be a reverse image to mechanically comprehend the opposite behavior.

As stated earlier, violence is salient and, as compared to nonviolence, it generates stronger reactions. As such it is natural that its consequential cognitive representation be far more vivid, strong and elaborate than that for nonviolent acts (ibid.). Helping and nurturing by nurses receive less attention than visible scars and broken bones in a gang fight. In other words, reversing violence and nonviolence does not mean changes in the attributes of equal magnitude in both directions (Box 1.1). Conceptually, an attempt to do so to represent both violence and nonviolence on a continuum might even cause appearance of gray areas where it would be hard to judge if the act was violent or nonviolent (Figure 1.1 shows the overlapping gray area between nonviolence and violence). When the followers of a peaceful march disobey prohibitive orders for further movement and break the police cordon on the road, they are called "militant protesters". Consider sit-ins that physically block movement of people or Rosa Park's refusal to leave her seat in the bus.

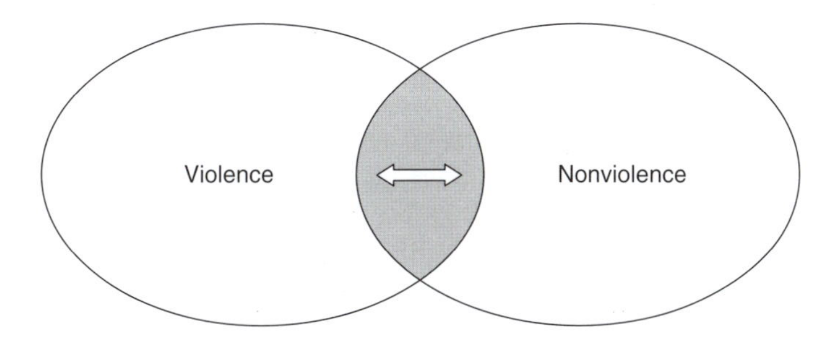

Figure 1.1 Violence and nonviolence: Overlapping gray area

In sport, especially those involving intense physical contact, such gray areas of confusion, that is, labeling behavior as violent or nonviolent, often makes a referee's decision very difficult and even controversial. In baseball or cricket, pitchers often target the ball on the bodies of the strikers and intimidate them. Transgressions of behavior are also difficult to judge in American football as it is not easy to determine when a tackler crosses the line of fair play. I believe that there are lessons to be learned from researches in sports psychology. The transformation of a competitive nonaggressive behavior into an act of aggression may be best understood in terms of "bracketed morality" (Bredemeir, 1983, 1994). This concept explains how moral forces respected in everyday life are suspended during a competitive sport. Supporting this conclusion, Stephens and Bredemeir (1996) reported that the competing teams tended to create an atmosphere that favored willingness to aggress.

A joint study of violence and nonviolence will often lead us to scenarios of ambiguity. In case of sport, only the athlete can tell if his/her act was intentionally aggressive. Referees follow the rules and deliver their judgment, but the real reality is contained in the intention involved in the behavior of the person. The "aggressor" athlete often protests to the referee that his/her offense was not intentional, but his/her repeated requests for reversal of judgment are rarely obliged. Research studies have also supported similar conclusions for criminals who tend to underestimate the magnitude of their crime in sharp contrast to the assessment of harm reported by their victims (Baumeister, 1999).

The ultimate source of understanding any transformation from violence to nonviolence or vice versa is rooted in the analysis of intention of the "aggressor". Unfortunately, intentions are intervening variables that are not easy to put to empirical examination and hence considered useless by psychologists like Skinner (1987). Far from such extreme viewpoints offered by hard-boiled psychologists, scholars like Bandura (1977), Staub (1990), Baumeister (1999) and others have consistently held that understanding behavior along with cognitive processes would be beneficial for psychology. In his succinct analysis of violence, Baumeister categorically stated that the evil intentions of the perpetrator and the perception of its impact by the victims are important sources for judging the magnitude of violence. Summarizing the research findings on this subject, he concluded that although the perpetrators tend to underestimate the impact of their ill intentions as compared to the victims, any evidence of intentional harm would define the range and magnitude of aggression. The perpetrators often use methods to minimize the impact of their aggressive behavior by offering excuses such as being in a bad mood or being drunk.

Gene Sharp (1973), a noted Harvard University scholar, stated that it was not easy to define a multidimensional concept such as nonviolence. In its simple form, Sharp defined nonviolence as "... noninjury in thought, word, and deed to all forms of life" (p. 134). Actually this definition represents an ideal view of nonviolence practiced by many Buddhists and Quakers. Such a principled form of nonviolence is not acceptable to many others who prefer to adopt nonviolence as a strategy to resolve conflicts. According to Sharp, such individuals do not adhere to nonviolence as a precondition or are guided by an ethic of nonviolence but, as a matter of their training and experience, use noncooperation, civil disobedience and other means to demonstrate that nonviolence is a better alternate to violence.

According to Sharp, there are six different categories of individuals who reject violence on principle:

1. *Nonresistance*: Such groups of individuals, while maintaining their own beliefs regarding nonviolence, avoid resisting violence (for example, Mennonites and Amish).
2. *Active reconstruction*: For example, Quakers who indulge in social reconstruction and building goodwill.
3. *Moral resistance*: This category includes individuals who believe that evil should be resisted through moral and peaceful means. They refuse to participate in war. During the 19th century, peace societies in New England followed moral resistance.
4. *Selective nonviolence*: A group of individuals, for example, Jehovah Witnesses, acted selectively in participating in violent conflicts like war.
5. *Gandhi's Satyagraha*: Satyagraha means adherence to truth and right actions. It aims at reforming the society by setting personal examples and thereby minimizing the disparity between individual and social good.
6. *Nonviolent revolution*: Individuals adhering to this belief opt for revolutionary change but only through cooperative and egalitarian methods.

On the other hand, Sharp classified three types of nonviolence that do not involve strict adherence to the principle of nonviolence: passive resistance, peaceful resistance, and nonviolent direct action. This last one, nonviolent direct action, will figure prominently in our discussion as it deals with issues of civilian defense like organized protest, and so on. From the point of view of modern social psychology, these approaches to study nonviolent behavior in the absence of a belief system are more concrete and visible while they represent the action domain of behavior. According to Hare (1968), the motivation of activists in such cases is based on a short-term goal to use nonviolence as a tool to resolve a conflict. On the other hand, a study of nonviolence in the form of principle raises problems. According to Flanagan (1991), there is no single ethic that binds moral behavior and therefore there is no common purpose moral algorithm suitable for understanding moral problems. In short, a study of moral behavior, as related to nonviolence, is more complicated than what appears to most people as a straightforward, simple relationship.

Borrowing from the work of Leary (1957) and Bales (1968) who had presented an elaborate analysis of interpersonal behavior in the clinical and nonclinical settings, Hare (1968) presented a three dimensional analysis of interpersonal behavior as applied to the understanding of a nonviolent actor:

1. Dominant (upward)–submissive (downward) domain
2. Positive (right)–negative (left) domain
3. Forward (goal oriented, conforming)–backward (deviant) domain

Citing the position of a nonviolent actor in the three-dimensional analysis, Hare posited that the direction taken by the nonviolent individual would be in the direction of submission. But this submission should not be misconstrued as cowardice behavior. The actor would use submission as a strategy to communicate with the adversary. To be sincerely on the side of nonviolence, the actor would take the positive route instead of a negative one, because in order to be constructive he/she should forge a healthy relationship with the opponent. The third dimension, forward (goal oriented, conforming)–backward (deviant) is somewhat complicated. By taking the course of downward–backward pattern, a nonviolent actor would identify with power to help the underprivileged and shape into a champion of the underdog. A positive-forward approach would lead to optimism, idealism and love but might arouse dislike for others.

Factor analysis of the data, according to Hare, supported the classifications emanating out of the various combinations to account for the behavior of the nonviolent actor. According to Hare, "If the actor did play the submissive-positive part, he should 'pull' a dominant-positive response from the opposition which would lead to the desired change" (p. 524). He further wrote, "Thus, it is apparent that when the demonstrators can maintain their Downward-Positive-Backward role under the influence of their leaders, the campaign goes as planned" (p. 527).

An important feature in the classic work of Hare is the support it draws from Homans' (1961) theory of social interaction. Both violence and nonviolence tend to emerge in the context of some relationship between two or more individuals and thereby representing an exchange of activity costing more, equal or less to individuals involved in the interplay. Each party that tends to maximize its profit and the exchanges, in addition to being material in nature, might be perceived as rewarding in the form of approval or help. Although an old theory now, Homans work is still relevant because it sought to explain the behavior in terms of "distributive justice", a topic that is currently widely studied in social sciences (Deutsch & Coleman, 2000; Folger & Baron, 1996). Distributive justice refers to the discrepancy between what a person actually receives and what he deserves. Whereas perception of disparity in distributive justice is a source of violence, the nonviolent actor prefers a settlement by proposing some form of exchange to the opponent to resolve the dispute in the allocation of resources.

Hare further contended that the nonviolent actor is often involved in action on behalf of a third party. The white peace protesters would champion the cause of blacks, without any grievance to themselves as individuals. This dimension represents the social side of nonviolence. Focusing on the meanings of nonviolence in the individual and the social context, Theodore Herman (1993), of Colgate University, identified seven forms of nonviolence:

Personal/individual	**Group**
1. Transformation or psycho-spiritual change	5. Nonviolent struggle and civilian-based defense
2. Pacifism or non-retaliation	6. Conflict resolution
3. Reconciliation	7. Removing causes of violence
4. Respect for mother earth	

In terms of action, Herman (1993) defined nonviolence as follows:

> Nonviolence is both an attitude and a course of action that leads both an individual and a group of people to resist tyranny and injustice other than by physical force, and to build a community of caring by the reconciliation of adversaries. It also has a positive meaning as people strive to remove the causes of violent conflict, both human and environmental. (p. 269)

In the book review journal of the American Psychological Association, *Contemporary Psychology*, Goldstein and Pawel (1996) reported that Herman's definition and classification were practical, worth generating new ideas and capable of identifying attitudes and behavior related to nonviolence. If the concepts of peace and nonviolence are to be used interchangeably—and in fact they bear resemblance—then Anderson's (2004) definition of peace has an added value for defining nonviolence:

> Peace is a condition in which individuals, families, groups, communities, and/or nations experience low levels of violence and engage in mutually harmonious relationships. (p. 103)

Since Anderson explains peace as a social process that involves groups and for our purpose we refer to nonviolence on the part of an individual as his/her attitudinal and behavioral characteristic to minimize the use of force, the classic difference between the two social psychologies—one that is cognitively based with a focus on individual and the other dealing with the role and influence of social institutions—may present some difficulty to the reader in judging the focus of this book. As I stated earlier, this book is about the psychology of nonviolence. Whether we deal with peace issues in terms of processes or products of international or cultural conditions, our focus throughout this book will be the individual: How he/she understands and interprets issues concerning nonviolence and translates them, as a matter of choice, into behavior. In the traditional sense, this difference in psychological literature may also sound similar to anxiety as a trait or a state, that is, whether an individual is anxiety-prone in all situations or only during specific conditions. Similarly, those who follow nonviolence as an ideology will bear the trait of nonviolence as compared to those who, guided by the situational influences, prefer nonviolence as a technique for resolving a conflict.

Anderson (2004) stated at least two issues within the definition of peace. First, in the West the term is mostly used in the negative sense, that is, absence of war or conflict. Quoting from the *Oxford English Dictionary*, Anderson reported that the word peace means "freedom from, or cessation of, war or hostilities" (p. 102). On the other hand, in the eastern cultures like India and China, the word has a relatively stronger positive tone. The Sanskrit equivalent of peace is "shanti" or inner calmness. In Japan, peace refers to a distinct culture involving the concepts of quietness and harmony. In non-western languages like the Hebrew and Arabic, the words for peace have roots in "shalev" which means "whole" or "undivided".

The other argument offered by Anderson (2004) concerns the inability of researchers "to develop valid, reliable, and useful measures" (p. 101) of peace. In its classic document on "Culture of Peace", the United Nations General Assembly (1998) identified eight components to promote peace (nonviolence, human rights, tolerance and solidarity, equality of women and men, sustainable development, democracy, free flow of information, and peace education), but nowhere was a definition of peace presented. In fact, at a follow-up conference on this document of the UN, the scholars at the Clark University concluded that the notion of peace and the notion of culture of peace have different implications and the two should not be mixed together (Anderson, 2004). Sensitive as this matter is, I simply warn the reader that there are problems in overlapping concepts, such as aggression and violence or nonviolence and peace, but to the extent such concepts supplement each other in raising the level of our understanding and promoting insights into solving conflicts, the contribution of social sciences should be regarded as mutually inclusive rather than exclusive.

Nonviolence: A psychological perspective

Most of the psychological literature on nonviolence and peace emerged from the opposition to war or its destructive consequences, not through any concerted scientific effort to study nonviolence and peace *per se*. In fact, in the famous article written by the founding father of modern psychology, William James (1910/1995), *Moral Equivalent of War*, the title itself was about war but the article itself is very futuristic. Let's see what he had warned a century ago—and which is so true even today:

> It may even reasonably be said that the intensely sharp competitive preparation for war by the nations is *the real war*, permanent, unceasing; and that the battles are only a sort of public verification of the mastery gained during the "peace" interval. (p. 19)

According to Smith (1986), like other disciplines, psychology also felt the impact of the two World Wars. World War I put psychology on the map through its contribution in the fields of intelligence testing and personnel selection. World War II saw a mature psychology contributing in vital areas such as human factors engineering and clinical psychology. In fact, wrote Smith, psychologists residing in each belligerent country were called upon to serve in whatever ways they could, the only exception being Jews in Germany for obvious reasons. Thus, when everyone served the country, how could psychologists not join the mainstream surge of patriotism? In fact, most psychologists entered the mainstream ideology of their time.

The destruction caused by the two World Wars raised the conscience of many psychologists from different backgrounds and various schools of thought in interpreting, analyzing and, in some cases, actively opposing war efforts. Table 1.2 shows the names of psychologists who, in terms of their association with a school of thought in psychology, had written about peace and nonviolence, albeit their primary focus was opposition to war.

In the early 20th century, the discipline of psychology grew very rapidly. Since issues of war and human survival were cardinal and the public looked at the academic community, including the psychologists, for answers, it is very obvious from Table 1.2 that psychologists from various schools of thought addressed the issues of war and peace. Even those who did not show any direct concern were drawn into it owing to public pressure and the saliency of the issues.

While leading the psychoanalytic school, Freud was writing about the dark side of the human mind with id forces craving for the fulfillment of repressed desires, he did not elaborate upon issues of peace and war. In his letters to Einstein (1933), he first focused on the destructive nature of war. His concept of the death instinct is representative of the destructive forces that govern the human mind. His theory of aggression is discussed in Chapter 2.

The behaviorist, while championing classical and operant learning, did not write much about war and peace issues to any significant extent. Skinner's book, *Walden Two*, is probably one effort that can be conceived as helpful in "programming" and building nonviolent patterns of behavior ideally suited to a peaceful community. In fact, in Twin Oaks Community in Louisa, Virginia, an experimental community was patterned after Skinner's ideas but it did not last long because its members could not define what constituted an ideal behavior (Hunt, 1993).

Tolman led the cognitive revolution in psychology and is regarded as the leader in legitimizing its status at a time when die-hard behaviorists were skeptical about mentalistic concepts. Unfortunately, Tolman did not write to any significant degree about issues of nonviolence and peace, but when he did as an activist, he suffered professionally.

Table 1.2 Psychologists contributing to peace/nonviolence

Functionalistic
William James (1899, 1910/1995)

Psychoanalytic
Freud (1930, 1933)
Erikson (1969)
Frank (1984)
Lifton (1986)

Humanistic
May (1972)
Maslow (1954)
Rogers (1961)

Cognitive
Tolman (1942)

Behavioristic
Skinner (1987)

Others
Cognitive-Developmental
Kohlberg (1981)
Gilligan (1984)

Cognitive-Social
Bandura (1959, 1977, 1997)

Experimental
Guthrie (1950)

Social/conflict resolution
Allport (1945), Cantril (1949), Klineberg (1956), Murphy (1945), Stagner (1961), Osgood (1962), Deutsch (1983), White (1986), Feshback (1986), Kelman (1965), Smith (1986), Schwebel (1965), Staub (1990, 2004) and Blight (1986). This list is long and only a few representative names and years of publication are reported here.

For details on the historical perspective, the reader is referred to Jacobs (1989) and Kool (1993).

Offering a firm explanation of healthy and constructive human nature, the humanistic movement grew as a third force in psychology. Its leaders, May, Maslow and Rogers, held that human nature is neither negative problem-focused, as depicted by the psychoanalytic school, nor neutral, as shown by the behaviorists, but all individuals inherently seek to enhance their potentials and realize their capacities during their lives. Looking at the history of scientific psychology, humanistic psychology has been viewed with suspicion, as its core concepts are considered to be loosely defined and pose actual problems in measurement. However, it is also true that they paid greater attention to positive forms of behavior than any other group of psychologists. An outcome of humanistic psychology is the growth of positive psychology (Sheldon & King, 2001). Although distinct from the traditional humanistic psychology, positive psychology also focuses on how individuals develop, retain and broaden positive forms of behavior that contribute to their well-being. In Chapter 4, I have shown how it is relevant for our understanding of nonviolence.

Now that almost all the schools of psychology have disappeared in their original form, splinter groups consisting of a combination of one or more have emerged, giving the science of psychology a more pragmatic character than ever before. It is not uncommon now to combine different viewpoints to explain behavior. For example, while Skinner believed that learning cannot take place without reinforcement, cognitive psychologists contended that reinforcement is not necessary for learning (Bandura, 1977).

With the understanding of the above-mentioned conceptual framework of nonviolence, its definition and nature have become clearer than ever before. However, there is still a dearth of suitable models or theories to account for nonviolent behavior. As a science of behavior, psychology should be certainly interested in studying nonviolent form(s) of behavior, but it lacks a sound theory or model that would best describe the nonviolent behavior. For a discipline to become a tacit form of knowledge, it must possess sound theories or, in its absence, sustainable models. Astrophysics is a weaker science as compared to many physical sciences because our knowledge of the universe is scant and with each discovery in the galaxy, new conceptualizations emerge, offering new interpretations to the understanding of the composition of the universe. Psychology, time and again, lives at a similar threshold, especially when new discoveries in biological sciences tend to influence our interpretations of behavior, but fortunately, it has survived even those times when Helmholtz declared that psychology would never become an independent science (Hunt, 1993).

In the absence of a theory, a model tends to bridge the gap between different sets of beliefs that would have normally strengthened the base of a science. Models are analogies that serve a useful function in the growth of a science. A computerized chess player helps us understand how an individual thinks and makes his/her decisions. Unless we have tangible methods to study the working of the human brain, we need to rely on such artifacts (computerized models in this case) to study the functioning of our brain. In short, until such time a comprehensive theory emerges, a model is a very handy tool in plugging the gaps between various concepts used in a science.

During the past 25 years I, along with coworkers (Kool, 1990, 1993; Kool, Diaz, Brown, & Hama, 2002; Kool & Keyes, 1990; Kool & Sen, 1984, 2005), have been studying the correlates of nonviolence. Our collaborative work (Kool & Sen, 1984) resulted in the development of a nonviolence test (NVT) that has been used in several countries and translated into many languages. This test is reported at the end of this chapter. Based on our findings and the material that I surveyed in the scientific literature on nonviolence, I have concluded elsewhere that there are three key components involved in the understanding of the psychology of nonviolence (Kool, 1993):

1. *Aggression (intention to harm)*: Nonviolent individuals avoid the use of force and/or think of it as the last resort (see Chapter 2).
2. *Moral concerns (justice and humanitarian concerns)*: Nonviolent individuals adhere to justice and humanitarian orientations, but in most cases find themselves in a difficult position, because approaching justice may minimize humanitarian concerns or vice versa (see Chapter 3).
3. *Power (controlling and manipulating)*: Nonviolent individuals use integrative power that belongs to people, and is shared with them, not just confined to the gratification of their own selves (see Chapters 3 and 4).

Given the above-mentioned scenario, a nonviolent individual would occupy the following position in Figure 1.2: Low on aggression, high on moral concerns and shares power that belongs to people with whom he/she shares it. This is in contrast to the violent individual who is high on aggression, low on moral concerns and is self-oriented in using power. The above model is a dispositional view of nonviolent behavior that focuses on the characteristics of individuals. On the contrary, the current trend in research, however, favors studying behavior in the context of the situation (Zimbardo, 2004). My arguments to substantiate the dispositional contention were based on the relationship of the above-mentioned three components with the scores of subjects who responded to the NVT and with the assumption, one that is rightly held by many personality psychologists like Mayer (2005), that individuals would respond to situations in some cases but not to others. While the aggression and power components correlated negatively with the NVT, the moral components showed only a weak relationship. Further

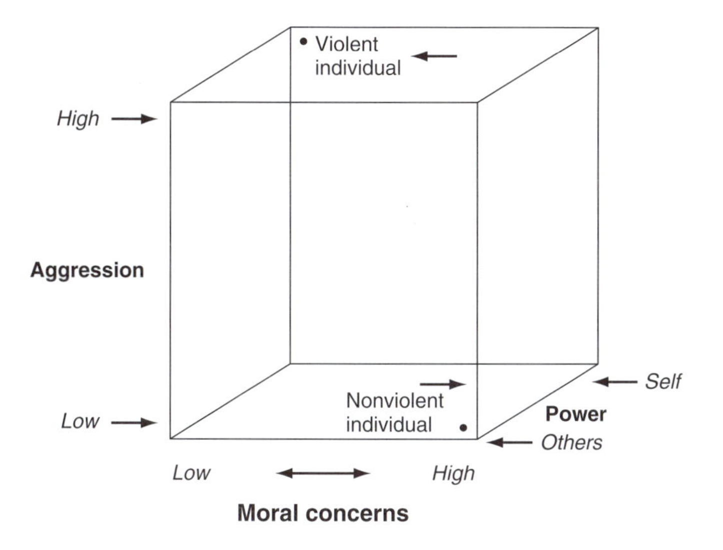

Figure 1.2 A three-dimensional model of nonviolence

research, focused mainly on delineating and identifying specific moral components, sharpened our understanding of the relationship between nonviolence and moral concerns. Commenting on the relationship between nonviolence and the above-mentioned three components, I stated:

> The "genes" of psychology of nonviolence are formed by moral components which determine the features of aggression and power, and the operation of these genes is controlled by intentions. The significant role of intentions in moral responsiveness of individuals is important in understanding the structure of human cognition. Developments in the field of psychology of nonviolence will be a major step in this direction. (Kool, 1993, p. 17)

I offered three arguments in favor of a conceptual framework of the psychology of nonviolence. First, if there is a legitimate field of study of violent behavior, there should be no objection to the study of nonviolent behavior as well. However, the psychology of nonviolence should not be misconstrued as the inverted mirror image of violence. Just as truce does not mean the end of war, a peaceful state does not mean creation of peace. Violence can keep peace but it does not "create" peace. The driving forces between violent and nonviolent behaviors have different roots and origins.

Second, the development of the psychology of nonviolence is linked to the exploration of psychological variables that correlate with it. Nonviolence is a multidimensional concept, a concept that will be understood in the form of an interface of several psychological characteristics. In our model, we argued that, at the minimum, we need aggression, power and moral concerns as core psychological components to develop a conceptual framework of the psychology of nonviolence.

Third, consistent with and following the cognitive revolution in the discipline of psychology, it would be appropriate that psychologists should explore the cognitive processes involved in nonviolence; otherwise, concrete explanations of nonviolent behavior, in the absence of intentions and attitudes, will remain a black box. Studies based on the analysis of cognition of nonviolence are needed to understand this form of behavior. In short, it was concluded:

> Three years before his death, Skinner (1987) published an article in which he made an attempt to explain the behavior of Gandhi with the help of his popular theory of reinforcement. I find now that from Skinner, a hard boiled psychologist, to May and Maslow, both soft boiled psychologists, and from William James to information processing in moral reasoning, there has been a direct or indirect, passive or active interest to develop and understand the psychology of nonviolence which, unfortunately, has not grown to any significant proportion as compared to the psychology of violence. The proposed metatheoretical analysis of the psychology of nonviolence is expected to help us investigate the psychological structures that are vital for our understanding of nonviolent behavior. (Kool, 1993, pp. 21–22)

As I stated earlier, a preference for nonviolence or violence is a matter of choice that may be deliberate or spontaneous, planned or unplanned, or simply a defensive reaction during a moment of opportunity. How do people react to such conflicts? One way to look into the preference for nonviolence or aggression is to examine the response of an individual in a conflict setting, for example, does he/she approach or avoid a target. In his seminal work using rats, Miller (1944) found that the animals moved faster in aversive conditions than in approach conditions. In adapting to changing conditions, Helson (1964) reported that decisions of individuals were more context-driven than those based on absolute judgments. The experience of his subjects changed as per their exposure to the levels of hot or cold stimuli presented to them, rather than being simply determined by absolute criteria. Based on such findings, we may argue that acts, whether emerging from some deliberate effort or as a product of an individual's state, represent an individual's preference to cope with a situation. Preference of nonviolence or aggression is one such dimension of human action.

According to Baumeister (1999), most people who perpetuate evil know where to stop. In other words, they opt for violence as a means to satisfy their urge and hence such behavior is based on a pragmatic choice, rather than one emanating out of a moral consideration. And yet, Baumeister wrote, no theory explaining violent behavior is sound enough to encompass all forms of violence. What is appropriate in explaining a serial killer's behavior, an extreme case of violence that accounts for less than 1 percent of 1 percent crime, is unfit to explain general violence. If this is the result of several decades of research on violence, imagine the limits of explaining nonviolent behavior that has received poor attention from psychologists around the globe. Needless to say that the choice of maintaining nonviolence is far more strenuous, time-consuming and restraining than the suddenness and immediacy that appears consequential in violence.

Nonviolence and prospect theory

In the following discussion, I will focus on the application of prospect theory as advanced by Daniel Kahneman and his coworkers (Kahneman, 2003; Kahneman & Tversky, 2000; Kahneman, Fredrickson, Schreiber, & Redelmeir, 1993). This theory is considered relevant for individual choices, but its popularity has grown to the extent that it has been advanced to show the implications for international mediation during conflict and violence (Levy, 1992; Milburn & Isaac, 1995). Basically, prospect theory was developed in the context of economic behavior to explain how subjects become risk-aversive and what drives them to avoid loss, ignoring the perceived gains. Consider the following quote from Kahneman (2003):

> A good is worth more than when it is considered as something that could be lost or given up when it is evaluated as a potential gain . . . . Loss aversion also contributes to the well documented status quo bias. (p. 705)

In a conflict situation, we often think about whether nonviolence would result in potential gain, and when we fail to decide in its favor, believing that it would bear high cost, we return to the baseline, that is, maintaining the *status quo*.

Table 1.3 Two cognitive systems

Perception	Intuition system 1	Reasoning system 2
Process	Fast	Slow
	Automatic	Controlled
	Effortless	Effortful
	Emotional	Neutral
	Associative	Rule-governed
Content	Stimulus-bound	Conceptual
	Percepts	Past, present and future

Source: Adapted from Kahneman (2003).

Applying prospect theory to a general framework of human behavior, Kahneman stated that two ideas of his theory are relevant for social-cognitive psychology:

1. Accessibility of ideas, and
2. Nature of processing information.

Table 1.3 describes the basic components of this theory. Accessibility of ideas may differ, some ideas being easier to retrieve than others. For making judgments or responses, several factors mediate in determining the level of accessibility, for example, saliency of the stimulus, selective nature of attention, specific nature of training, and so on. One popular concept of this theory is framing that has been used in international negotiations (Milburn & Isaac, 1995). In simple terms, framing refers to the way in which information is presented. Therefore, one example of a frame is the manner in which the instructions for negotiation are presented and an individual evaluates his/her gains or losses within that context. Bullock, Wyke, and Williams (2001) described how framing took place through the content and prevalence of media images depicting the poor and such illustrations might lead to violence against them. More specifically, framing may involve portraying some reality to make the observation look authentic, suppressing important information, constructing a story, developing a moral message or context, and even offering remedies for the problem.

Referring to the work of Stanovich and West (2000) regarding cognitive processes operating at Systems 1 and 2 in Table 1.3, Kahneman argued that these two systems have implications for the way we handle incoming information. In System 1, the information is governed at an intuitive level that requires a faster, automatic, effortless, or even emotional response. On the other hand, System 2 requires controlled, effortful, flexible or even neutral response. Note the two underlined words in Systems 1 and 2, emotional and neutral, respectively, as they have implications for our understanding of aggression and nonviolence. At the level of intuition in System 1, the operation is guided by impressions, not simply by the attributes of an object. Even language can evoke such intuition if the mental operation is not monitored appropriately.

The hallmark of System 2 is its slower processing, controlled nature, flexibility, effort, and neutrality while consciously monitoring cognitive tasks. In dual task operations, in which the subject has to perform an additional task simultaneously, a breakdown is likely to occur as we do not have unlimited cognitive capacity to focus on multiple tasks at the same time. In his earlier research, Kahneman (1973) had pointed out that an individual's limited capacity to do several tasks at the same time is an indication of one's limits to the allocation of mental resources. Performance tends to suffer when demands of a task exceed one's capacity to allocate mental resources. When mental operations are overloaded, the cognitive system uses short cuts (heuristics). Other useful concepts offered by Kahneman and coworkers will be discussed later in the book (for a detailed description of prospect theory, see Kahneman, 2003; Kahneman & Tversky, 1979; Tversky & Kahneman, 1992).

The question before us is the usefulness of System 1 and System 2 in understanding choice behavior when nonviolence is an option. Remember the two underlined words, emotional (System 1) and rational (System 2), reported above and look at the features of System 1 and System 2 in Table 1.3. When cognitive processes operate at faster and emotional levels as in System 1, it is likely that the quality of a decision, unless well rehearsed and experienced on prior similar occasions, is likely to be narrow and poor. In his popular work reported in *Prisoner's of Hate: The Cognitive Basis of Anger, Hostility and Violence*, Aaron Beck (1999) showed how "primal thinking" provides economy in thought processes in situations of genuine or imagined threat and may trigger, fuel, and maintain conflict. Those driven by hate and anger display low levels of thinking and are likely to operate at System 1. This statement does not imply that violent individuals do not operate at the level of System 2. In a threatening situation where an instant behavioral response is required for one's survival, flight or fight are the likely options. You cannot make friends among hungry tigers who are looking for their meal.

Citing examples of how elite students at Princeton University gave wrong answers to a simple problem because of their low levels of cognitive functioning (Box 1.2), Kahneman further argued that System 1 might not always be monitored by System 2 that is effortful and rule-governed. So, what happens when there is a breakdown between System 1 and System 2? Here is what Kahneman (2003) answered:

BOX 1.2 LEVELS OF THINKING

A bat and a ball cost $110. The cost of the bat is $100 more than the ball. What is the cost of the ball? Did you answer $10? Wrong. You are not alone; even elite students at Princeton University made the same error. The correct answer is $5 (the cost of the bat is $105; add $5 for the ball). Such questions are part of Cognitive Reflection Test.

Adapted from: Kahneman (2003).

> The anthropomorphic phrase "System 2 monitors the activities of System 1" is used here as shorthand for a hypothesis about what would happen if the operations of System 2 were disrupted. (p. 699)

As per our discussion on nonviolence above, if self-control and patience are the cardinal properties of nonviolent behavior, System 2 should better monitor the activities of System 1. Ruth Linn (2001) categorically stated in her analysis of moral issues involved in a war that "spontaneity has no place in a moral decision as one has to think about it" (p. 343). With quick and sudden decision-making, there are chances of the failure of System 2 which, in turn, may result in errors, misjudgment and misinterpretation even when the knowledge base is sound but not adequately monitored or remains inaccessible. Table 1.3 also shows that the processing level in System 1 consists of emotional attributes that may involve in a natural assessment of whether to approach something good or avoid something bad. This influence of a "primordial" evaluative system may lead to formation of attitudes and preferences that people may adopt which, in turn, may later pose a risk for System 2 in monitoring the processes in System 1. Not surprisingly, violence, accompanied with hedonistic behavior, tends to reduce the level of monitoring by System 2. Baumeister (1999) reported that in the pursuit of their sadistic pleasure, criminals tend to lose self-control. In short, we see the potential of prospect theory in explaining aggressive and nonviolent behavior.

Measurement of nonviolence

Owing to the multidimensional nature of the concept and its varied definitions, it is not easy to measure nonviolent behavior and attitudes. Psychological testing also requires adequate standards for establishing the validity and reliability of its measures. The question regarding validity of a measure, that is, if it is measuring what it is supposed to measure, has always been a critical issue, especially with complex concepts, such as love and nonviolence, in psychological research. One way to establish validity is by demonstrating a high degree of relationship between measures and differentiation from those concepts and measures that are believed to represent the opposite end of a continuum. For example, if various measures of nonviolence have positive relationships in addition to their negative relationships with measures of aggression, it reflects favorably on the validity status of a psychological measure.

The issue of reliability is not as difficult as that of validity, but nevertheless it is essential for the measurement of nonviolence. There are various ways of establishing the reliability of a test, for example, by retesting the subjects, developing a parallel test, or splitting the same test. As nonviolent attitudes and behavior change over time, reliability scores may sway and appear to weaken its index. A robust test should have higher levels of validity and reliability to qualify as a sound measure.

Mayton and coworkers (2002) ran a Psylit search for references on nonviolence between the period 1974 and 2001 and identified 180 publications, including five measures of nonviolence. These five measures of nonviolence were classified by Mayton and coworkers into two groups

1. Tests of attitudes and behavior
   a. The Pacifism Scale (PS)
   b. The Nonviolence Test (NVT)
   c. The Teenage Nonviolence Test (TNT).
2. Tests of nonviolent tendencies and behavior
   a. The Gandhian Personality Scale (GPS)
   b. The Multidimensional Scales of Nonviolence (MSN).

Developed by Elliott (1980), the PS consisted of 55 items in the Likert-type format and two forced-choice items (total 57 items). Divided into the following three categories, the items in the scale were prepared on the basis of Gandhian ideology:

a. Physical nonviolence (avoidance of any physical harm): 24 items
b. Psychological nonviolence (open and direct communication): 28 items
c. Active value dimension (value orientation): 5 items

On the basis of advanced statistical analyses, including factor analysis, Elliott established the presence of the above-mentioned three components. However, the test was considered unsuitable for samples across cultures (Heaven, Rayab, & Bester, 1984).

Kool and Sen's (1984) NVT was primarily designed to identify violent and nonviolent subjects and to study the differences in their behavior in a Milgram-type of experiment in which a subject gave shocks to the learner (actually, a confederate). It consists of 36 items, with each presented in a forced-choice format inviting a respondent to endorse either a nonviolent or a violent orientation. With the endorsement of all nonviolent orientated items, a subject receives a maximum score of 36. The remaining 29 items in the scale are filler items. All the items of the NVT are reported in Appendix A at the end of this chapter.

In their study, Kool and Keyes (1990) found that, compared to Buddhists and Quakers with a mean score of 31.86 on the NVT, the delinquent adolescents from a residential facility in Wisconsin scored the lowest (19.83). The NVT not only showed significantly negative relationship ($r = -0.43$) with the Buss–Durkee scale (BD), but also with each of the subscales measuring physical aggression (–0.51), verbal aggression (–0.28), negativism (–0.34) and irritability (–0.30). It also correlated significantly but negatively with power orientation of deceit and flattery as measured by the Mach scales. As mentioned earlier, nonviolent people do not use power for their own selfish ends but share it with others to promote justice, harmony and peace.

The NVT has been used in several countries and has also been translated into many languages including Japanese (Matsumoto, 1993). Mayton and coworkers (2002) reported that the NVT has been very effective across the samples. Based on the factor analysis of NVT data, Kool and Keyes (1990) identified seven factors in nonviolence in which self-control emerged as the strongest (Chapter 5 reports all the seven factors).

The TNT test, developed by Mayton and coworkers (1998), was designed to measure the nonviolent attitudes of teenagers. With 55 items written in a Likert-type format, this test consists of six subscales:

1. Physical nonviolence: 16 items
2. Psychological nonviolence: 16 items
3. Active value orientation: 4 items
4. Satyagraha (truth/soul search): 10 items
5. Tapasya (dedication): 4 items
6. Empathy: 5 items

Both reliability and validity indices of the test were reported to be satisfactory. The test correlated significantly positive with the NVT.

Among the personality-oriented scales, Hasan and Khan's (1983) GPS was based on Gandhian ideology. It consists of 29 items presented in a 7-point Likert-type questionnaire. Unfortunately, the factor structure of the test did not correspond to the Gandhian ideology, resulting in its weak psychometric utility.

Johnson and coworkers' (1998) MSN began with a solid promise by addressing the multidimensional character of nonviolence. The designers of this test conceived six different components of nonviolence: direct nonviolence, system level nonviolence (for example, religious basis), compassion, opposition to oppression, respect for life and environment, and spirituality. The developers of MSN recorded a significantly positive correlation between MSN and the NVT scores of the subjects, but as in the case of the NVT, a negative correlation with the BD scale of aggression. In spite of its breadth, some concerns have been raised about the consistency of the subscales of the MSN.

Mayton and coworkers presented a comparative analysis of the above-mentioned scales and concluded that "... the NVT (Kool & Sen, 1984) has the best-documented validity and has a record of effective use cross-culturally" (p. 351). Additionally, the NVT has been used as a tool for establishing the psychometric properties of several measures of nonviolence. From the statistics reported in the literature, the correlation indices (*r* values) of the NVT with other measures of nonviolence were highly consistent (Table 1.4). As stated above, the NVT has been used in several research studies to demonstrate the nature of aggression (Sen, 1993), attributions (Baumgardner, 1990), dogmatism (Hammock & Hanson, 1990), moral exclusion (Kool & coworkers,

Table 1.4 Correlations between the NVT and other measures of nonviolence

Other measures of nonviolence	NVT
MSN	0.56
TNT subscales	
Physical nonviolence	0.57
Psychological nonviolence	0.53
Satyagraha	0.39
Tapasya	0.34
Empathy	0.42

All *r* values reported here were significant at the 0.05 level or above.

2002), and aging (Matsumoto, 1993). We will refer to these and other studies later in the book.

In addition to the above-described measures of nonviolence, several questionnaires were designed earlier to study attitudes toward war (Droba, 1931; Stagner, 1942). Levy's (1995) measure of "Restraint in the Conduct of War" is a 27-item questionnaire that assesses opposition to war. Factor analyses of the data obtained for the scale extracted two clear components: opposition to war and humane treatment. For our purposes, both the components are useful in our description of nonviolence. Herr (1992) also developed a scale for measuring attitude toward nuclear disarmament. Nelson and Milburn (1999) assessed militaristic attitudes and offered suggestions for peace education.

In Germany, Cohrs and Moschner (2002) developed a 10-item questionnaire based on several scales published earlier to measure attitudes toward war and related issues. In particular, they contended that psychological research measuring attitudes toward war and nuclear issues could be divided into three categories: general attitude toward war, specific attitude toward a war (Iraq War), and attitudes toward fictitious war scenarios. Grussendorf, McAlister, Sandstrom, Udd, and Morrison (2002) developed a Peace Test, based on Bandura's concept of moral disengagement, that is, a tendency to seek moral justification for using force and/or an obligation with no choice but to attack. Formatted in a Likert-type five-point scale that ranges from "strongly agree" to "strongly disagree", this 10-item test measures resistance to moral disengagement in support of using force on the adversary. Examples of such moral disengagement involve using force when military actions can save the lives of innocent people, when there is no risk to our soldiers, when there is possibility of attack by another nation, and so on. The results based on this test show that females resist moral disengagement more than men and that people of India, China and the USA exhibit lowest resistance.

McAlister's (2001) "Nonviolent Norm Questionnaire" also measures moral disengagement, but it is more comprehensive than Grussendorf and coworkers' (2002) research that was confined to military action. McAlister's test employs values of cooperation, forbearance, avoidance of conflict, assertion and self-aggrandizement as variables in the study of moral disengagement.

Other methods of measuring nonviolent attitudes and behavior, such as projective technique like the TAT (Asthana, 1990) and psychobiography (McAdams, 1988) will be described later in this book. Owing to practical problems in conducting experiments and collecting data through other common methods employed in research, narratives in the form of telling stories based on one's experiences have been found to be useful in many applied settings such as conflict resolution. For example, this method was recently used to heal the problems between Jews and Germans (Albeck, Adwan, & Bar-On, 2002). The two groups were invited to meet initially at Ben Gurion University in Israel and their conversations were recorded through notes, transcriptions, tape recordings, and so on; later the contents were analyzed with the help of trained but independent professionals. The approach in this situation was shown to be similar to that between a patient and an individual therapist involved in dealing with trauma.

The measurement of nonviolence suffered for a long time owing to lack of suitable tests and the notion that those scoring low on aggression measures would be supposedly high on nonviolence. Bonta (2001) suggested that we would need to focus on nonviolent people *per se* if we want to measure nonviolence and not simply on those low scorers on other tests. For example, he emphasized that if people value nurturance and look down at competition that is adversarial, and also downplay violent acts both explicitly and implicitly, it would be a healthy beginning for the testing of nonviolence.

SUMMARY

In this chapter, I attempted to describe the nature of nonviolence vis-a-vis violence and offered available definitions of nonviolence. I also stated categorically that research in the area of psychology of nonviolence has been meager as compared to its counterpart. Citing complexity of the concept itself and unfavorable political climate in the USA among the many reasons for poor research on the subject, the chapter focused on a model of nonviolence that I proposed in the early 1990s consisting of (lack of) aggression, power and moral concerns as core components in explaining nonviolence. A review of prospect theory was also presented, hoping that this theory is likely to provide us a greater insight in understanding nonviolent behavior. The chapter ended with a description of several psychological measures that have been used in research on nonviolence. Kool and Sen's test of nonviolence is presented in the appendix section of this chapter.

SUGGESTED READINGS

Jacobs, M. (1989). *American psychology in the quest for nuclear peace*. New York: Praeger.

Kool, V. K. (Ed.). (1993). *Nonviolence: Social and psychological issues*. Lanham, MD: University Press of America.

Mayton, D. M., Susnjic, S., Palmer, B. J., Peters, D. J., Gierth, R., & Caswell, R. N. (2002). The measurement of nonviolence: A review. *Peace and Conflict: Journal of Peace Psychology, 8*, 343–354.

APPENDIX: THE NOVIOLENCE TEST (NVT)

1. A car driving through a parking lot splashes water on you. You feel like
   a. making him apologize and pay for damages
   b. telling him to be more careful in the future.
2. The more I think of how bad someone's actions or thoughts are
   a. the more I try to understand how to get along with that person
   b. the more I get irritated and want to tell that person off.
3. My reaction to groups is
   a. I like the feeling of belonging to a social group
   b. for some reason I really don't like groups.
4. If someone keeps bothering me even though I ask him/her to stop, I will
   a. lose control
   b. control myself.
5. I think of myself first of all as
   a. an individual person
   b. a social being responsible to society and those like me.
6. When a stranger hurts me I believe
   a. forgive and forget is the best policy
   b. a tooth for a tooth and an eye for an eye is the best policy.
7. Workers on an unlawful strike should be
   a. approached and a compromise should be negotiated
   b. fired without notice.
8. Being different from my friends
   a. makes me feel uncomfortable
   b. does not bother me; I like it.
9. When someone is rude to me I want to
   a. be rude back to that person
   b. overcome the temptation to be rude.

10. I am inspired by
    a. ideas
    b. some people.
11. If I were in charge and some high officials were found guilty of taking bribes, I would
    a. pardon them with minimum punishment if they apologized
    b. publicly humiliate and physically punish these people.
12. If someone breaks something that belongs to me
    a. I will probably become enraged
    b. I understand that accidents happen.
13. I consider myself to
    a. be like everyone else
    b. be different from everyone else.
14. Judgments about me
    a. should be made on my own merits
    b. should be made according to the people I associate with.
15. Lawbreakers must be
    a. brought to justice, yet be dealt with mercifully
    b. severely punished.
16. I am
    a. loyal
    b. independent.
17. A boy was very mischievous and would beat up other boys. I would
    a. kick him out of the group
    b. try to change his habits.
18. I am responsible to
    a. other people, those I love, and those who depend on me
    b. myself, my ideals, and my ambitions.
19. When I hold a poor opinion of a person
    a. I do not try to hide the way I feel
    b. I try to hide my feelings and improve them without their knowing.
20. Criminals that are physically abused
    a. deserve it
    b. should not be abused.

21. My reaction to crowds is
    a. I dislike crowds
    b. I enjoy the excitement of crowds.
22. If an employee refused to follow orders I would
    a. threaten to fire him unless he did what he was told
    b. persuade him to do what he was told.
23. I admire
    a. no one very much
    b. some people, and would not question their opinion.
24. I see myself as
    a. an important person
    b. a social person.
25. A person who commits a murder should be
    a. placed in a rehabilitation program and given minimum punishment
    b. put on death row.
26. I like to
    a. get to know people
    b. be alone.
27. Governments should deal with rebellious people by
    a. punishing them
    b. treating them in a humane way.
28. I like a person
    a. to say he/she is a good person provided they are
    b. to be modest, even if they are good.
29. When someone does something bad to me
    a. I will get back at them if I can, just because of the principle of the matter
    b. I do not get back at them, but try to show them their mistakes.
30. I have confidence in
    a. myself
    b. things I and others like me represent.
31. When a person makes fun of me, I
    a. try to convince the person that it is not always good to make fun of others
    b. retaliate.

32. I live for
    a. the good of everyone else
    b. myself.
33. If someone criticizes me, I
    a. do not criticize them back; rather, I defend myself with good arguments
    b. I find it is best to criticize the person back.
34. Sex crimes such as rape and attacks on children deserve
    a. imprisonment and psychiatric care
    b. more than mere imprisonment, such criminals ought to be physically punished or worse.
35. When a friend does me a favor
    a. I feel that I must return the favor
    b. I do not feel that I must return the favor.
36. Sometimes, when my parents scolded me I
    a. showed resentment
    b. tried to reason with myself to understand whey they acted as they did.
37. I like to
    a. give gifts
    b. receive gifts.
38. When I am disturbed by another, say, while studying,
    a. my first reaction will be to get angry
    b. I will explain to the person I do not want to be bothered.
39. The majority of my schoolwork involves
    a. reading
    b. writing.
40. If a person skips me in line
    a. I will pass him and stand ahead of him
    b. I will persuade him to go back.
41. When I was younger
    a. I did not care to be a member of a crowd or gang
    b. I was always a follower.
42. If students misbehave in school, the teachers should
    a. punish them as needed
    b. think of things they may have done to cause the behavior.

43. If a teacher grades me unfairly I will
    a. complain to my friends
    b. seek an explanation.
44. If someone harms my family, and me I will wait for an opportunity to
    a. retaliate
    b. make them understand what they did.
45. If my friend has a problem I would like to
    a. counsel that friend on his problem
    b. recommend that my friend see a counselor.
46. I like
    a. team sports
    b. individual sports.
47. If a judge were found guilty of corruption, I would recommend
    a. a stronger penalty for him than for a common citizen
    b. the same penalty for him as for a common citizen.
48. I am
    a. forgetful
    b. organized.
49. Our nation's history is glorified by
    a. great fighters and conquerors
    b. great writers and social reformers.
50. I follow
    a. ethical standards
    b. my conscience.
51. All citizens should be allowed to carry weapons
    a. only when there is a war
    b. to defend themselves.
52. My attitude about groups is
    a. I do not join groups
    b. I am proud to be in some groups.
53. If a teacher is involved in a sex crime involving a student, s/he should be given
    a. harsher punishment than usual to set an example for other teachers
    b. the same treatment as someone who was not a teacher.

54. I look forward to social events with
    a. parents and relatives
    b. friends and neighbors.
55. I like instructions to be
    a. general
    b. specific.
56. A good social system needs
    a. rugged and tough discipline
    b. people who can tolerate others.
57. A clergyman who is involved in immoral behavior should
    a. be allowed to return to his position in the church after he repents and changes his ways
    b. never be allowed to return to his position in the church.
58. I appreciate
    a. music
    b. art.
59. When I see a parade go by I
    a. enjoy watching it but have no desire to be in it
    b. wish I could be in it.
60. When I am in a bad mood I
    a. feel like smashing things
    b. relax and tell myself things will get better.
61. People who drink and drive should
    a. be imprisoned and severely fined
    b. undergo counseling and education on the effects of drugs and drug abuse.
62. I would rather watch
    a. mystery movies
    b. humorous movies.
63. If someone I know is engaging in deviant behavior I feel I should
    a. tell him that what he is doing is wrong, then talk him out of doing it
    b. let him do what he wants as long as I am not affected.

64. If a country is supporting terrorist acts, I think the country should be

    a. attacked by military action until these acts end
    b. persuaded through negotiations to withdraw their support of terrorism.

65. People who try to force their religious beliefs on others should be

    a. ignored until they are ready to listen to others' beliefs
    b. asked to leave and threatened if they refuse to go.

The NVT code sheet

1. B
2. A
3. FILLER
4. B
5. FILLER
6. A
7. A
8. FILLER
9. B
10. FILLER
11. A
12. B
13. FILLER
14. FILLER
15. A
16. FILLER
17. B
18. FILLER
19. B
20. B
21. FILLER
22. B
23. FILLER
24. FILLER
25. A
26. FILLER
27. B
28. FILLER
29. B
30. FILLER
31. A
32. FILLER
33. A
34. A
35. FILLER
36. B
37. FILLER
38. B
39. FILLER
40. B
41. FILLER
42. B
43. B
44. B
45. FILLER
46. FILLER
47. B
48. FILLER
49. B
50. FILLER
51. A
52. FILLER
53. B
54. FILLER
55. FILLER
56. B
57. A
58. FILLER
59. FILLER
60. B
61. B
62. FILLER
63. A
64. B
65. A

NOTE: A or B = nonviolent orientation = 1
Filler = Irrelavant item.

Human Aggression

OUTLINE

Like nonviolence, defining aggression is not easy. According to Geen (1990), aggression refers to a number of behaviors that might not mean the same thing. For example, animal aggression that is predatory in nature is not the same as intentionally harming another human being. In the psychological literature, approximately 250 definitions of aggression were available by 1980 (Harre & Lamb, 1983). Even in its extreme form, for genocide, which is very tangible in inflicting harm, scholars disagree in accepting a common explanation and definition (Charney, 1999; Mork, 2003). The definition adopted by the UN that genocide refers to "acts committed with intent to destroy, in whole or part, a national, ethical, racial or religious group, as such" (p. 1, Article II), has been considered too narrow by many scholars. The careful splitting of Tutsi and Hutu tribes in Rwanda by the Belgians or even adoption of black children by the whites has also been considered as genocide.

The complex nature of human aggression

Do you consider any of the following acts as aggression (Benjamin, 1985)?

"A spider eats a fly"
"Two wolves fight for the leadership of the pack"
"The warden of a prison executes a convicted criminal"
"A physician gives a flu shot to a screaming child".

The answers to the above and many such statements are negative, and yet when presented, subjects deliberate in detail and differ in classifying such behaviors as aggression or not. Generally speaking, aggression involves delivery of a noxious stimulus to the victim, but such behavior will be considered as aggression if it involves:

a. intention to hurt the victim
b. aversive consequences are expected
c. given the opportunity, the victim might have avoided the harm.

Many social scientists do not accept the above definition of aggression offered by the psychologists. Instead, they consider such a definition too narrow and even prefer to use the word "violence" over aggression. Violence is generally used in an institutional or a group context, but aggression is narrowly restricted to an individual context (Kool, 1993). For example, Barak (2003) defined violence as an action or structural arrangement leading to physical or nonphysical harm to one or more victims. Because there is a focus on the structural component that includes social systems or networks, including the distribution of rewards, the definition goes beyond the conventional limits of psychology that primarily deal with cognitive, affective and behavioral factors. For all practical purposes, here in the text, we will prefer aggression instead of violence owing to our focus on the psychological issues. The reader may then consider this to be an anomaly, as we prefer "aggression" instead of "violence", but not "nonaggression" instead of "nonviolence". The reasons for our preference are very obvious. Nonaggression is neither a common word nor does it connote any specific form/s of behavior except absence of aggression; whereas, nonviolence is well documented and researched, albeit with controversy, as stated in Chapter 1.

Types of aggression

Aggression is best understood in its different types. Buss (1961) presented a classification of aggression in a 2×2× 2 matrix consisting of eight categories: physical and verbal aggression, each with subclassification of active/passive and direct/indirect aggression. Table 2.1 shows these eight forms of aggression. Applying this classification in a job setting, Folger and Baron (1996) gave examples of each type of aggressive behavior. Thus, an example of direct/active/physical aggression will be assault; direct/passive/physical, intentional slowdowns; indirect/active/physical,

Table 2.1 A typology of human aggressive behaviors

	Active direct aggression	**Active indirect aggression**	**Passive direct aggression**	**Passive indirect aggression**
Physical aggression	Hitting the victim	Playing practical jokes on victim	Staging a sit-in	Refusing to do something
Verbal aggression	Using insults to hurt the victim	Engaging in gossip about the victim	Refusing to speak	Refusing permission

Source: Adapted from Buss (1961).

sabotage; and indirect/passive/physical, reporting late at work. For a similar classification of verbal aggression in each category, see Table 2.1.

The relevance of such a typology of aggression is that it represents the choices that an individual makes to show the level and range of his/her aggression. People often avoid direct, physical aggression owing to fear of retaliation and law and order problems, and tend to scale it down to the indirect, verbal level. Theoretically, it may sound as if direct, physical aggression is the highest in magnitude and indirect, verbal aggression the lowest, but nonetheless just as beauty lies in the eyes of the beholder, perception of harm also lies in the eyes of the beholder. Sometimes a couple have an argument using words that sting harsher than the bite of a bee. The social movements involving nonviolence as an strategy (not as a principle), you may recall, very often employed some of the indirect, passive forms of aggression, for example, sit-ins, work slowdowns and failure to report at work. No wonder, many forms of nonviolent protests such as defying assembly of people, rallies, and so on, have been labeled as aggression of a milder form and represent the gray areas of Figure 1.1 where it is hard to tell where nonviolence ended and aggression began. Would you classify Rosa Park's refusal to leave her seat in the bus much against the prevailing social norms or the defying of British law in India regarding the making of salt by Gandhi, as aggression?

Instrumental versus emotional aggression

Aggression is also explained in terms of rewards that are associated with one's behavior or, in the absence of such rewards, grows out of emotional components including anger and hostility. The former form of aggression is known as instrumental aggression in which reinforcement of behavior is the primary goal of the aggressor. The bandit has no interest in harming the girl at the teller in a bank so long as he gets the money. His goal is to seek the reward for his effort. This form of aggression involves coercion and is often mediated by problems of self-esteem. Generally speaking, instrumental aggression appears to be a more cognitively controlled form of aggression as compared to emotional aggression.

Emotional aggression, on the other hand, is driven by negative arousal, anger and hostility and is often mediated by provocation or revenge. The goal in such aggression may not be focused on a reward leading to material gain but merely confined to harming the target. In the domain of psychology, this form of aggression has been more widely studied as compared to the instrumental aggression that is mainly a focus of study by the sociologists and other social scientists. Figure 2.1 shows the difference between instrumental and affective aggression and also separates both of them from assertive behavior that is often confused with many forms of aggression. Defying the conventional norms, an assertive woman at work may be perceived as "aggressive", whereas a male exhibiting similar behavior will be considered assertive only. Assertive behavior involves unusual effort and legitimate force. Analyzing the differences between instrumental aggression, emotional aggression and assertive behavior among athletes, Cox (1998) reported that in sport, it is very difficult, at times, to identify if the behavior is assertive or aggressive (overlapping gray areas in the Figure 2.1). Analyses of behavior in sport often involve "bracketed morality", a behavior that is at the fringe of moral and legitimate boundaries (Bredemeir, 1994; Stephens & Bredemeir, 1996). If a batter covers his body over the strike zone, writes Cox (1998), an assertive pitcher is invited to throw a fastball inside the plate. Would you call it aggression if the ball hits the batter?

Research has shown that some form of emotional aggression might be spontaneous, for example, sudden, seizure-like, and pathological. According to Geen (1998), this type of emotional aggression is a precondition or predisposing variable and does not constitute the reactive nature of aggression in which "explanations for aggression must be built on considerations of intervening processes that connect the investigating condition to the aggressive

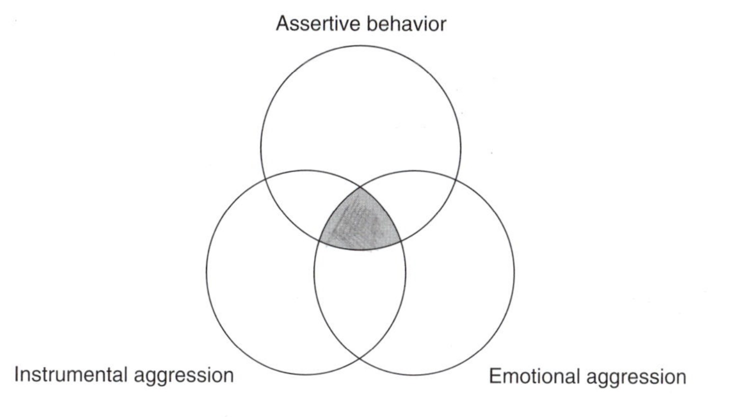

Figure 2.1 Assertive behavior, instrumental aggression and emotional aggression

response" (p. 2). In other words, the social psychological analysis of aggression focuses on the negative affect, such as provocation and arousal, as an instigating condition leading to an aggressive response. The role of biological factors, such as testosterone and brain pathology, is viewed as a predisposing factor only. The dividing line between a psychological approach and a biological approach is a prior existing state or situational context of a variable that ultimately causes an aggressive response. For the purposes of psychological analyses, according to Geen (1998), aggression might be understood in two ways:

1. A joint product of instigating conditions and pre-existing biological factors, and
2. A sequence of events in which instigation or provocation is viewed as a causal factor leading to an aggressive response.

Most of the psychological research is devoted to the latter approach.

Given that emotional aggression is mediated by an unpleasant situation, managing or minimizing such aggression is related to socialization practices, experiences and training of individuals. However, developmental psychologists have recently noted that by as early as six months an infant shows symptoms of anger, but it does not accompany all the behavioral symptoms like compressing its lips (Izard as quoted by Benson, 2003). Whereas adults use language and know the cultural context of anger, the infants don't because the cognitive context of anger is missing. In a "peek-a-boo" game, the infants looked less at the sad faces in comparison to expressions of anger (Montague and Walker-Andrews as quoted by Benson, 2003). Owing to its complexity and increased differentiation, aggressive behavior does not appear in infants until much later in life (for example, the well-known terrible age two of the infant). Based on the results of such findings, it is argued that with the management and control of negative emotions children learn to express nonviolent behavior. Reinforcement of such behavior in socialization practices is a key for understanding how aggressive or nonviolent behavior is encouraged or discouraged in a culture. Differences in reinforcement of males and females that begin at infancy and continue until their death simply show the high levels of direct, physical aggression levels of men, as compared to those of women. For example, the percentage of homicide rates between men and women was 91 and 9, respectively, during the last ten-year survey 1991–1999 (Kenrick, Neuberg, & Cialdini, 2005).

Theories of aggression

Why do we show aggressive behavior? Is aggression biologically programmed in our brain? Is it learned? To answer these and related questions, psychologists have offered different theories to account for human aggression: biological, drive, and social learning.

Biological theories

The biological theories stem from the notion that aggression is preprogrammed at the biological level. It is there in our genes and as we grow older, the genetic program unfolds itself in interaction with the environment.

The classic view that behavior is guided by innate forms of predisposition, called instincts, also contends that aggression is an instinct. For Freud (1920), instincts of life and death (Eros and Thanatos) were cardinal, the former guiding behavior for preserving life and the latter for its destruction. Whenever an individual faced conflict, his energies moved either inward or outward. When libidinal impulses were blocked, aggression resulted in an outward form of energy leading to destruction and killing. Although Freud' psychoanalytic school gradually faded from the scene of psychology owing to its untested concepts like id and ego and absolute reliance on sex, in some respect, at least, it is still considered useful. The reduction in the levels of aggression due to release of energy in some form of behavior, that is, catharsis and displacement, is still popular with many psychologists.

BOX 2.1 CATHARSIS

Aristotle recommended that people should watch tragic plays to release their negative feelings. Taking a clue from his views, Freud believed that if people were not allowed to express their feelings of hostility, their anger would accumulate over a period of time and the energy would find an outlet in the form of some mental illness or express itself in an act of extreme violence. Brill, in the USA, advocated Freud's ideas and advised his patients to watch prizefights periodically to purge their anger (Bushman & Anderson, 1998). In order to avoid such an undesirable condition, he recommended that aggressive behavior should be allowed expression in socially approved conditions. In other words, expression of aggression in some acceptable form tends to reduce the occurrence of its expression in harmful way, that is, catharsis will take place.

However, several scholars (Bandura, 1965; Berkowitz, 1993) have presented contrary evidence to show that engaging in aggression might in fact increase, not decrease, the level of aggression. Russell (1993), a sports psychologist, observed that the level of hostility increased among spectators as the game progressed and their negative feelings lasted for several hours after the game had ended. Geen (1990) reported a number of studies that show that rather than reducing its level, continued aggression tended to increase the intensity of the aggression.

Adapted from: Kool and Agrawal (2006).

Unlike Freud, the neo-Freudians recognized the significance of social factors and the demands external factors placed on the individual. Adler, who was an important follower of Freud, established his own school of individual psychology that laid more emphasis on social urges than on unconscious processes (Hunt, 1993). His concept of social interest is particularly important because it highlighted the innate potential for cooperation. His emphasis on individuals' ability to orient their behavior toward the future pushed traditional psychoanalytic approach from the dark side of human nature to a positive view. Jung, while emphasizing the role of collective unconscious that contains the cumulative experiences of the past generations, showed how opposing forces within an individual increase the capacity to maintain the unity of his/her self. Horney (1937) was mainly concerned with the growth of the neurotic personality and believed that the masochistic attitudes of women do not originate from biological sources but have roots in social forces. So, with many followers of Freud breaking away from him, the impact of biological factors gradually weakened in psychology.

The aftermath of Freud and other followers of the psychoanalytic school resulted in the creation of some popular conceptions regarding aggression. Ardrey (1976) proposed that human beings are territorial and suffer from xenophobia, a tendency to dislike outsiders. They needed weapons for their survival and at heart became brutal. Aggressive behavior shows our fascination with violence that outstripped our capacity to deal with it in reality. The joy and the thrill associated with violence become overwhelming with its experience. Fromm (1959) was particularly concerned with the "anatomy of human destructiveness" in which negative resources overtook the positive resources in coping with the demands of life. In short, while Freud was not so serious about his formal theory of aggression until he corresponded with Einstein (Einstein & Freud, 1933), psychoanalysts, irrespective of their affiliation, later began to portray the tendencies that characterized human aggression and showed how social factors contribute to its uncontrollable form.

Offering a different perspective on aggression, Anthony Storr (1968) believed that aggression plays a positive role in enhancing our survival. Aggression contributes to spacing, sexual selection and defense of young and promotes affiliation and competition as well. Commenting on the negative side of aggression, Storr argued that when an inadequate resolution of aggressive drive takes place, aggressive behavior emerges in a pathological form; otherwise, aggression is after all not as negative as has been depicted in the literature. One example of a positive form of aggression is proactive aggression that is unprovoked but stems from the need to dominate and influence others. Leadership and a sense of humor are often linked to this type of aggression. In addition, proactive aggression is linked to formation of friendship and groups in the classroom (Marcus & Kramer, 2001).

The above shift in the biologically oriented thinking of aggression in the mainstream of psychology, on the one hand, and the impact of Darwin's theory of evolution on social sciences on the other, led to the emergence of at least two more views on aggression: sociobiological and ethological.

Taking a clue from Darwin's natural selection and adaptation as key components in evolution, Wilson's (1975) presented a very systematic account of a sociobiological approach that described behaviors associated with emotions:

1. *Personal survival* is enhanced by *hate and aggression*
2. *Love* aids *reproduction*
3. Altruism: *Helping and cooperating* versus feelings of *guilt* associated with non-helping behavior

From the psychological point of view, each emotion is attached to a category of behavior and is adaptive. For example, male baboons tend to put themselves in dangerous positions and fight to allow others in the group to eat. When we tend to be altruistic, we enhance the survival of others at the cost of our own fitness. In short, the sociobiological approach maintains that aggression tends to maximize the fitness of individuals. In a psychological perspective, it means that there is a useful motive involved in aggressive behavior, that is, enhancing our survival.

Lorenz (1974), an ethologist, who studied animal behavior in natural settings, considered that animal aggression was instinctive. In line with the evolutionary view, Lorenz believed that aggression served three useful purposes: dispersed members for even distribution of resources, strengthened genetic selection and helped survival of young ones. The five key components of his theory are:

1. Aggression occurs naturally and builds up periodically in the form of energy.
2. It is discharged in the presence of a specific stimulus.
3. It shows characteristic motor expressions and behavioral rituals.
4. Animals avoid excessive harm and show appeasement gestures after a ritual is established.
5. Aggression is not reactive. It is inevitable.

The impact of Lorenz's work was so great that he was awarded the Nobel Prize for his scholarly work. Unfortunately, his theory could not hold for long, as criticism began to mount showing that aggression indeed is reactive in nature and is modifiable. Even his major contribution regarding behavioral rituals did not receive much support because it was found that rituals among the same species varied considerably and most rituals are not as rigid as described by Lorenz. His tendency to draw parallels between human and animal characteristics, that is, anthropomorphizing, was also excessive and unscientific.

Current evolutionary view does not support Lorenz's contention that human beings are programmed or pre-wired for aggressive behavior. Rather than focusing on individual survival, the evolutionary approach rests on genetic survival that is the essence for the continuation of species. If aggression is instinctive, as Lorenz argued, aggression should have been equally strong for both biological and adopted children, but the statistics is vastly disproportional, the cases of abuse for adopted children being 70 to 100 times higher than for the biological ones (Daly & Wilson, 2000).

The application of principles of evolution in psychology led to the emergence of a relatively new area of research, called evolutionary psychology. It seeks to employ the knowledge and principles of evolutionary biology in the study of human behavior. In essence, evolutionary psychology is a way of thinking about the functioning of the human mind, that is, how human cognition works in conjunction with neural development. In its relatively simple form, it consists of reciprocal influences between adaptive problems and the cognitive system, the latter interacting reciprocally with the neurophysiological system in the brain. For example, adaptive problems lead to searching for solutions (for example, when we face stressful conditions) and the cognitive system, in turn, interacts with neural networks that may enhance or limit the sequence of action (Box 2.2). Evolutionary psychologists tend to look backwards as they seek answers to the problems that human beings solved in the past and use this information to depict the architecture of the human mind. In contrast, when an engineer designs a product, he/she would study the problem and then draw a plan for the product. Therefore, evolutionary psychology remains a way of thinking and not a study that is traditionally designed to study our senses or perception.

BOX 2.2 THE NEURAL BASIS OF AGGRESSION

The prefrontal lobe, located behind our forehead, is the executive center of the brain. In the course of evolution this center developed to control the activities of the lower centers of the brain. Located in the lower part of the brain is an area called the Limbic System that controls several motivational and emotional responses. Within this area, a center known as amygdala handles emotions and a variety of information that is threatening for our survival. The prefrontal lobe controls and monitors the activities of the amygdala. The activation of the amygdala and failure of the prefrontal lobe to control its activities causes aggression especially in situations in which a sudden response is required to meet the threat. In other words, when the amygdala can override the inhibitory mechanism of higher centers in the brain, the consequence is likely to be seen in some form of aggression.

A classic example of how the amygdala can override the inhibitory control from the upper centers is the Tyson–Holyfield fight in which Tyson bit the ear of Holyfield. With the prefrontal lobe handling the working of an individual and the amygdala housing the brain's emotional memories, Tyson, reminded of his earlier humiliating defeats, became violent and defied all the rules in boxing. Goleman (1998) aptly calls this episode as "an amygdala hijack". Although the link between the amygdala and the prefrontal lobe is compared to that of a super highway connection, exigencies of time and situation might still demand an immediate response. This is possibly the best explanation for some of the most cynical and violent acts committed by otherwise "nonviolent" individuals, who had lived their entire lives peacefully with no history of violence.

BOX 2.2 (cont'd)

There are, however, limits in determining the relationship between neural activation and aggressive behavior. Owing to individual differences, Kosslyn and coworkers (2002) showed through their research that there was a problem in demonstrating the neural correlates of behavior. For instance, in case of threat leading to aggression, cortisol levels do not rise consistently and fail to correlate with aggressive behavior.

Additionally, evolution is not intentional. It does not foresee future needs (Buss, 2004). Adaptation in evolution served those inherited characteristics that emerged from natural selection. Such needs arose out of survival needs created in a situation that fluctuated from shortage of food to shelter. Birds that lived primarily in bushes with nut bearing trees needed stronger and better beaks for nut-cracking; otherwise their survival was threatened. Those who survived passed on their genes to the offspring.

Modern evolutionary psychologists believe that adaptation tells only a part of the evolutionary process and we need another concept "exaptation" to account for the by-products that emerged in the course of evolution. Thus, for example, feathers help birds in thermal regulation, but these feathers also help them to fly, a different function added to the adaptive process. "According to this distinction", writes, Buss and coworkers (1998), "the term adaptation would be properly applied to the original thermal regulation structure and function, but the term exaptation would be more appropriate for describing the current flight-producing structure and function" (p. 539).

Is war or heightened aggression a product of exaptation? Some evolutionary psychologists offer an affirmative answer. Gould (1991) believes that the large size of the human brain is an example of exaptation, a mechanism that was not the product of the original biological function of selection, but subsequently served a new function akin to the flying behavior of birds. To illustrate further the role of exaptations, Gould argued that the mechanism might be conceived as spandrels, a concept derived from an architectural design of a bridge that tends to leave gaps between its pillars to support the bridge. These gaps between pillars of a bridge are used by homeless people for shelter, although spandrels are not designed for housing the homeless. The oversized brain is a very complex design that developed in evolution with spandrels housing such activities as religion, fine arts and war.

As mentioned earlier, in the traditional theory of aggression, personal survival and territoriality were served by aggressive behavior. When one aspect of aggression, that is, emotional aggression, became burdensome in creating friendship, aggression of another type, namely, proactive aggression emerged to enhance prosocial behavior (Marcus & Kramer, 2001). In this form, the survival value of aggression led to the establishment of leadership and the development of a satisfying nature of friendship. For example, the quality of friendship varies remarkably between children exhibiting proactive and emotional aggression (Poulin & Boivin, 2002). Lore and Schultz (1993) concluded that aggression is an optional strategy in animals which is determined by their experience and understanding of the social context. Based on their experiments on rats, they observed that the response to an intruder rat's threat varied in a cage. One dominant rat (Alpha) launched a vigorous attack on the intruder, but others remained calm. Another rat, called the Beta rat, which was otherwise submissive, would take over the role of a dominant rat, if needed. The third type of relatively smaller rat, the Omega, remained submissive and bedraggled. Thus, aggression is one of the many survival mechanisms and even animals have strong inhibitory mechanisms that restrict them from aggression if it promotes their survival.

Drive theories

The concept of drive refers to a noninstinctive motivational force. It tends to increase in magnitude if conditions supporting the motivation such as hunger and sex are not satisfied. Human beings engage in behavior that leads to the termination of such deprived states. In the classic literature in psychology, reduction of drive meant reinforcement (Hull, 1943) or the probability of occurrence of a response (Skinner, 1953).

There are many conditions in which we remain deprived and feel frustrated, that is, the drive state is not terminated. When we fail to reach our goal, it results in frustration, a state caused by the thwarting of an ongoing goal directed behavior (Baron & Richardson, 1994). To account for what such frustration does to elicit aggression, Dollard, Doob, Miller, Mowrer, and Sears (1939) presented a theory called "Frustration–Aggression Hypothesis" (FAH) with the following two tenets:

1. Frustration is the root of aggression.
2. Frustration always leads to aggression.

Unfortunately, when many studies did not support the above contention of FAH, the theory was promptly revised stating that frustration does not always lead to aggressive behavior. One critical variable overlooked by the FAH was the fear of punishment that might inhibit aggression even when the individual was frustrated. In general, frustration may also accompany behaviors like escape or withdrawal from the scene, attacking another target (displacement of aggression), and inhibition of aggression following cultural beliefs. Based on the results of his experiments, Miller (1948) presented a significant finding that the inhibition effects are not identical for and against aggression. The instigation to aggression, not the inhibition, decreases slowly and, as a result, its effects tend to prolong.

Berkowitz (1993) extended the implications of the FAH to show that an unpleasant stimulation will cause aggression if it results in arousing unpleasant

Table 2.2 Frustration–Aggression Hypothesis and its revision

Original version	**Revised version**
Frustration	Frustration, pain, heat, unpleasant experiences
Causes	Negative feelings
Aggression	Emotional aggression

Source: Adapted from Kenrick et al. (2005).

feelings. What do you think of a man in the elevator who is belching hard with lots of garlic smelling around? According to Berkowitz, it's not just frustration alone, but any unpleasant situation that may lead to negative feelings causing emotional aggression. As mentioned earlier, emotional aggression involves inflicting harm for its own sake without necessarily expecting control over reinforcement. Table 2.2 shows the FAH and Berkowitz's model of aggression.

In their classic experiment, Berkowitz and LePage (1967) showed that certain stimuli in the environment could act as cues to aggressive behavior—cues associated in an environment, such as the presence of a gun, that might lead to aggression. Berkowitz (1993) made a famous statement that it is not only the finger that pulls the trigger, but it is the trigger that also pulls the finger. Aversive stimuli and cues in the environment contribute to the formation of negative affect leading to an aggressive response.

Another landmark contribution in the understanding of aggression is that of Zillman (1994) who believed that the key to understanding aggression is arousal. With the increase in the arousal level, the excitation level increases and this may cause aggressive behavior. According to Zillman, arousal is the excitement of the sympathetic autonomic system with symptoms of increase in heart rate and blood pressure, gastrointestinal motility, perspiration, and so on. For example, arousal may be caused by biking or watching pornography, but it will lead to aggression if a cognitive cue is mislabeled. Thus, after biking for a long time, the chances for retaliation to a provocation are higher than after finishing a sedentary task. In essence, Zillman's excitation-transfer theory contended that arousal from one source may combine with another source and cause increase or decrease in aggression in terms of interpretation of the cues involved in the provocation.

The following sequence shows Zillman's (1988) contention:

High arousal → interference with cognitive processes → intense aggression
Moderate arousal → available cognitive inhibition → control of aggression

In short, Zillman's analysis offers an insight into the consequence of physiological arousal in interaction with the type of emotion—positive or negative—that is involved. With low arousal and positive emotion, aggression tends to decrease, but with high arousal and negative emotions, aggression greatly increases. Table 2.3 presents a summary of such increase and decrease in aggression.

Table 2.3 Role of arousal and type of emotion in aggression

Type of emotion	Low arousal	High arousal
Negative	Increasing aggression	Greater increase in aggression
Neutral	No effect	Increasing aggression
Positive	Decreasing aggression	Increasing/decreasing?

Are individuals driven with excessive competitiveness, achievement striving, and exaggerated urgency easily aroused by poor time management, tardiness, and omissions? In the psychological literature, individuals with symptoms of such nature are identified as Type A personality versus those who are laid-back and tolerant of deadlines (Type B). Baron (1989) studied the behavior of Type A managers and found that they had more conflicts with their subordinates and were less accommodating in conflict management. Now imagine how a Type A would behave during traffic jams or tailgating. A newly discovered phenomenon, called road rage, is a correlate of Type A personality because the patience of a Type A driver runs thin very quickly under extreme conditions of traffic jams. In the crowded streets of India, driving is not easy and more so for the Type A individuals who are known for rough driving. Type A bus drivers, in a study in India, were involved in accidents and received reprimands more than their counterparts, Type B (Evans & coworkers, 1987). On the flip side, controlling arousal, especially with negative affect, is the hallmark of nonviolent behavior, but it does not mean that they are any less competitive or poor managers of time. As stated in Chapter 1, tolerance is the essence of nonviolence (Box 2.3).

BOX 2.3 ROAD RAGE

The terms road rage and aggressive driving are used interchangeably. With the number of automobiles and congestion on roads increasing, deaths, injuries, hostilities and negative affects have also increased. According to Deffenbacher (as cited by Dittman, 2005), of the Colorado State University, road rage has risen at a rate of 7 percent each year during the past six-year period. Deffenbacher characterized those showing road rage as high in risk taking and identifying themselves as high-anger drivers. As per American Automobile Association records, between 1990 and 1996 the death toll caused by road rage was 218 while 12,610 people suffered injury.

Psychologists have constructed several measures of road rage: Propensity for Angry Driving Scale, called PADS (DePasquale, Geller, Clarke, & Littleton, 2001); and James and Nahl's Scale (2000). Aggressive drivers indulge in aggressive self-talk, loss of self-control, impulsiveness, excessive honking, switching lanes without signaling, tailgating, and obscene gestures. Simply speaking, it's failure to regulate one's behavior as a consequence of impulsivity.

Social learning theories

Although Skinner himself stated that theories in psychology are unnecessary, ironically his work on reinforcement became one of the most popular theories in the history of psychology. For Skinner, all behavior, including aggression, is learned when reinforced. With suitable changes in the intervals and ratios of reinforcement, the behavior can be shaped to the desired target. In his book, *Walden Two* (Skinner, 1948), he claimed that through reinforcement, children could be conditioned by rewards to become cooperative and sociable. Not only his theory, but his general comments later raised a lot of controversy (Box 2.4).

BOX 2.4 WHAT DO YOU THINK ABOUT SKINNER AFTER READING THE FOLLOWING PASSAGE?

On his first TV appearance he posed a dilemma originally propounded by Montague—"Would you, if you had to choose, burn your children or your books?"—Skinner said that he himself would burn his children, since his contribution to the future would be greater through his work than through his genes. (Hunt, 1993, p. 269)

According to Hunt (1993), he was a provocateur and a superb publicist.

Bandura disagrees with Skinner's overemphasis on reinforcement and contends that reinforcement is important but not necessary for learning. His classic experiment using a cartoon character that was earlier watched by children demonstrated clearly that learning might take place through imitation and observation, and also without reinforcement (Bandura, Ross, & Ross, 1963). Bandura also states that the "aggressive drive" need not be mediated through anger or other negative emotions. Mercenaries or hired assassins show violence without being upset or angry. Further, Bandura (1997) argued that in many situations, an individual may find better options than aggression, for example, when the cost of aggression is high and other nonviolent solutions are available. With such mitigating factors present, it is likely that an individual will prefer to remain nonviolent rather than opting for aggression.

According to Bandura, social learning of aggression involves three components: acquisition, instigation and regulation. Acquisition of aggressive behavior takes place with the contribution of biological factors and learning, including reinforcement and observation. Aggression is instigated by aversive stimulus, incentives, cultural beliefs, and other factors and is conducted through self-regulatory mechanisms such as guilt and pride, and external rewards and punishment.

A comparison between drive and social learning theories shows that whereas the former was developed to explain emotional aggression, the latter is most suited for instrumental aggression. In between, reinforcement theory may be considered useful for maintaining and sustaining aggressive behavior, but the range of learning aggressive behavior can probably be best understood through Bandura's work. It is generally believed that a comprehensive theory of aggression should encompass several variables as no single theory covers the multifarious factors that are involved in aggression.

Anderson's (1997) GAAM model (General Affective Aggression Model) is a composite effort involving inclusion of a wide range of variables to account for aggression. Beginning with the analysis of input variables, such as frustration and irritability, the mediating factors leading to aggression are: arousal, affective states and aggressive cognitions. Although the flexibility of this model is excellent, there are problems in adequately explaining aggression. For example, the impact of media violence in raising the levels of violence has been a major controversy around the globe. In spite of the pioneering work of psychologists like Bandura, Berkowitz, Huesmann, Donnerstein and others and the efforts of the American Psychological Association, there is not much agreement regarding the harmful effects of media violence on children (Eron, Gentry, & Schlegel, 1996). For further reading on the controversy, the reader is referred to Kool and Agrawal (2006). Also, Anderson and Bushman (2002) presented an excellent review of research on aggression.

One comprehensive and useful way of looking at the learning of aggressive behavior is to examine it in the context of uncontrollable environmental changes on the one end, and when control is possible, at the other end. Under such scrutiny, both biological and learning theories would unite and offer a reasonable explanation for human aggression. Kimble (1994) emphasized that behavior should be "understood in terms of adaptation and coping" (p. 514), as they tend to promote survival. When human beings find that control is possible, they exhibit operant conditioning to enhance coping with the environment. On the other hand, when environment changes beyond the control of the human being, adaptation is the only choice for survival. Kimble cited examples for adaptation in the form of classical conditioning and coping in the form of instrumental behavior (Table 2.4). Thus, if a bee approaches our eye, the natural

Table 2.4 Adaptation and coping

Classical conditioning	**Instrumental conditioning**
Elicited response	Emitted response
Reflex response	Voluntary response
Habitual response	Problem solving
Declarative memory (remembering what)	Procedural memory (remembering how)
Automatic processing	Effortful processing
Helplessness	Competence
External locus of control	Internal locus of control
Submission	Dominance
Obsession	Compulsion

Source: Adapted from Kimble (1994).

response is winking by closing the eyelids, but classical conditioning increases our adaptation if we wink by hearing the sound of the moving bee much before it actually hits the eye. Now, closing the eyelids is an instance of adaptation, but not a wise one, for the bee can still hurt you by biting. Given the time and availability of a gadget, one would want to kill it (instrumental conditioning). During friendly fire in war, soldiers mistakenly fire at their fellow soldiers simply at the sight of a threat (classical conditioning) without any time supposedly available for further processing of the information about this threat that could have otherwise helped them better cope with the situation.

During the course of evolution, the complex ways in which adaptation and coping have made an impact on the individual such that the original function is also accompanied by an auxiliary task is better understood; as stated above, in the post-Darwinian analysis. Future research in the psychology of aggression needs to continue to align with the fundamental principles of psychology—in this case the learning of aggressive behavior.

Measurement of aggression

There are several difficulties in measuring aggression. First and foremost, it may not be safe to measure this concept in a laboratory setting. When a subject is frustrated or angered, it may not be easy for an experimenter to control the behavior of an aggressor. Second, there are problems with the concept, as psychologists do not agree on the nature of aggression. In laboratory measures of aggression, aggression is often defined in terms of the nature of operations through which aggression is measured. Obviously, aggression is narrowly defined and studied in a limited way through laboratory procedures.

Among the nonexperimental procedures that are used to measure aggression, the archival method, self-reports and personality measures, and natural observations are very common. Among the popular experimental methods, Buss and Milgram's procedures have been widely employed by researchers.

The archival method involves reviewing past data and records. There is little chance of bias in this procedure but the researcher is often not sure regarding the purpose for which the data were collected or records were prepared. In his seminal work, Anderson (1989) showed how elevation in the temperature is linked to increased aggressive behavior. With the temperature rising, a significantly positive relationship with (a) crime rate and police calls and (b) the number of players hit by wild pitches in baseball and errors increased. Nisbett (1993) reported that the southern culture of honor in the USA developed out of the predominantly herding economy in which the crop had to be defended from the poachers. Under the circumstances they developed a relatively more violent culture than the northerners. One possibility for increase in the levels of aggression of southerners was temperature that was hotter than that of the northern region (Anderson & Anderson, 1998).

Self-reporting methods employ questionnaires to measure aggression. They may measure a situational effect caused by provocation or irritation or relatively stable characteristics of personality. For example, the Conflict Tactics

Table 2.5 Sample items from the BDHI

Assault: Whoever insults me or my family is asking for a fight
Indirect: I sometimes show my anger by banging on the table
Irritability: I lose my temper easily but get over it quickly
Negativism: When someone is bossy, I do the opposite of what he asks
Resentment: I don't seem to get what's coming to me
Suspicion: I know that people tend to talk about me behind my back
Verbal: When I disapprove of my friends behavior, I let them know it
Guilt: I sometimes have bad thoughts which make me feel ashamed of myself

Scale is a measure that enlists increasingly higher levels of aggression and solicits the response of family members engaging in such behaviors (Baron & Richardson, 1994). Among the most popular questionnaire measure of aggression is the Buss–Durkee Hostility Inventory (BDHI) that was briefly mentioned in Chapter 1 (Buss & Durkee, 1957). The scale is divided into two parts: Five kinds of aggression including assault, indirect aggression, irritability, negativism and verbal aggression; and two types of hostility: resentment and suspicion (Table 2.5). As mentioned in Chapter 1, this scale correlated negatively with the test of nonviolence (Kool & Sen, 1984, 2005).

A revised BDHI, called the Aggression Questionnaire (Buss & Perry, 1992), measures four factors: physical aggression, verbal aggression, hostility, and anger. Caprara and coworkers (1984) developed another measure of aggression consisting of the following three subscales:

1. *Irritability*: It is reflected in short temper and readiness to explode with provocation.
2. *Emotional susceptibility*: Feelings of inadequacy, discomfort, and vulnerability.
3. *Dissipation and rumination*: Retaining anger for considerable time after being instigated.

Observing behavior in a laboratory is a very safe procedure for studying a dangerous behavior like aggression. With carefully trained judges who can code behavior into various response categories, the behavior in such laboratory conditions, though not as natural as in a free environment, is still spontaneous and not overly restricted by the nuances of the experimental procedures. Among the best-known experiments conducted using this procedure is Bandura and coworkers' (1963) study of young children in a free play situation. These children watched a cartoon character that acted in many aggressive ways, for example, assaults against a Bobo doll. Following a movie, the behavior of children was observed and compared with those who had not seen this movie. The study concluded that for the children in the movie group, the cartoon character became a model as they repeatedly behaved in the same way as did the cartoon character. This study has been criticized on the ground that in such aggression, no one is actually hurt. Is this real aggression? Answering to such criticism, Bandura (1977) remarked that a distinction must be made between learning and performance and that such situations demonstrate how many forms of aggression are learned without even hurting the victim.

In the scientific literature on psychology of aggression, laboratory procedures involving the independent variable (simply referring to stimulus manipulated by the experimenter) and dependent variables (simply referring to the responses of the subject) and linking cause-effect relationships have greater credibility than other procedures. Buss (1961) pioneered a laboratory procedure to measure aggression in which a subject was invited to shock the learner (victim) for errors. The shock levels varied on the aggression machine, the dependent variables being the duration of the shock, the intensity of shock that ranged from low to high, and the duration × intensity yielded the total aversive stimulation score. Since Buss developed this technique, hundreds of studies have employed this procedure to measure aggression and the aggression scores of subjects correlated significantly with several self-report inventories of aggression (Baron & Richardson, 1994).

By far the most popular, albeit controversial, is the procedure devised by Milgram (1974). On his aggression machine too, a subject delivered shocks to the victim but the dependent variable was designed differently to measure aggression of the subject. Each subject was categorically told that it was mandatory to increase the level of shock each time the learner made a mistake. In other words, this procedure demanded compliance from the subject when showing aggression. His experiments, popularly known as obedience to authority studies, showed that all his subjects, with the exception of a few, obeyed the instructions to raise the level of shocks to dangerous levels until they felt uncomfortable and wanted to withdraw from the experiment. In normal life, no sane person will give shocks to any one, but why did Milgram's subjects continue to raise the level of shock? For Milgram, the answer was our tendency to obey, much the same way as the henchmen of Hitler participated in the genocide of the Jews in Germany by blindly following his orders and without realizing the consequence of their actions (Box 2.5).

BOX 2.5 MILGRAM'S WORK AND ITS IMPLICATION

When social psychologist Milgram (1974) studied the aggression levels of students from Yale University and the ordinary citizens from New Haven, CT, he was intrigued by the fact that irrespective of the level of education or age range, these people delivered unusually high shocks to a confederate in a laboratory setting. The prestige of a Yale University professor and the lab setting of a renowned institution, known as the Yale University, convinced the participating subjects that they were supporting the scientific cause for which this professor was working. However, in doing so they were delivering lethal doses of electric shock that would make them liable for criminal proceedings. Such is the power of obedience to authority.

BOX 2.5 (cont'd)

From our parents, teachers and significant others, we learn to obey. Such obedience, if mistakenly guided for gruesome acts as shown by Hitler and others, may lead to catastrophic consequences. A sad example of such blind obedience is the self-sacrifice of many adolescents and children who are blowing themselves up in the acts of terrorism.

Aristotle, the father of psychology, and Freud, as mentioned earlier in this chapter, recognized the significance of reduction of aggression through release of energy in some form. We can vent our anger by punching a bag or by expressing anger over a trivial matter embarrassing the younger brother. However, not all social psychological studies reported similar results indicating that catharsis had not occurred. The expression of aggression might lead to escalation of aggression, but not its reduction as Aristotle and Freud originally proposed, and many empirical studies have supported this contention. Using a Milgram-type of experimental procedure, Sen (1981, 1993) reported an experiment in which her violent and nonviolent subjects, as selected on the basis of their scores on the Nonviolence Test (NVT), were given an opportunity to aggress under two conditions: (a) annoyed condition in which the subjects were provoked but had to wait before they could aggress (wait-annoyed condition), and (b) wait-shock condition in which they were allowed to shock another victim during the wait period (catharsis condition). The results clearly supported the catharsis hypothesis. There was a significant decline in the aggression scores when the subjects got a chance to shock during the wait condition. However, this effect was observed in the case of violent subjects only; the nonviolent subjects did not show any significant change in their aggression scores under wait or no-wait conditions (Figure 2.2). The latter remained unprovoked and hence the decline in their scores was not expected. It appears that, by and large, the catharsis effect appears to be genuine, but personality and other factors tend to mitigate or even reverse its effect.

There are several other experimental procedures for measuring aggression in the laboratory conditions, but it is not intended to review them all here. A brief summary of five laboratory procedures widely used in psychological research on aggression is reported in Table 2.6.

Berkowitz's (1962, 1993) procedure required an assessment of a written solution and delivery of aversive stimulus (shocks). Although widely used in many research studies, his procedure is flawed owing to the eliciting of defensive reactions, not aggression *per se* (Baron & Richardson, 1994). Another procedure, designed by Taylor (1967), involves competing on a reaction time type of task in which a subject responding slower than his opponent receives the shocks. If the accomplice of the experimenter raised the level of the shock, the opponent

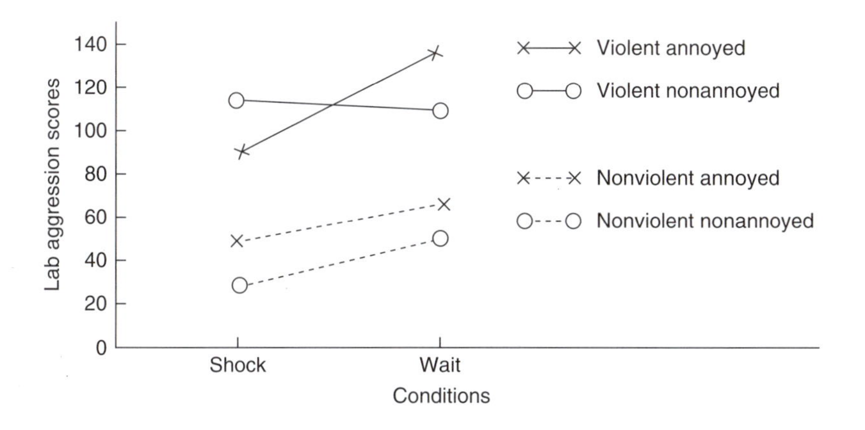

Figure 2.2 Aggression levels of nonviolent and violent subjects

Table 2.6 A comparison of five laboratory procedures for measuring aggression

Feature	Buss	Milgram	Diener	Taylor	Berkowitz
Material	Machine 1–10 shock	Machine higher shock	Harmless objects	Machine shocks	Problems shocks
Procedure	Deliver shock	Deliver shock	Throwing	Instigating	Shock A => S
Dep. variable	D x I	Shock +	Harmful +	Instigation	Shocks
Comments	Artificial	Compliance	Violence	Ethical	Defensive

D = Duration; I = Intensity; Dep. = Dependent variable.
For further details, see Baron and Richardson (1994) and Geen and Donnerstein (1998).

retaliated by increasing the aggression levels or vice versa (Richardson et al., 1986). None of the above procedures actually involved harm to the subjects (the button delivering the shock remained switched off), but sensing this limitation in measuring aggression, Diener (1976) used real objects, like foam bricks, and other similar materials, to measure direct physical aggression. The procedure was criticized when, in some cases, it became difficult to control the physical aggression of the participating subjects.

Social scientists in general and many psychologists in particular are very skeptical about measuring aggression using laboratory procedures such as the types described above. Therefore, Bushman and Anderson (1998) raised the important question: "Do different laboratory measures of aggression measure the same underlying conceptual variable?" (p. 27). Fortunately, using dependent variables as criteria (for example, intensity, duration and frequency of shock delivery), the correlations between the procedures were positive and statistically significant (Carlson & coworkers, 1989). The laboratory scores also correlate significantly positive with questionnaire measures of aggression (Kool & Sen, 1984/2005).

Table 2.7 Laboratory versus real world examples of aggression

Type of aggression	Real life examples	Laboratory Examples
Direct physical	Body injury	Delivery of shock
Indirect physical	Damage property	Loss of money
Direct verbal	Derogating/cursing	Negative evaluation
Indirect verbal	Spread rumors	Negative expression

Source: Adapted from Bushman and Anderson (1998).

Another issue addressed by Bushman and Anderson (1998) is related to the similarity between laboratory examples of aggression and "real world" aggression. For this purpose they compared examples of direct and indirect physical and verbal aggression as per Buss's classification vis-à-vis aggression in our real life. Table 2.7 shows how real life examples of aggression match those identified in the laboratory procedures. It's ok so far. But, how about the active versus passive dimension of aggression described in $2 \times 2 \times 2$ typology of aggression that we mentioned in the beginning of the chapter (Table 2.1)? Unfortunately, the passive types of aggression in laboratory procedures were not operationally common and hence no firm conclusions could be drawn in classifying them in experimental studies. As I mentioned earlier, such passive aggression represents the gray areas of research in aggression.

There are other problems and limitations in depending on laboratory procedures alone in measuring aggression of the subjects. When invited to participate in an experiment, the subjects have knowledge that they are participating in an experiment. Therefore, it's not the same behavior that we normally show in naturally occurring conditions that elicit aggression. Further, reporting to an experimenter in the laboratory setting creates a mindset that we are a part of an experiment and it is desirable to respond to the demands of a situation. This phenomenon is known as the demand characteristic of an experiment that elicits a response of a subject as per the experimenter's expectation. Many of Milgram's subjects complied with the instructions for delivery of shocks, but later had nightmares and regretted their participation in the experiment (Milgram, 1974).

For a better understanding of human aggression, psychologists would need measures that apply equally well to their laboratory conditions and in the real life. It reminds us of Lewin's famous statement regarding the value of a psychological theory that enhances with its robust applications.

SUMMARY

Violence and aggression are used interchangeably in social science research, but psychologists prefer the term aggression to focus on an individual's behavior. While unpleasant effects like anger and hostility mediate aggression, its nature is intriguing because it has a prosocial function as well. The chapter began with a description of the nature and types of aggression and reminded the reader that the definition of aggression might change with its classification.

Among the existing theories of aggression—biological, drive, cognitive and evolutionary—a special reference was made to the survival value of aggression and how it has been viewed in the post-Darwinian era. The last segment of this chapter dealt with the measurement of aggression, with particular emphasis on the laboratory procedures developed by Buss and Milgram.

SUGGESTED READINGS

Anderson, C. A., & Bushman, B. J. (2002). Human aggression. *Annual Review of Psychology*, *53*, 27–51.

Baron, R. A., & Richardson, D. R. (1994). *Human aggression*. New York: Plenum Press.

Geen, R. G., & Donnerstein, E. (Eds.). (1998). *Human aggression*. New York: Academic Press.

Krahe, B. (2001). *The social psychology of aggression*. Howe, England: Psychology Press.

Cognition and Self-control: The Engine and Brakes of Nonviolence

OUTLINE

Gifted with the most complicated structure that developed during the course of evolution, the human brain, its capacity to use symbols is extraordinary as compared to other species. We are capable of extracting meaning from people, objects and events in countless ways. And yet, a small provocation derails our capacity to think subtly and to control our feelings. Not surprisingly, it is the loss of a wedding ring, not the loss of a job that causes unusual violence at times.

"We obtained our capacity for violence along with our ability to reason abstractly, to see things, like gravity or threats that are not materially there. We are the only species capable of aggressing because of the beliefs we hold" (p. 20), wrote Goldstein (1986) to highlight how a neutral stimulus like the colors of the flag of an unknown nation, after identification, raises our emotional response to that flag. In Chapter 1, I had mentioned that when alternate responses to aggression are not available during conflicts, fight and flight often remain the only significant options.

When the impact of behaviorism swept through the science of psychology in the middle of the previous century, social psychology was not as much under its influence as were many other fields of psychology. Thus, most social psychologists have no difficulty in accepting a metaphysical concept such as mind or cognition, that is, what goes on in our mind and how we think about and understand ourselves and other people. But others, especially in the field of experimental psychology, were not so fortunate. As late as in 1960, George Miller, a noted experimental psychologist, reported that conducting research in the area of cognition was rated as an act of defiance. Had he not received the support of scholars like Jerome Bruner, at Harvard University, to set up a center for research on cognition, some of his trend-setting work would not have been possible.

Directly or indirectly, cognitive processes are involved in nonviolence—whether it is a genuinely spontaneous and altruistic response to the needs of a baby in distress or a cool, calculated strategy to win the adversary through tolerance and forgiving. Beginning with the application of a computer-based approach to study cognition, that is, the individual-focused information-processing approach, this chapter will follow it up to examine the social side of cognition, for example, the application of social identity theory (SIT). Do nonviolent and violent individuals differ in their causal analysis of scenarios in which they are placed? Are there nonviolent cultures? If yes, how are people in these cultures different? Having our focus on cognition, we will examine these issues along with recent research in self-control and moral dimensions as relevant for our understanding of the psychology of nonviolence.

Information-processing approach to study cognition

In this section of the chapter, we will focus on how nonviolent and aggressive behaviors are mediated by cognitive processes that connect biological and situational factors. More specifically, we will show how we receive information and what happens after receiving it. This approach is based on the information-processing model that follows an analogy of computer functioning as applied to the understanding of cognition.

Schemas and scripts

Studies on social cognition are a relatively recent trend in the history of psychology. It refers to the way we receive, interpret and remember events and people.

The core concept in social cognition is schema, that is, a mental framework in which we keep information and understand it. When we organize information about ourselves, it is called self-schema. Similarly, organizing information about our work as a professor is called role-schema, about an event as an event-schema, and so on. In short, schema represents a broad, macro level knowledge about a concept and its attributes. Upon linkage of several schemas, a script is prepared. A script serves as a guide to behavior as well as generates beliefs regarding future events. We have a script for boarding a plane that involves a sequence of events that is different from when we board a train. Similarly, dining in a restaurant is different than eating in a fast food facility. The available scripts vastly influence our social behavior and examples of scripting in violence and nonviolence are cited in Box 3.1.

BOX 3.1 SCRIPTING VIOLENCE AND NONVIOLENCE

Scripting of violence

Moerk (2002) analyzed several episodes of violence including the US invasion of Iraq, antecedents leading to the two World Wars, and the Pearl Harbor incident. Here are two examples:

1. Hitler would develop a well-rehearsed script—such as, starting from today, we will be shooting back—a ploy for attacking the enemy.
2. In case of Pearl Harbor, the Americans would prepare a script by placing two ships in harm's way and then waiting for the enemy to attack. This scenario would make Americans look like defending themselves.

Scripting of nonviolence

- Bondurant (1965) referred to many episodes of Gandhi's technique of scripting nonviolence. Each participant (called a satyagrahi) in the nonviolent movement would rehearse a set of action plans consisting of keeping a firm posture of fearlessness while being beaten by the police, restraining from showing anger or retaliation, keeping on chanting the slogans and remaining on fast after arrest.
- Other examples of nonviolent scripts used by the participants in the slavery movement are cited by and referred to in this book in Chapters 4 and 5 (also see Cooney & Michalowski, 1987).
- When Nelson Mandela found that his adherence to Gandhian methods of nonviolence was unsuccessful in demolishing apartheid in South Africa, he approved both violence and nonviolence. In other words, when a script fails, people develop alternate scripts. Quoting many historians, Presbey (2006) contended that by mixing the two methods, freedom became more elusive and got delayed in South Africa.

BOX 3.1 (cont'd)

- For more illustrations on nonviolent movements (how activists scripted the sequence of their action plan) the reader is referred to the works of Katz (1990), Sharp (2005), Ackerman and DuVall (2000), and Ackerman and Kruegler (1993).

Moerk (2002) concluded that scripting has been playing an important role in the survival of a group. For example, the primitive herd needed a strong leader for defense to deal with any threat from outside and created folklores to honor their leader's bravery. Considering its value for survival, such scripting is not likely to go away soon and will probably "reign" during the new millennium as well, albeit, the cost of such scripting might involve sacrificing countless lives. According to Moerk, although we admire Lincoln, Wilson and Roosevelt and glorify them in our writings and speeches, their actions caused enormous suffering as well.

Priming

A study of social cognition will help us to understand how retrieval of a script is involved in an aggressive or nonviolent behavior. Retrieving any information depends on the saliency of the information and the context in which it was stored (encoding). If you meet Bill Clinton at the Heathrow airport, you will remember this information when you will be at the Heathrow next time. Had you met an insignificant passenger at this airport, you might not recall him. The context and the saliency of the stimulus are important sources that help in the retrieval of a script. But how is a thought process activated? If we see a documentary on animals and subsequently are given a word completion task, it is likely that we will perform better on El_ _ _a_t (Elephant) than when we do not watch the film. Once we perceive something, it triggers an action that lasts for some time in our mind and such activation of a thought process may facilitate subsequent input. Medical students, who study diseases in their classes, often suffer from "medical student syndrome", that is, misinterpreting their minor health problems and labeling them as serious. While studying a course on abnormal psychology, I felt many of those symptoms haunting me and planting a seed of doubt in my mind regarding whether I was a normal human being (and still doubt my normalcy). Increased availability of information, say recently used words or ideas, leads to priming. No one understands it better than those in the advertisement business because their ultimate goal is to prime your thoughts for their products and goad you into buying them.

Mental heuristics

Finally, the cognitive system operates in terms of parsimony, that is, attempting to conserve mental resources. Imagine what will happen to me if I have to remember each time afresh the classroom, the building and the faces of students when I go to my class. Mental operations follow heuristics that provide economy in our mental life. If a person bears a resemblance to the members of a group, we may mistakenly identify him as a member of that group or community (representative heuristics). Another heuristic, called, availability heuristics, depends on availability of information. When students were asked if words beginning with the letter "k" were more than those with the words that have "k" as the third letter, most of them favored the former in spite of the fact that the English language has three times more words with letter "k" in the third position. "What is readily available" guides the heuristics that are involved in making judgments (Tversky & Kahneman, 1982).

Later work in cognition showed that facilitation in decision-making is not the only function of heuristics. In fact, Rothman and Hardin (1997) showed how the availability heuristic tends to influence the quality of decisions. For example, when we make judgments about our own group, we use a different set of rules than when judging outsiders (in-group versus out-group). In judging our group, we tend to rely on facts (more relevant information), but in judging others, we tend to rely on feelings and emotions. Why? It is easier to focus on feelings and emotions than to collect facts about others and process them in detail. No wonder that hostility and aggression are easily evoked for out-groups but not for the in-groups. We will discuss in-group versus out-group evaluations further later in this book.

It is not intended here to catalog research on cognition and for details on this subject, the reader is referred to sources elsewhere (Baron & Richardson, 1994; Huesmann, 1998; Krahe, 2001). Nor do we intend here to enlist the problems in applying the information-processing models. Our goal here is to figure out how the information-processing approach has helped us in our better understanding of nonviolence and aggression. For example, Wendy Josephson (1987) invited second- and third-grade schoolboys to watch violent and nonviolent movies and subsequently they played a hockey game in the school gymnasium. The critical variable in the study was the walkie-talkie that was used in the violent movie. Its presence primed aggressive behavior in the violent movie group. For the nonviolent group, this critical variable, walkie-talkie, was not present. In the absence of such priming, the latter group was found to be less aggressive. In another study, Carver, Ganellen, Froming, and Chambers (1983) gave jumbled sets of four words to their subjects who were asked to make sentences by picking up three words. One group of subjects had word sets, 80 percent of which made only violent sentences, as compared to the other group that had only a few such word sets. When both groups were given a chance to aggress using a Buss-type aggression procedure, those subjects who had made more violent sentences tended to score higher on aggression than their nonviolent counterparts. The violent group was already primed by the exercise involving violent sentence construction. Summarizing the impact of priming, Berkowitz (1993) wrote:

> What is especially important is that the primed thoughts are apt to bring a certain kind of conception, or interpretative schema, to mind and that this schema will determine how relevant information is understood. (p. 106)

The question before us is therefore: If aggressive behavior can be primed, as in the case of the studies reported above, is it possible to prime nonviolent behavior? After all, we show nonviolent behavior in our daily routine most of the time. We go to church, learn not to call others enemies, follow our religious scriptures to remain honest and truthful, and so on. According to Berkowitz (1993), in spite of being reminded of ethical and exemplary behavior from various sources, "our nonaggressive ideals aren't always fully in mind" (p. 112). Berkowitz further elaborated on this topic by mentioning how displacement of responsibility onto others could rationalize one's behavior. Thus, the priming effects could be attenuated easily if we do not hold to our beliefs in a timely manner. During the well-known Nuremberg trials, when the Nazi generals were asked why they had acted in those inhumane ways, they responded that they were simply following the orders and that they were in no way responsible for those brutalities. In other words, the Nazi generals had developed "self-regulated internals standards", that is, they were not evil until they themselves initiated those violent acts. As mentioned in Chapter 1, such mindless acts take place at a very primordial level, confining them to Stage 1 in Kahneman's prospect theory. Huesmann and Guerra (1997) described such behavior as regulated by normative beliefs that was, in the case of Nazi generals, unconditional obedience to authority. In Germany, loyalty to the Fuhrer and to the nation was considered a cardinal virtue.

On nonviolent cultures: Nonviolence as normative and internalized

Do we have cultures that are nonviolent and foster internalized standards and normative beliefs that restrain violence in any form? That, in spite of being repeatedly provoked and made angry, children in such cultures are taught to remain nonviolent. In his seminal work, Ashley Montagu (1976, 1978) reported that nonviolent societies did indeed exist and with the help of other research collaborators identified those cultures. Later, Bonta (1993, 1997) also identified at least 23 cultures around the world that are nonviolent. Among the nonviolent societies that Bonta (1997) mentioned in his article published in the *Psychological Bulletin*, a few are described below:

1. *The Amish people*: They are mostly located in rural America and Canada. Although changing rapidly from their traditional system, they still maintain their life style, for example, they use horse-drawn carts and resort to the minimal use of technology. They do not resist authority and take pride in their commitment to peaceful living.
2. *The Balinese*: Located in the Indonesian island of Bali, the community is best known for its self-control and suppression of conflict. Although there have been reports of violence, a typical family lays unusual emphasis on peacefulness. The population shares Hindu and other regional beliefs.

3. *Birhor*: A nomadic tribe located in the central part of India, members of this community are known for their love for peace, and crime is exceptionally rare among them. Hindu by religion, they believe in harmonious relationships with the local people.
4. *Chewong*: They live in the mountains of the Malay Peninsula. The most amazing aspect of their culture is the absence of words for quarrelling, aggression or warfare. They have no mythology of violence.
5. *Ladakhis*: They reside in the northern parts of India and in the Himalayan region. Following Buddhism, they adhere to nonviolence very seriously and avoid conflicts.
6. *Hutterites of the central plains in the USA*: While resembling the Amish and the Mennonites in their beliefs, they differ from the Amish in their use of modern technology. Any open conflict is resented among the community members, but modernization is having its impact on their traditional living.
7. *Tristan Islanders*: They are located in the western region of the Republic of South Africa. After prolonged observation, the only incidence of quarreling recorded among them was an occasional abuse of a wife by her husband. Basically, it is a very peaceful community where tensions are avoided or settled very soon through interpersonal cooperation.

BOX 3.2 THE AMISH WAY OF FORGIVINGS

When Charles Robert held several children as hostages at gun point in a school near Lancaster, Pennsylvania, killed many among them and finally shot himself to death on 2 October 2006, the Amish people, unlike others, did not ask for tightened gun laws or increased security. Instead, they looked inward believing that their children had gone to heaven and were resting peacefully. The Amish community called for forgiveness to the killer and went on to raise money for the family of the killer to spread the effect of healing on both sides—to the family of the killer, for whom they raised thousands of dollars, and to their own by pardoning the killer.

Adapted from: Observer Dispatch, 6 October 2006.

Although there is a vast amount of variation with regard to the nonviolent attitudes and behavior shown by the people in the above cultures, they nevertheless, tend to follow cultural practices that ingrain and promote nonviolence among their children. Some of their practices may sound unique or funny to us, but they are designed to keep nonviolence salient in their culture. Here are some of the ways they adapt to ingratiate, nurture and elaborate their focus on nonviolence:

1. The child-rearing practices in nonviolent societies are distinct and the socialization of a child in nonviolent ways begins fairly early in life. The child in some cultures, for example Paliyan in the southern part of India and Semai in Malaysia, is the center of attention until around two years of age. The infant's needs are readily attended to with overwhelming attention and love, but all of a sudden, between two and three years, the child is made to feel that he or she is no longer special. Rather, children are taught to love and respect others instead of dominating over them. The message is clear to them that without the support and goodwill of others, they have no place in society. Surprisingly, children learn fast and adapt themselves to the normative practices of the culture.
2. Play is very important in understanding social rules. Paliyan parents teach their children to play quietly without fighting. Similarly, children belonging to Kadar in India, !Kung in Namibia and Botswana, and Chewwong in the Malay Peninsula play games without competition and aggression and for sheer pleasure leading to their enjoyment. Research in psychology has clearly shown that competitive games increase the likelihood of aggression among children. Peace-loving cultures tend to inhibit such competitive sport.
3. Parents teach values that inhibit misbehavior. Children are clearly taught not to be assertive and aggressive but to be sensitive to the needs of others. The Ifaluk of Micronesia instruct their children that a ghost will trouble them if they misbehaved. The Inuit of the central Canadian Arctic also teach their children to inhibit their aggression.
4. Individual achievement is often discouraged in such nonviolent cultures. Highly ambitious individuals are left alone, as they are perceived to threaten the stability of the community. The Tahitians, Amish, Mennonites and Inuit are modest about personal achievements.
5. Competition is discouraged among the Buids, Piaroas and Ifaluks because they believe that competition brings violence. If a child is praised a lot for his achievement, it is considered an embarrassment among the Hutterites. Such cultures internalize opposition to violence and do not permit any violence during play.
6. There is an extraordinary emphasis on cooperation and interdependence. Children tease each other when they act selfish and genuinely believe that a cooperative mind will not easily become violent.

What kind of schema and scripts children of such nonviolent cultures would generate as compared to the Joes and Janes of our modern culture who are exposed to exceptionally heavy doses of violence on television—8000 murders and 100,000 other episodes of violence by the end of elementary grade (DeAngelis, 1993)? Needless to say, this level of exposure to violence is being offered at an alarming proportion, as compared to nonviolence. This scenario is certainly not conducive for fostering nonviolence.

Research studies conducted by Denton (1968), Robarchek (1979), Bonta (1997) and others show that unlike the western view of dichotomized cooperation versus competition, the nonviolent societies conceive cooperation and competition unitarily but regard aggression as an antithesis of cooperation. Robarchek (1979) administered a self-concept test to the members of the Semai that required sentence completion. Most of them responded that, for solving problems, they would work with others instead of trying to solve them alone. In addition, good and bad did not mean the same to them as it does to us. Whereas good means interdependence and nurturance, bad refers to destroying group cohesiveness, aggression and anger. In other words, if the group norms have been internalized to the extent that aggression is conceived as being opposite to cooperation, such cognitive representation will inhibit any or all the tendencies that maintain and sustain aggression. Going back to Berkowitz's statement that "nonaggressive ideals aren't always fully in mind", it is noted here that when they do, they attenuate those priming effects as well as activate aggressive thoughts. Conversely, what would happen with a weaker cognitive representation of nonviolence? In the words of Berkowitz (1993):

> We are not always thinking about the values we hold and the codes of conduct we try to follow, and thus they aren't necessarily operative on a given occasion. On a Sunday a churchgoer can truly believe that we ought to "turn our cheeks" to the blows delivered by our enemies, and yet, the next day, caught up in the very different world of business, he might want revenge for the unfair treatment he believes he received at the hands of a competitor. (pp. 112–113)

There is more to Berkowitz's major contention, as stated above, regarding nonviolence. Social psychologists have long been concerned with the issues of social behavior as a product of forces outside, as well as inside, the individual. Since cognition mediates between the biological forces and adaptation to the external forces, it is important to understand how violence and nonviolence are represented in our cognition. In Chapter 1, we mentioned that understanding and explaining an act of violence and nonviolence was not a problem for the subjects (Kool, 1993). War, as an example of an act of violence, is a categorized form of behavior with somewhat clear normative identification (Table 3.1). And so is an act of nonviolence, for example, a sit-in. Violent and nonviolent acts are not very categorical and they are inferred in the context of one's personal orientation. Because violence is salient and threatens our survival, aggressive acts are readily recalled and identified, but this does not seem to hold true for the nonviolent acts. The representation and retrieval of nonviolence in our

Table 3.1 Acts of violence and nonviolence versus a violent act and a nonviolent act

Act of violence: War	*Act of nonviolence*: Sit-in
Violent act: Kicking a chair	*Nonviolence act*: Caring for animals

Source: Kool (1993).

cognition may have superior normative value but they definitely seem to have weaker availability and retrieval than violence (for more details, see Kool, 1993).

Did you ever notice the difference between the following two expressions:

You are a colored person.
You are a person of color.

The semantic values of the two statements differ, being negative for the former and positive for the latter. This difference was not there some centuries ago, but as we became more sophisticated, we learned the subtle nature of expressions that became desirable (or not at all) in a psycho-historical context. Calling eta in Japan, a nigger in the USA or a Sudra (untouchable) in India is now considered offensive and demeaning. As I mentioned in the opening paragraph of this chapter, our enormous capacity to generate symbols is a gift of nature, but the same gift will become a curse if the aggressive symbols bear the capacity to outweigh nonviolence, a point William James (1910, 1995) made in his famous essay, *The moral equivalent of war.*

In another experiment, Kool, Diaz, Brown, and Hama (2002) asked their American and Japanese subjects to evaluate a number of people, objects and events, for example, Hitler and Gandhi in terms of whether they are being active or passive. The results showed that, while the Japanese rated nonviolent concepts conspicuously high, their American counterparts did not differ any significantly on the evaluation of both violent and nonviolent concepts (Figure 3.1).

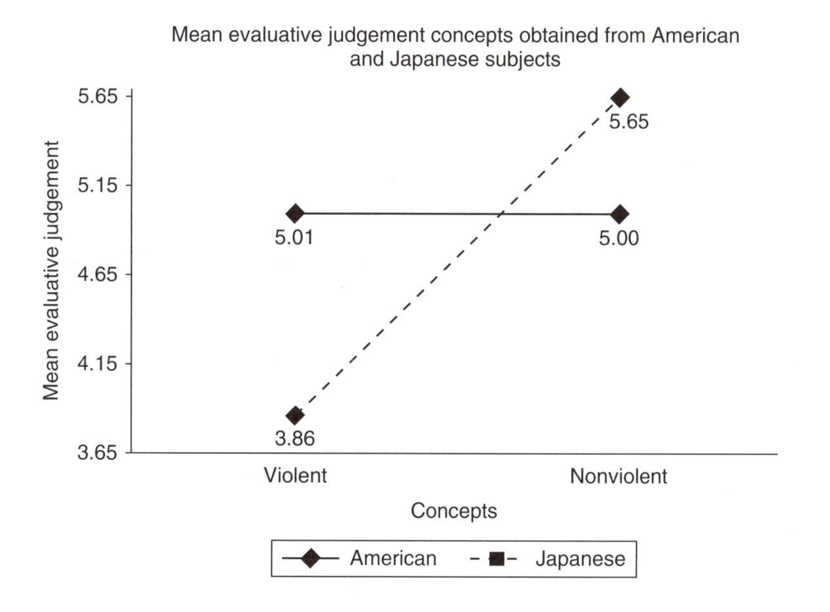

Figure 3.1 Evaluation of violence and nonviolence

The orientation of a culture, that is, individualistic or collective, has its impact on the self-concept of its members. In individualistic cultures like the USA and Great Britain, the socialization of members takes place with an emphasis on maximizing their personal goals through competition and self-enhancement. On the contrary, in collectivist cultures, like the East Asian cultures of Japan, China and India, group goals and obedience are more important than personal accomplishments. Both cultures have a basic difference in terms of how members relate with each other—collectivists being more interdependent and individualists more independent.

The schemas of members of individualistic and collectivist cultures develop differently. Kitayama, Markus, Matsumoto, and Noraskkunkit (1997) observed that the same sport in these two cultures might generate an entirely different conception. In contrast to the Japanese who take volleyball very seriously at the court, Americans find it a relaxing and enjoyable activity. Miller (1984) compared the American and Asian Indian children to find out the causes they attribute for their success and failures. Whereas Americans made more attributions related to their personal dispositions, the Indians made more situational attributions. Also, as compared to the American students who rate themselves more different than others, the Asian Indian students report themselves as being more similar to others.

Social identity theory (SIT): Tracking the social side of the cognition of nonviolence

Although William James was considered a functionalist who emphasized the adaptive features relevant for understanding human behavior, he was also very eclectic. The psychology that grew after James in the USA emphasized reductionism, mainly because of behaviorism led by Watson and Skinner. Away from the above-stated information-processing approaches in social cognition that focused primarily on an individual's cognitive processes, another major development in social psychology focused more on the group or social phenomenon as represented in cognition. This view is known as the Social Identity Theory (SIT) that emphasizes development of social identity as a result of self-categorization, that is, awareness of one's membership in a group. In a clever experiment, Tajfel, Billig, Bundy, and Flament (1971) showed a series of dotted slides to high school students in Bristol, England. In the second phase of the experiment, these students were divided into two groups supposedly based on their overestimated or underestimated scores or even a trivial criterion such as the flipping of a coin. Tajfel's argument was that these were "minimal groups" with no prior history of competition, rivalry or antagonism. And yet, given the opportunity, these subjects tended to favor the members of their own group by allocating more resources to them. Thus, any arbitrary categorization based on identification of in-group or out-group has an accentuating effect and fosters intergroup differences.

Tajfel's work is germane to understanding social behavior. By allocating more resources to the unknown members of the group, what is it that an individual is trying to accomplish? According to SIT, in doing so an individual seeks his membership in the group and achieves distinctiveness by opposing the other group. For example, Arndt, Greenberg, Schimel, Pyszczynski, and Soloman (2002) noted that one's need for affiliation with his/her own group increases during his/her heightened thoughts of mortality. Under such conditions, Christian targets were rated superior by Christian participants, while the ratings awarded to the Jewish participants were substantially inferior. These results were interpreted as supporting the Terror Management Theory (Pyszcznski, Greenberg, & Solomon, 2002) that shows how anxiety affects behavior and leads to changes in judgment.

In their classic work on the authoritarian personality, Adorno, Frenkel-Brunswik, Levenson, and Sanford (1950) showed how authoritarians show their prejudice toward women, minorities, homosexuals and others and that many authoritarian tendencies were related to aggression. Prejudice consists of negative evaluations of others and is likely to contribute to the negative affect. If you remember the disparaging comments that were made against the Muslim community immediately after September 11, 2001 (known as 9/11), such a negative response was fuelled by the "out-group" hostilities led by a select group of terrorists but not by the majority of peace loving Muslims. In their recent popular work on terrorism, Pyszczynski et al. (2002) employed the SIT to explain the hostile behavior of Americans after 9/11. In short, the SIT explains how self-pride is enhanced by seeking and maintaining one's membership in a group and how one's self-esteem is boosted through in-group favors.

In an article published in *Peace and Conflict: Journal Peace Psychology*, Suleiman (2002) examined the implications of SIT in the context of the Israeli and Palestinian conflict. For this purpose, he analyzed the identity patterns of Palestinians living in Israel and noted that the self-categorization of these Palestinians is divided into their civic identity as residents of Israel on the one hand, and their Palestinian ethnic values on the other hand, that make them appear anti-Israel. By adhering to Israel's norms, these Palestinians tend to elevate their status and self-esteem, but also feel marginalized when they do not get their adequate share of power and acceptance in the community. In addition, their ethnic identity is diluted as they stretch themselves away from the normative standards of their own group. Thus, while confronting this "double marginality", they face problems in categorizing themselves—whether they belong to Israel in the true sense or not. In short, SIT helps us to understand not only our categorizing of others but also of ourselves, and ultimately explains how individuals become groups.

In collectivist cultures, the in-group bias, as stated above, is not encouraged. Rather, they tend to make disparaging remarks to minimize their biases toward out-groups. However, Capozza, Voci, and Licciardallo (2000) did not fully support this contention and argued that collectivists too manifest such out-group bias, albeit some differences exist between the two cultures. Generally speaking, in collectivist cultures, such as some of those described earlier in the chapter, there is an emphasis on cooperation and tolerance and the group discourages any negative expression of anger, hostility or aggression. Self-criticism is considered a cardinal virtue that is more important than degrading others.

The SIT has implications for understanding the cognition of nonviolence. How do individuals categorize themselves as nonviolent? According to Schwebel (2001) and McLernon and Cairns (2001), children get plenty of opportunities to learn about violence, but peace remains undefined for them. What they know best is absence of violence (negative peace) but not much about positive peace (peace-building), that is, promoting harmonious relations.

Not much research has been conducted to study children's conception of nonviolence. Peter Verbeek and Frans de Waal (2001) studied the behavior of preschool children in the natural field setting during preconflict, conflict and postconflict settings. They focused on the conciliatory behavior among children preceded by their aggression. Here is an example:

> YL pushed YF from the tire swing. While YF attempted to flee from the scene YL kicked her. YL then immediately apologized to YF, hugged her, and invited her to come back to the tire swing. The two girls resumed peaceful play, taking turns in pushing each other on the swing. (ibid., pp. 14–15)

A significant finding of their study was that preserving a harmonious relationship was considered important among friends, and reconciliation took place mostly within five minutes. In other words, young children have a sense of positive peace, that is an active process of peacemaking and they realize that while being a member of a group (in-group) they need to minimize aggression, decrease tensions and promote harmonious relations. In contrast, among non-friends, peacekeeping was considered adequate and no special need for peacemaking was expressed. de Waal (1996) and Roosmalen (de Waal & Roosmalen, 1979) have been studying the behavior of primates for a long time and noted that postconflict reconciliation is common among many chimpanzees and other ape species. It promotes survival of the group. Peacemaking therefore, has significance from the evolutionary point of view and seems to be an old form of behavior.

Let's recapitulate the material presented so far in this chapter. Human cognition can be understood in terms of processing of information in the brain, for which purpose a computer analogy-based information-processing approach to cognition was presented. Such a view assumes that our capacity to receive input, its storage and retrieval are needed to view the nature of cognition. Research studies show that availability of aggressive or nonaggressive cues, the nature of priming and scripts help us in the understanding of our cognition. On the other hand, the SIT explains the social aspect of our cognition. Mere information regarding our affiliation with a group, even in the absence of any reward, leads to unusual responses, for example, in-group bias. Citing some evidence from animal studies and research on preschool children, it is argued here that keeping membership in a group and enhancing harmonious relationships with the members in it are natural processes that orient us toward resolution of conflicts. This latter approach, if pursued from the social psychological point of view involving the role of culture, interpersonal situation and social context, will be referred to as "Social psychology of cognition of nonviolence", whereas

Table 3.2 Nonviolence and cognition

Cognition of social psychology of nonviolence	Social psychology of cognition of nonviolence
Approach	
Concepts developed for nonsocial objects tested for social objects	How people assign meaning to events: Other people are taken into account
Sample of content	
Script of nonviolence	Context
Priming	Culture
Automatic processing	Influence of interpersonal situation
Level	
Thinness—micro	*Thickness—macro*
Nonviolent behavior	

the former will be known as, "Cognition of social psychology of nonviolence". Together, they represent the thickness and the thinness of human cognition, respectively, one dealing with the "outside" influence on cognitive processes and the other describing the microlevel processing that characterizes human cognition (Table 3.2).

In a slightly different way, I had approached this subject elsewhere (Kool, 1993, 1994). At the macro level, studies on the psychology of nonviolence will benefit from the findings in the social sciences such as sociology, political science and anthropology. On the other hand, concentrating on the individual, the microlevel studies should focus on how our understanding of nonviolence takes place, what we retain and execute, and the ways in which biological mechanisms play their role.

Attributions and nonviolence

Heider (1958) believed that all human beings are intuitive scientists, for they tend to seek causal relationships between events. We engage in attribution quite often, surmising why events are happening the way they are happening. All this can happen without knowing the facts, for example, blaming the instructor for the poor grades, a blonde getting a very prestigious job, a referee's decision in judging a player out, and so on.

Table 3.3 Examples of internal and external attributions in nonviolence

Internal	External
We did not adhere to nonviolence	The police firing caused our violence
We lack will power	We did not get public support
I let the nonviolent movement fail	They were more organized than us

Such attributions have internal or external sources, as stated above. An internal attribution involves seeking the cause in oneself, whereas an external attribution places the reason on the situation.

Do nonviolent individuals attribute differently than their violent counterparts? Do we rationalize violence and nonviolence differently, irrespective of our preference for violence or nonviolence? Several empirical studies conclude that indeed there is a significant difference in the attribution styles of nonviolent and violent individuals. In an elaborate study, Baumgardner (1990) contended that nonviolent individuals tend to blame wrongdoers to a lesser extent because by taking self-blame and suffering they can transform evil into good. He used the NVT (Kool & Sen, 1984) to classify high- and low-scoring nonviolent subjects and hypothesized that the cause, responsibility and blame among violent and nonviolent individuals would differ with respect to their judgments on rape victims. He tested both groups on the rape scenarios and attribution measures and analyzed their overall judgments for the rapist and the victim. Summing his findings, Baumgardner stated that his nonviolent subjects assigned more responsibility and blame to their victims than their violent counterparts. He concluded, "Present results add to the construct validity of the Nonviolence Test by showing differences in attribution judgments between violent and nonviolent persons, as defined by the test. Such differences increase the meaningfulness and salience of a violence/nonviolence dimension in people's judgments or violent acts" (pp. 61–63).

Using the NVT, Hammock and Hanson (1990) also examined the role of attribution of intentionality and dogmatism (close-mindedness). They began with the premise that the response of an individual, violent or nonviolent, would be influenced by the attribution of the intent of the actor. Their high- and low-scoring subjects on the NVT clearly showed that with the increasing malicious nature of intentions, there was an insignificant endorsement of nonviolent alternatives to conflict. Using a Dogmatism Scale based on Rokeach's work, they also noted that with the increase in scores on dogmatism, the preference for nonviolent solutions declined significantly.

In his research based on a projective test, the TAT, Asthana (1990) compared the responses of his violent and nonviolent subjects based on the NVT scores. Commenting upon the attribution mechanism of his nonviolent subjects, he concluded, "The attribution of blame is mainly on oneself. The fault is perceived to lie in one's own imperfection. There is a readiness to own responsibility, unless otherwise indicated" (p. 51). Asthana noted further that the need for aggression was low in his nonviolent subjects, but other needs like nurturance, succourance and affiliation were significantly higher among them as compared to their violent counterparts.

Sanderson and Darley (2002) contended that we tend to think of ourselves as genuinely moral while others are moral because of external pressures. Thus, the "I am moral but you are deterred" expression embodies the difference in the attributions made by the violent and the nonviolent individuals. In other words, we make a fundamental attribution error by overestimating the role of personal dispositions (for example, personality characteristics) in explaining the behavior of others, but for our own behavior, we tend to blame the situation (external factors). During the normal peace period, we seek causes in the situation, but when it is disturbed, we begin to blame people who contributed to its failure. Mayton (2001) argued that when violence is counteracted with nonviolence, it is considered as an unusual response and hence it becomes questionable to begin negotiation. However, in such a scenario, the effect of the fundamental attribution error is reduced because by not retaliating, the nonviolent actor offers a peaceful solution to the problem. He/she then appears genuinely interested in resolving the conflict.

Researches in social cognition have identified a number of concepts regarding the functioning of our self. We present, monitor, regulate and enhance our self and adapt to changing situations. When coping with imagined or real problems, we sometimes show dysfunctional attitudes and behavior. The self-handicapping strategy, a pattern of behavior designed to sabotage one's own achievements, is an example of the dysfunctional mode. The problem with such concepts in social psychology, according to Sheldon and King (2001), is that they represent the traditional bias of psychology that focuses on pathology rather than on positive resources such as resilience, optimism and positive emotions. Second, there is a dearth of empirical studies that show how attitudes and behavior related to nonviolence are monitored, regulated and enhanced. In short, we know little about the forces that restrain violence.

Self-control: The brakes of nonviolence

Provocation, anger, jealousy, envy and other factors contribute to aggressive impulses but we have an amazing capacity to deal with them and keep our aggression in control. Imagine what would happen if our brakes to control aggression fail? Thanks to our capacity to regulate behavior, aggressive behavior is displayed only occasionally. Self-control (also called self-regulation) is necessary for curbing aggression. However, it is not easy to display self-control because it requires hard work and patience to seek alternatives to violence.

An important function of self-control is that it alters the expression of our action for meeting our goal. Mayer (2005) reported that self-control is related to an individual's success and crucial for occupational and marital adjustment. When exerting self-control, people have an option: to change the situation or change themselves. In the case of marital disharmony, one may either change personally or seek divorce. Depending on what one does, the consequence in the form of action by the individual reflects one's personality.

Self-control is a central issue in understanding aggression and nonviolence. According to Baumeister (1999), "Violence starts when self-control fails" (p. 263). The NVT (Kool & Sen, 1984, 2005), reported in Chapter 1, has several items that measure self-control (Table 3.4).

Factor analysis of the NVT data yielded the emergence of a very strong component of self-control (Kool & Keyes, 1990), that is the individual's capacity to keep internal restraints against aggression. If you take away the inhibitions for aggression, there would be plenty of fighting all over the world. Once we are

Table 3.4 Three items from the NVT showing self-control

1. When a stranger hurts me, I believe
   a. forgive and forget is the best policy
   b. a tooth for a tooth, an eye for an eye is the best policy
2. When a person makes fun of me, I
   a. try to convince the person that it is not always good to make fun of others
   b. retaliate
3. When I am in a bad mood, I
   a. feel like smashing things
   b. relax and tell myself things will get better

placed in a conflict situation—to aggress or not—we orient ourselves to regulate our behavior through internal standards (Bandura, 1997) and normative beliefs (Huesmann & Guerra, 1997).

In their book, *A General Theory of Crime*, Gottfredson and Hirschi (1990) stated that most crimes in the world are the result of low self-control, that is, a lack of inner discipline, available opportunity and impulsivity. The two scholars' backgrounds being in the field of criminology, it is surprising to note that such a handy concept available in the backyard of psychology was discovered not by psychologists but by criminologists. In developing their theory, they contended that some people have chronic problems in self-control. Based on the analysis of impulsive, unplanned and unskilled nature of crime, they also exposed the myth regarding criminals specializing in only one type of crime. Criminals with poor self-control, reported Gottfredson and Hirschi, do not specialize in one or a few crimes as popularly believed, but indulge in multiple types of crime owing to their lack of self-control in a situation and lack of respect for the law.

If self-control serves as brakes for violence, how long would such brakes last? Roy Baumeister (1999) and coworker (Mauraven & Baumeister, 2000) believe that like financial expenditure, mental resources too have their limits. The prolonged use of self-control can deplete the limits of tolerance. It's like using a muscle while exercising: the more you use it the more you feel fatigued. In a clever experiment, Vohs and Heatherton (2000) placed very tasty snacks near dieter and non-dieter subjects under high temptation and low temptation conditions. As expected, the dieters under high temptation conditions had to employ their self-control the hardest. Further research by them showed that the self-control did not last long and the dieters gave up quickly to their strong craving.

Mauraven and Baumeister's (2000) further work on self-control is particularly noteworthy. It was designed to study how self-control diminished while the subjects were instructed to hold a handgrip and keep it squeezed. After the subjects had seen a film on sick and dying animals ("Mondo Cane"), the behavior of the subjects was studied under three conditions: Amplification (express emotions), Suppression (inhibit any expression) and Control (no instructions). The dependent variable in the study was the length of time the subjects squeezed the handgrip. The results of this study confirmed the hypothesis that under

Table 3.5 Loss of self-control

	Time: Handgrip persistence	
	Before movie	**After movie**
Amplification	High	Low
Suppression	High	Low
Control	Medium	Medium

Source: Mauraven and Baumeister (2000).

Amplification and Suppression conditions the subjects would lose their willpower to hold the handgrip, but no such effect would be significantly noted in the control condition (Table 3.5).

In another clever experiment, Baumeister, Bratskvsky, Mauraven, and Tice (1998) tested the willpower of their subjects in what was apparently a taste perception study. All participating subjects did not eat for at least three hours and were divided under radish- or chocolate-eating conditions. Both groups were given difficult puzzles after they had eaten radish or chocolate chips. Subjects who ate radish only but not the chocolate chips lying in the vicinity gave up earlier on the difficult puzzles than those who ate the tasty food. The researchers concluded that resisting willpower to eat tasty food depleted the energy level of the subjects and it was expected that they would quit the experiment early.

Self-control can be more complex than we normally think, for the more we apply and think about it, the more we may also worry about its failure. Try *not* to think about something, but ironically, it keeps popping up in our mind. It's like a double-edged sword—whichever side you fall, you are likely to get hurt. By applying self-control, we think that we will conserve our energy, but it is not necessarily so in all cases. In a very interesting experiment, when Daniel Wegner (1994) asked his subjects not to think of a white bear for the next 30 seconds, they reported that the image of the bear kept on intruding very frequently. Further, the image of the bear would appear even more frequently if we try to suppress the image strongly. The implications of suppressing thoughts are vital for mental health problems such as depression and post-traumatic disorders (Purdon, 1999). When we control our aggression, we are also constantly reminded of our limits of being perceived as helpless or as a coward or simply wait for the time when we aggress to teach the wrongdoer a lesson.

We believe that self-control is like a moratorium, a temporary suspension of aggression. How temporary is this suspension? It all depends on our inner resources for restraint and the situation that places demands on our behavior. While self-control is considered a desirable quality in church where we receive sermons, nonaggressive thoughts may not be in our mind outside the church (Berkowitz, 1993). Precisely, because of this reason, William James (1910/1995) was concerned about the moral equivalent to war, a situation that serves as a constant reminder of how vulnerable we are in detracting from the path of peace. Not everyone among us is a saint capable of imagining the whole society as an extended church.

Fortunately, there is a plethora of empirical research in social psychology that points out to the conditions under which self-control is weakened or lost. First, when we are focused on things we are doing, it may get involved in private self-consciousness, that is, a tendency to focus on our own inner thoughts and feelings, or public self-consciousness, that is, to focus on our public image. People with high private self-consciousness choose self-descriptive statements and fill incomplete sentences with first-person pronouns. According to Zimbardo (1970, 2004), loss of private self-consciousness leads to deindividuation, a state in which internal restraints break down and uninhibited behavior occurs. When subjects were kept under a condition of anonymity (head covered by a brown bag), they delivered higher levels of shocks than when their identity was known. Soldiers in their uniform and crowds in a sport event tend to become unusually aggressive because they have little chance of being identified. Among other reasons for the loss of self-control are our inability to employ clear-cut and consistent internal standards (Baumeister & Heatherton, 1996), use of chemical substances (Browning, 1992), failure to delay gratification (Shoda, Mischel, & Peake, 1990) and situation or opportunity (Gottfredson & Hirschi, 1990). Commenting on the role of self-control in curbing violence, Baumeister (1999) wrote:

> The immediate, proximal cause of violence is the collapse of these inner restraining forces. This point is crucial, because it means that many of our efforts to understand violence are looking at the question the wrong way. To produce violence, it is not necessary to promote it actively. All that is necessary is to stop restraining or preventing it. Once the restraints are removed, there are plenty of reasons for people to strike at each other. (p. 263)

Moral dimension of nonviolence

The "genes" of the psychology of nonviolence, wrote Kool (1993), are formed by moral components and the operation of these genes is controlled by intentions. The significant role of intentions in the moral responsiveness of individuals is important in understanding the structure of human cognition. This section on the moral dimension is reproduced here, with some additions/modifications, based on the author's earlier article written elsewhere (ibid.).

Prevention of violence often calls for moral concerns that may be due to social concerns or self-worth or a combination of both. It grows out of interaction with the members of a society. Although psychologists have reported the stages of moral development of the individual, recent developments in moral psychology show that both personality psychologists and social psychologists need to integrate their efforts. An individual may have several virtues but they may not be useful for social purposes. Refusing to participate in a war may be considered a personal virtue, but what if it brings defeat, death and humiliation to the members of the group?

The psychology of nonviolence is essentially based on the components of moral representation in our cognition. The moral concerns of individuals are mediated by a complex set of psychological dispositions. It is not easy to find an ethic guided by a single principle that integrates both the social and individual good. And yet we tend to look at the common components of a moral individual in the form of maturity in resolving conflicts within and without the framework of social norms, something of a personal ethic over and above the commonly accepted modes of behavior in many situations (Flanagan, 1991). At this point, moral psychology as an area of empirical research becomes an uphill task for a psychologist who may discover that moral judgments, moral behavior and moral feelings may not necessarily lead to the same conclusions. We believe that honesty is the best policy and yet we continue to cheat in our tax returns.

Moral judgment and behavior are supposed to be governed by moral rules that are based on moral reasoning. At least this is the stand most psychologists have taken to form an empirical base of their research. For example, beginning with the studies by Piaget (1932), psychologists have argued that a pattern of rules develops in the moral reasoning of all children and that these rules become more harmonious, autonomous and independent with change in age and social interaction.

At least five major trends in the growth of moral psychology may help us in the understanding of behavior and judgments of nonviolent individuals. These have been mentioned below.

Piaget's contribution

Piaget (1932) focused on the roles children follow in their interaction with other people and his studies led him to conclude that, as compared to the first stage of moral development in which rules are considered as unchanging properties of the world, the second stage shows awareness of children in judging an actor's intentions. As described earlier, intention is a key element in judging aggressive behavior because even young children use a wide variety of cues to judge the intention of an aggressor. Nelson (1980) reported that kindergarten children used the facial expressions of the transgressors to judge the intentions involved in a harmful act. When a mother is dusting a doll, a three-year-old child may misunderstand her mother's behavior as punishment to the doll for not being clean. The child is likely to say, "Mom, don't beat her. She can't take a bath." Every child, then, becomes a nonviolent individual as soon as s/he develops awareness of intentions and rules involved in an act.

Piaget made two major contributions to the field of moral psychology. First, development of rules helps a child make a conceptual adjustment to the environment. His observation of children's behavior led him to postulate that children have a system of mental structures that evolve in a series of developmental stages. Second, he provided an empirical, albeit nonexperimental, base for the study of intentions that had no place in the rigorous behaviorist psychology. Although

Piaget's theory faded in the 1960s and 1970s owing to its failure to identify the age levels involved in the judgment of intentionality, it has returned to show us once again that rules are the essence of morality and to emphasize that the moral interpretation of events in a child's mind is "bathed in rules."

Kohlberg's stages of moral development

The second major impact for the understanding of moral judgments and behavior was offered by Kohlberg (1976) who believed that a moral person is one who reasons with, and acts on the basis of, principles of justice and fairness. Using imaginary cases like the Heinz dilemma in which Heinz's wife is dying but the pharmacist would not lower the cost of a drug, Kohlberg cited moral development at three levels, preconventional, conventional, and postconventional, explaining how each one of the two stages at a level is characterized by a shift from external to internal control of behavior. Although the stage 6 at level III represents the highest growth of moral development, it has remained an elusive, ideal stage in Kohlberg's system because no case has been found in this category. The stage 5 at level III characterizes the next highest level of moral development in which fewer than 10 percent of the individuals entered only after about 20 years of age (Colby et al., 1983). I wonder at this point what would be the nature of aggression of individuals who belong to this category.

There are two examples for moral reasoning at each stage in the Kolhbergian system: one that supports Heinz's theft of the drug and the other that he should not do it at all. I believe that subjects who adhere to nonviolence in its principled form and reach the Stage 5 are not likely to use violence to steal the drug. On the other hand, those who will endorse stealing the drug and are at the Stage 5 may use aggression directed either at the pharmacist in a controlled form or upon themselves in the form of a hunger strike or other self-punishment methods. In any case, no one in the Stage 5 is expected to endorse heightened aggression because it may save Heinz's wife but may cost the life of the pharmacist.

It is reasonable to argue here that there is no such thing as an overall moral personality, because all individuals, highly moral or ordinary, do not have similar experiences or socio-moral environments. Parents tell us not to steal but they do not normally teach us what to do in a Heinz type of situation, that is, how to get medicine for a sick wife at a time when one can't pay for it. In short, confronting individuals with moral problems may not be the only diagnostic test of moral personality because adhering to a single set of virtues is not the only way to describe a moral person. The relationship of nonviolence and morality, then, becomes a matter of one's cultural learning and a compromise between one's personal ideal and his/her social ideal. At an advanced stage of moral development, people often think that what is right for them may not be right for the community. Many pacifists during World War II debated if any war could be called a "just war" and reluctantly participated in it. They were, I am sure, in the Stage 5 of Kohlberg's analysis and believed that Hitler's genocide was impossible to stop without war, although personally they remained opposed to war.

Like Piaget, Kohlberg believed that a child does not passively learn moral rules but tends to restructure them in terms of his/her experiences. However, he differed from Piaget in the sense that an individual's moral development is not a matter of two stages but rather it is a long, continued and complex process that expresses itself in several stages. Describing moral development is like teaching rules of grammar. After learning the rules of a language, an individual can construct simple sentences. However, one will comprehend the deeper levels of the language only when one can express the same idea in different sentences. I believe that the interaction of moral judgments and nonviolence refers to a similar type of deep structure to embody alternatives to violence (Table 3.6).

Flanagan (1991) argued that the presence of only six categories in Kohlberg's theory does not provide enough space for explaining moral development. Patterns of moral reasoning and the behavior of Gandhi, King, Muste, Tutu and several others during the 20th century alone will need a variety of moral categories in order to mirror the relationship between nonviolence and moral development. Ruth Linn (2001), of Haifa University, Israel, is very critical of Kohlberg's contribution because there has been a major focus on moral competence in the stages of development but there is no examination of the moral position of the individual. It amounts to "I see an evil and I do not see an evil"—a bystander who simply watches the wrongdoing, but fails to act. Kohlberg did not address this issue in his formulation of the stages of moral development. In other words, Kohlberg's focus on moral competence failed to account for activism that constitutes a highly significant component of nonviolence. Soldiers learn obedience and discipline and remain patriotic. They evaluate war objectives (*jus ad bellum*) and are also taught how to conduct war (*jus in bello*). When Benhardt refused to shoot in My Lai during the Vietnam War, Kohlberg interpreted his behavior as a just response and placed him at the post-conventional stage of morality, but the moral development does not stop here. One step further in moral dimension is an effort to take responsibility to intervene such that others also do not kill unarmed, helpless people. Echoing the same sentiment, Walzer (1988) remarked, what is so good about a moralist who failed to intervene and remained a silent spectator.

Table 3.6 Stages in the moral development: Kohlberg

Preconventional (age 4–10): Moral values basically related to one's own needs
Stage 1: Obedience to avoid punishment
Stage 2: Instrumental purpose and exchange: You hit me, I hit you
Conventional (age 10–13): Observing others/some internalization
Stage 3: Seeking approval: Am I a good boy or girl?
Stage 4: Social system and conscience: Follow social order
Postconventional (age 13+): Decision to follow social order or not
Stage 5: Understanding conflict between social order and change
Stage 6: Development of universal ethics: Doing what is right

Gilligan: caring and justice perspectives

The third major contributor in the relationship between nonviolence and moral judgment and behavior is Carol Gilligan (1982) who, by pointing out the flaws in Kohlberg's analysis, like the lack of female samples, proceeded to show that moral reasoning alone is not enough to understand moral development. Instead of focusing on the justice perspective, she argued for a caring perspective that sees people in terms of their connectedness and concern for others. For her, moral requirements were not merely confined to fairness and justice but emerged from the particular needs of people with whom we connect. She produced empirical data to show that women, more than men, orient to ethics of care that make them function "in a different voice". According to Flanagan (1991), Gilligan created two moral psychologies—one for men and the other for women.

The main argument for offering a hypothesis of two distinct voices is that all children experience inequality and attachment during the course of development. In a neo-Freudian account, Gilligan highlighted the role of powerlessness and inequality at the one end, and attachment, at the other end, a situation that prepared the groundwork for two moral versions of justice and care. As children grow older, they tend to develop a self-concept, which is reinforced by their gender roles. Because in most cases the mother is the caregiver in the family, girls, more intensely than boys, learn to value empathy, connectedness and interpersonal communication.

Gilligan believes that the two ethics—of justice and caring—are competing in nature and tend to divide an individual much like a vase–face illusion. Faced with a moral dilemma, says Gilligan, an individual will oscillate between justice and care orientations. Is there a way to unify the two perspectives? As far as Gilligan is concerned the answer is in the negative. When she started her work by asking the question, "What does morality mean to you?" and found that males and females differed in their orientations, she concluded that a new dimension of psychology in relation to ethics had been discovered (ibid.). Avenues of the relationship between the psychology of nonviolence and morality will show that although Gilligan established a landmark for the psychology of nonviolence by concentrating on the justice and care dichotomy, her focus gradually became unidimensional in an effort to reify the gender differences.

I recall here a factual event dramatized in the movie *Gandhi*. When Gandhi was charged for instigating the people of India to overthrow British rule and was brought into the courtroom, the British judge stood up to show his respect, categorically stated that the charge against Gandhi was beyond consideration in any court in the world, and yet, followed faithfully the rule of law by sending Gandhi to prison for several years. The judge had no doubt experienced the difficulty in focusing on the care and justice perspectives in this case, but in the end showed moral responsiveness in integrating both the justice and care perspectives. However, not everyone thought so (Box 3.3).

BOX 3.3 WAS GANDHI FLATTERED?

In his book, *Meek ain't meek: Nonviolent power and people of color*, Tom Hastings (2002) raised the issue of whether Gandhi felt flattered when the British judge stood up to honor the incoming prisoner, Gandhi himself, into the court. The behavior of the judge was by no means unprecedented and established his moral supremacy. After this episode, did Gandhi's approach soften toward the British rulers? Arun Gandhi (2004), Gandhi's grandson, believed that Gandhi was neither flattered nor could criticism bias him, as he removed the wall between us–them or friend–enemy categories forever—an essential step in educating nonviolence as reported in Chapter 7 of this book.

The psychology of nonviolence need not be built on extraordinary personalities. I recall here another incident to show how ordinary people integrate justice and caring in their lives. One day the clerk in my office lost an expensive gadget, for which the administration ordered him to compensate. It was beyond his means to replace the material or to raise the money. The chairman of the department, who was new to the place, paid all the money from his personal funds but made the clerk pay a very small amount. When I asked the chairman why he did not pay the full amount to take full credit for his philanthropic act, he said in all humility that he wanted the clerk to feel responsible for the negligence. He cared, but justice was served within the means of the clerk! In short, when people experience a dilemma caused by fluctuating care and justice perspectives, they tend to remember their childhood experiences, take clues from their holy and other important books, emulate their role models, and integrate these experiences with their own, to sharpen the level of their moral judgment. Critical studies show that an individual faced with a dilemma tends to integrate the two perspectives (Flanagan, 1991).

Piaget, Kohlberg and Gilligan developed their theories based on the studies of moral judgments of normal, mostly middle-class children. Researches on children participating in war or living in adverse conditions portray a different picture. The Graca Machel study, sponsored by the UN, reported that 300,000 children are being used in the armed conflicts and that they served in 31 armed conflicts that resulted in over two million deaths (Klot, 1998). In Guatemala and Angola, according to Wessels (1998), the entire generation grew in armed conflict. Children affected by war are stuck in the primitive stage of moral development, show aggressiveness, and suffer from emotional numbing and loss of empathy (Boyden, 2003). However, the brighter side of this traumatic effect is that many such children cope with adverse conditions through their resiliency. Among both boys and girls, the moral development of boys suffered more than that of the girls. Such findings call for further examination of the development of moral reasoning and behavior in human beings.

Erikson's work

Using a psychoanalytic model, Erikson (1958, 1969) presented a unique analysis for understanding the behavior of nonviolent individuals. His psychobiographical studies of Gandhi and King, with a focus on the development of identity, constituted the fourth major force in the psychology of nonviolence. So intense did he become in his analysis of one episode (the Ahmedabad, India event) that he could not help writing at the end of his book, *Gandhi's Truth* (1969): "... I sensed an affinity between Gandhi's truth and the insights of modern psychology" (p. 440). For Erikson, identity without affiliation had no meaning. He believed that identity is a "process located in the core of the individual and yet also in the core of his communal culture, a process which establishes, in fact, the identity of those two identities" (p. 266). Those who adhere to nonviolence understand the identity struggle of their own as well as of the members of the community they belong to in a very personal and representative way. Erikson also believed that nonviolence in any form would be successful only when moral considerations are replaced by ethical consideration. "Ethics", wrote Erikson, "is marked by an insightful assent to human values, whereas moralism is blind obedience... ethics is transmitted with informed persuasion... " (p. 251). In short, the psychology of nonviolence will grow with the understanding of how people solve different moral problems in different ways. An ethic of care will be difficult to understand without delving into the diverse conditions of fairness and justice. We cannot teach children justice in one context and caring in a totally different context.

Given the scenario that people learn the components of justice and caring in different ways, it is argued that the saliencies that describe the range of nonviolent behavior can be represented in a 2 × 2 matrix (see Figure 3.2) in the following four combinations:

1. Those who are high on issues of justice as well as caring are likely to consider what is most fair and compassionate in a situation;
2. Those who are high on justice but low on caring are likely to follow rules;
3. Those who are low on justice but high on caring are likely to show supreme compassion; and
4. Those who are low on both justice and caring are likely to be Machiavellian in their style, showing what is "good" must be implemented with or without care.

When issues of justice and caring become equally important at the same time, the two perspectives fluctuate in the mind of a nonviolent individual to give him/her the experience of "spiritual" schizophrenia. In this state he/she shows awareness of a problem, evaluates the consequences of a decision, and finally, chooses a path that is best in a given situation.

I do not claim that the above dichotomies related to justice and caring will encompass all that is salient in nonviolent personalities. However, there does seem to be an inherent claim in this approach to begin with an empirical base for

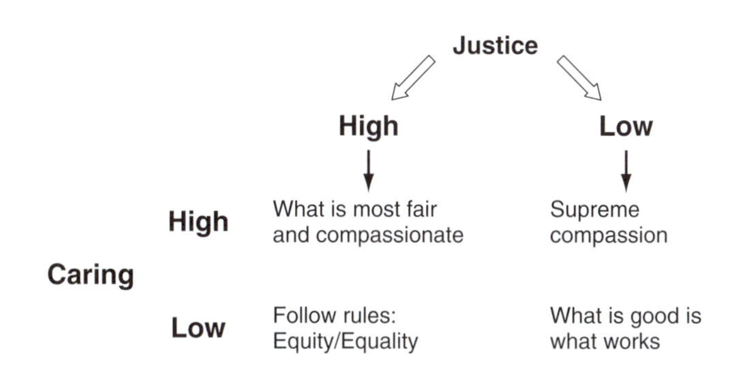

Figure 3.2 Justice and caring perspectives

the psychology of nonviolence by integrating the frontiers of moral and ethical sides of human judgment, feelings and behavior in searching the alternatives to violence. For a practical psychologist like Gandhi, nonviolence was experiment with truth and if the same truth was not tested again and again, it lost the virtue of being a truth. For a modern empirical psychologist, this truth consists of exploring what makes justice and caring considerations integrate so as to avoid violence, how an individual processes rules to understand fairness, and what happens to one's cognitions when one seeks better methods to resolve conflicts. To the extent that the above-mentioned four typologies help in understanding the broad nature of the psychology of nonviolence, it seems to be a reasonable head start (Figure 3.2).

Rest: The Defining Issues Test

The fifth significant support in the growth of the psychology of nonviolence may be found in the work of James Rest (1979) who was more concerned with the methodological issues than on refining the conceptual framework. Borrowing from the work of Piaget and Kohlberg, he constructed a test, The Defining Issues Test (DIT), in which subjects are given several moral dilemmas and asked what an actor should do in a given situation. Unlike Piaget and Kohlberg, he was not concerned with states of moral development but believed that individuals could operate at several stages at a time. For instance, he found that, with increasing age and education, people more often preferred higher concepts of justice, but these same people might use lower concepts of justice on several dilemmas. A very useful development in the DIT has been the creation of a "Utilizer" (U) dimension that is computed on the basis of correspondence between action choices of subjects and their concepts of justice. Whereas issues of justice constitute the principled (P) dimension of DIT, the U dimension is a moderator variable that gave insights into how subjects put their moral judgments into action (Kool & Keyes, 1990).

The P and U scores of 57 subjects were correlated with the NVT in a study by Kool and Keyes (1990). As expected, the correlations (0.20 for P; 0.20

for U) were positive but insignificant. Even the correlation between P and U dimensions was not high (0.33). It should be noted here that nonviolence is a wider concept than one's knowledge of issues of justice as measured by the DIT. Because people with nonviolent orientations weigh humanitarian concerns such as compassion, forgiveness, and anti-punitiveness in addition to issues of justice, they may ignore their concern for justice in favor of humanitarian concerns. Similarly, P and I dimensions may not show a strong relationship if the subjects show a wide gap between knowledge of issues of justice and its usefulness. In other words, "knowledge of moral issues and use of moral concepts may have related but different bases, but an individual may be guided by various social, religious and humanitarian considerations when deciding what is the most appropriate thing to do in a situation" (ibid., p. 31).

By and large, the above section was reported in my earlier work (Kool, 1993). I will now focus briefly on a few more recent and significant developments in social psychology that have enriched the psychology of nonviolence, especially in the context of work on the moral dimension.

Self-efficacy and moral disengagement

Bandura is popularly known for his seminal work on observational learning and for emphasizing the limits of reinforcement in learning. However, his work on self-efficacy (Bandura, 1997) has an important bearing on the psychology of nonviolence. Self-efficacy is an individual's perceived ability to cope with the demands of a situation. Thus, believing in nonviolence, the nonviolent activist knows what he/she should do to seek justice. Knowledge of one's potential, learning to allocate resources and determination to persist make an individual self-efficacious. Employing the NVT, we measured the correlation between the NVT and self-efficacy scores of our subjects and found that there is indeed a positive significant correlation between nonviolence and self-efficacy (Kool & Keyes, 1990).

Another significant contribution of Bandura is related to his concept of moral disengagement. It refers to a set of aggressive responses to inter-group conflict in which people excuse violence by dehumanizing victims and providing moral justifications for the suffering that they inflict (Bandura, Barbaranelli, Caprara, & Pastorelli, 1996). In other words, the perpetrator is simply looking for some moral ground to carve his evil intention.

When we are placed in a dangerous situation, it is the invocation of a moral "right" to respond aggressively to such threats. According to Baumeister (1999), soldiers learn early how ethical principles are limited by the demands of a situation and their first obligation is to obey the orders. In the face of a moral conflict, they simply ignore the ethical side and continue to indulge in brutalities. As stated in Chapter 1, Grussendorf, McAlister, Sandstrom, and Morrison (2002) used Bandura's concept of moral disengagement to develop their Peace Test and presented scenarios for moral disengagement.

Equality and equity

Deutsch's (1985) work on two kinds of fairness (justice), distributive and procedural, has provided insights into how we base our decisions in terms of equity (proportionality) and equality and whether the procedures used to determine guilt are fair. Research studies show that women prefer equality to equity, whereas men prefer equal ratios of outputs to inputs.

Following the pioneering work of Deutsch, at least four kinds of justice have been identified (Kool & Agrawal, 2006):

1. Distributive justice: What one gets.
   Example: An employee will be more concerned when he loses his job individually than collectively, as in a layoff situation.
2. Procedural justice: How one gets something
   Example: If an employee's viewpoints are ignored and personal biases of administrators are not checked, a perception of procedural injustice may emerge.
3. Interpersonal justice: Sensitivity in perceiving events
   Example: It will take place if managers ignore simple courtesies, distance themselves from the employees, and change interpersonal demeanor. Any layoff is an emotional situation, and it should be handled with sympathy, compassion and honesty.
4. Informational justice: Right to information
   Example: Informational injustice is perceived when employees feel inequity in the availability of information crucial for them to do their work.

Needless to say, a sense of justice is germane to the understanding of nonviolence. Violence at work or in schools is often the consequence of everyday injustice that victims perceive whether real or imagined. When Gandhi was asked why there was so much violence in the world, he replied that with enough resources in the world, its uneven distribution led to keeping people in poverty, which was the worst form of violence. With unfair distribution of resources continuing, violence would never cease in the world. Nonviolence is about mitigating the effects of such injustice.

Moral exclusion

Arising from the above analysis of justice is the concept of moral exclusion (Staub, 1990, 2004) that refers to viewing individual or groups as outside the boundary of the rules of justice (Oskamp, 1990). When people are viewed outside one's moral boundaries, it becomes easy to harm them. Perpetrators of violence who view members of other groups as unconnected to them tend to perceive their own group as moral (Deutsch, 2005).

The problem associated with moral exclusion is that we do not know whom we include and whom we don't. Should we include all forms of life? Should we include our own pet but not other animals? Should we include trees and the entire environment? Drawing an appropriate boundary is not easy unless we confine ourselves to members of the same species. The implications of moral exclusion for the psychology of nonviolence are vital. Nagata (1993) cited internment of people of Japanese origin in the USA during World War II as a classic example of moral exclusion. On the other hand, people of German origin were not arrested. For a detailed discussion on moral exclusion, the reader is also referred to the next chapter in this book and a recent publication (Abrams, Hogg, & Marques, 2005).

To sum up, moral concerns form the core of the study of the psychology of nonviolence. As in the analysis of aggression, intentionality plays a very important role in the understanding of moral behavior. The psychology of nonviolence has moved a long way claiming legitimacy with the early studies of Piaget who began by explaining the significance of intentions in a child's moral development. This pioneering work was followed by Kohlberg who traced it through several stages; Gilligan, by adding a caring perspective; Rest, by separating principle and utilizer components; and Erikson, by offering the role of identity and childhood experiences. Based on the above discussion we may conclude that nonviolent individuals do not approach various components like justice or caring, moral principle or its utilization, and aggression or nonaggression as isolated parts, but tend to view them as a Gestalt, a configuration in which the best of their intentions and conduct mirror the components of social harmony and welfare. While such individuals appear to be god-like, they may still show the flaws of an ordinary human being.

SUMMARY

The chapter initially focused on two approaches to study cognitive factors involved in nonviolence: *Cognition of social psychology of nonviolence* and *social psychology of cognition of nonviolence*. We began with an analysis of the information-processing approach to the study of human cognition. Of particular interest here is the way we receive, process, hold and retrieve information, how scripts develop and what primes them. Besides, this "thin" approach to study cognitive processes, we examined the implications of SIT in the categorization process. Further, we examined the behavioral characteristics of the members of the nonviolent cultures and how their internal standards guide nonviolent behavior.

Focusing on how we monitor our behavior, the analysis of self-control was considered central to our understanding of the psychology of nonviolence. Some recent empirical research work on self-control was also cited to show how it acts as a restraining force for our aggressive behavior.

Raising the argument that moral components are essential for building a psychology of nonviolence, the next part of the chapter dealt with the moral dimensions of nonviolence. A review of the works of Piaget, Kohlberg, Erikson, Gilligan, and others was offered to show how moral issues extend and limit the scope of our understanding of the psychology of nonviolence.

SUGGESTED READINGS

Bonta, B. D. (1997). Cooperation and competition in peaceful societies. *Psychological Bulletin, 121*(2), 299–320.

Kool, V. K. (Ed.). (1993). *Nonviolence: social and psychological issues.* Lanham & London: University Press of America.

Miller, A. (2004). *The social psychology of good and evil: Understanding our capacity for kindness and cruelty.* New York: Guilford.

Verbeek, P., & de Waal, F. B. M. (2001). Peacemaking among children. *Peace and Conflict: Journal of Peace Psychology,* 7(1), 5–28.

Motivation: The Fuel of Nonviolence

OUTLINE

Nonviolence involves restraint, whether mediated by one's own conviction (intrinsic) or by external group pressures such as rewards, norms or fear of punishment (extrinsic), and opting for reconciliation with, and avoiding injury or harm to, the adversary. While making any such choice, a cardinal question that often strikes us is: Why should I choose nonviolence? What's in it for me? Will it serve me any good? In short, it is in my self-interest to remain nonviolent? I am sure that everyone has gone through some experience in life that brought us to a point where we found ourselves at a critical turn: whether to take a violent or a nonviolent route.

Let's think of a scenario in which a two-year old baby, sitting in the cart and moving along with its mother in the grocery store, physically hits you and leaves a stain on your freshly laundered shirt. Obviously, your first reaction would be of surprise, with some unpleasantness at the minimum. Realizing that it's a young baby, and being reminiscent of how "terrible two year olds" behave at times, you might say, "Hi, enjoying your ride in the cart" or something like that, conveying the message that you find the behavior of the baby indicative of warm social interaction. If you become angry at this incident, it would probably not be in your interest, because others might think that you lack compassion and empathy for the young. You would be rated far short of the social norm that expects you to treat the little ones with tolerance and self-control. Alternately, you might also think of telling the mother of the child to teach appropriate manners to her baby or complain to her that the freshly laundered shirt was stained by her child's inappropriate behavior. There is a remote chance that someone might even ask for a compensation for the damaged shirt, but the probability of demanding a compensation would definitely be high had your car, not the shirt, been somehow damaged by the baby.

What's involved in the above example, simple as it is? Basically, it is about our self-interest, that is, not to be criticized for negatively reacting to the baby and, at the same time, seeking to recover loss from the mother, should it be perceived as significant (as in case of damage to your car). Violent or nonviolent behavior, therefore, is a matter of choice that is governed by our self-interest, material orientation, and our ability to manage positive emotions and affective processes. The more the self-interest, materialism and negative emotion involved, the greater the probability for preferring a violent route at a choice point, overriding all that we have learned from our parents, in schools and at holy places. With regard to violent behavior, both Aaron Beck (1999) and Roy Baumeister (1999) have written succinctly in their books, *Prisoners of Hate: The Cognitive Basis of Anger, Hostility and Violence*, and *Evil: Inside Human Violence and Cruelty*, respectively.

For those interested in nonviolence, they will find the flip side of violence and more to it in this chapter, focusing not on the starkly dark side of human behavior, but on the bright side within us. Borrowing from insights offered by the emerging positive psychology, recent research in empathy, role of self-interest, and need for power, this chapter is built around our capacity to refrain from violence and the development of an orientation toward the promotion of positive behavior, including nonviolence.

Self-interest

Thinking about oneself is a natural process that leads us to understand who we are, that is, our self-identity. Maintaining a positive self-identity is a very powerful motive in our lives. According to Carl Rogers (1961), one cardinal task in which we are engaged in our lives is developing "positive regard", a self-evaluation that keeps us in a pleasant state. The onset of such motivation takes place early in life with experiences in the family and then continues until our death.

In spite of a fervent appeal by Ernest Hilgard in 1949 during his Presidential Address to the American Psychological Association to retain the concept of self in psychology, doubts have been expressed regarding its usefulness, especially by the hard-liners who promote a very objective psychology. The fact that there are as many selves as there are individuals led to the use and abuse of this concept and acceptance of self as a viable concept, such as the one espoused by Rogers, has remained debatable in psychology.

Further, developing a suitable and standard measure of self has always been a problem. For example, the meaning of self is not the same in individualistic and collective cultures. Given the nature of self as unique and separate from others, western cultures encourage its members to prioritize their personal goals. The USA, Australia, Great Britain, Canada, Netherlands and France rank, respectively, high in their individualistic orientation (Hofstede, 1983). By placing the group goals before their own, the members of collective cultures focus on cooperation, self-criticism and lowered self-enhancing behavior, in sharp contrast to their western counterparts. According to Miller (1999), the formulation of institutions in the individualistic cultures is such that people naturally pursue their self-interest. It is there in schools, at work, and everywhere. When a teacher in the elementary grade school asks a question to her students, see how quickly the hands of children go up in the air, so as to be the first one to answer. Competition promotes the level of self-interest: The more the competition, the higher the inclination to look after one's own interest. Don't be surprised if a trader does not easily share the addresses of his clients with another trader.

In Chapter 3, I mentioned about several nonviolent cultures and how they followed normative practices to promote nonviolent patterns of behavior. The child, whether in a violent or in a nonviolent culture, does not know how to behave during a conflict, but by focusing repeatedly on what is expected in such situations, a culture provides signals expecting certain behaviors from the child. Summarizing his analysis of nonviolent cultures, Bonta (1997) wrote:

> To conclude, practices such as the child suddenly losing attention, the child destroying cuddly baby animals, parents teasing about hurting others, or the child developing fears about the intentions of others could all lead children to become resentful and violent rather than cooperative and peaceful. Why should these practices necessarily lead to cooperative, peaceful behavior? The answer seems circular in nature. These practices are carried out in societies that are already highly nonviolent. The Inuit child who is taunted with "Why don't you kill your brother?" to use Briggs's (1994) haunting example, only has one possible way of dealing with the issue and he or she already knows what society expects. (p. 303)

Indeed, children continuously receive signals from their culture regarding the expectations from the society. They know what to pursue, so that it is rewarding and is in their self-interest. Miller (1999) contended that when cultures support the norm of self-interest, individuals tend to maximize their positive emotions such as joy, and minimize negative emotions. Further, self-interest may operate as a motive because if I keep on sacrificing for others and do not do all that is needed for my survival, I would be deviating from the norm of self-interest in society. Thus, cultures, particularly individualistic in character, implicitly promote appropriateness of serving one's self-interest. Ratner and Miller (2001) further pointed out that when offering help to others was not in the self-interest of individuals, it elicited surprise and anger.

The moral obligation to help is considered important in many cultures. But what if one does not feel a personal obligation for it? Joan Miller, Bersoff, and Harwood (1990) tested Americans and Hindus from India, and after comparing their responses concluded that while Hindus regarded helping as an absolute moral obligation, the Americans were willing to apply the norm of social responsibility, that is, helping those who needed help. In another study, Baron and Miller (2000) reported a similar trend when the researchers noted that for bone marrow donation, the Indian students showed greater willingness as morally required, compared to their American counterparts who considered bone marrow donation a matter of one's choice. The tendency to help varies from culture to culture and is guided by the norm of self-interest attached to it.

Accepting the fact that self-interest is the norm of our society, we now need to know: What is the most critical implication of heightened self-interest for violence and nonviolence? Self-interest tends to change the moral position of an individual who might underestimate the impact of his/her action. According to Bandura (1999), moral disengagements are likely to be facilitated under the influence of self-interest. Heinous acts of killing and bombing could be underrated as surgical strikes. Self-interest leads us to rationalize our inhumane actions and pulls us further away from humanity. Obviously, self-interest will bring us closer to, or at a minimum, seeking support for violence.

The power of self-interest as a motive is so strong in our everyday lives that it influences our behavior as a self-fulfilling force. In fact, it is so pervasive that it correlates more strongly with our behavior than with our attitudes, something that social psychologists should cheer since such correlations are hard to find. For example, we may retain our anti-war attitudes and yet, with self-interest intact, still participate in war or war-like situations.

In everyday life, the broader impact of self-interest can be observed in the relationship between an individual and his/her social obligations. Called social dilemmas, the conflict between individual and group interest leads us to decision traps that are arguably harmful in the long run, but serve the immediate needs of an individual. For recycling purposes, the city has clear laws regarding the sorting out of paper, glass and plastic materials, but for our convenience, we dump all the stuff together in the bin. Here are a few more examples illustrating our self-interest:

- Not using the public transport, but driving a personal car that increases pollution.
- Over-population and having many children in the Third World to increase labor force.
- Health problems due to smoking but working for the same industry.
- National security and modernizing the military versus helping the poor.

Since Platt's (1973) pioneering contribution to this field, considerable research has been conducted to show how immediate self-interest leads to social dilemmas (Dawes, 1980; Pruitt & Carnevele, 1993; Seijts & Latham, 2000). In their research, Wildchut, Pinter, Vevea, Insko, and Schopter (2003) contended that when groups offer anonymity to its members, they tend to act in a self-interested and aggressive manner. With competition added to the situation, fear of loss and greed combine together to promote the levels of self-interest.

Summers and Morin (1995) conducted a study on self-interest as a factor in post-cold war demilitarization in Canada. When the National Defence Canada, a Canadian Government body, began to consider closing bases and reducing military expenditure in 1994, many people were opposed to these actions arguing that any reduction in maintaining armed forces and military needs would be suicidal. Who were those people? According to Summers and Morin, they were surely the ones who received income from the military. Such personal interests tend to defeat the appropriate economic conversion that balances the needs of a country, for the resources could easily be diverted to other important social causes in the absence of self-interest.

Gandhi remarked that the issue of poverty is central to the eruption of violence all over the world. He believed that there were enough resources in the world, but poverty exists because of the unfair distribution of such resources. Another example of conflict of motives is resource dilemma, that is, how two or more people share a limited resource. Resource dilemma is of two types: Commons dilemma and public good dilemma. With increase in consumption, deforestation, mining and preparation of luxury goods, our limited resources will soon be depleted. Thus, violence against nature must stop by controlling the self-interests of people.

The other dilemma is about public goods. If we do not contribute to the social causes in our community, many programs will suffer or shut down. Imagine if all of us decide not to donate blood, to litter our parks and public places, and to make no contribution to charities, our community would be deeply hurt. The power of self-interest, therefore, can be very devastating.

In Chapter 1, prospect theory and its relevance for understanding nonviolence and conflict resolution was presented. It was also mentioned how a negative frame could influence the outcome of a decision. De Dreu and McCuster (1997) argued that given a negative frame, that is, potential losses instead of gains, the orientation of behavior might change due to change in the apparent utility value. What are the options that one might take that would show change in the orientation of an individual? There are three possibilities:

1. Cooperative: Maximize joint outcomes
2. Competitive: Win in a situation
3. Individualistic: Maximizing one's own outcomes.

The findings of De Dreu and McCuster have practical significance. They found that with a cooperative orientation, the subjects tended to prefer cooperative choices even in a negative frame, but that was not the case when individuals' cooperative orientation changed to a competitive one. Individuals with both competitive and individualistic orientation preferred to defect in a negative frame and rejected the cooperative choices available to them. In short, personal interests guided by individualistic choices are oriented toward competitive, not cooperative, orientation. We all know how a sense of personal achievement and victory of the team, increases the level of aggression, as a sporting event proceeds. Also, members of the team that is losing show higher aggression than its counterparts do (Cox, 1998).

Self-interest is also related to self-presentation. Barring a few exceptions, no one wants to look bad. The need for self-presentation becomes all the more conspicuous under special conditions. The 9/11 attacks changed the USA and one symbol of this change was the sudden display of patriotism by the Americans (Prentice & Miller, 2002). Flags appeared everywhere and all citizens, in a show of solidarity, indulged in high self-presentation. Under such conditions, those who advocated against retaliation by the USA fell below the level of standard evaluation of patriotism. By displaying such symbolic things such as flags, people, including those from the ethnic group of the attackers, avoided alienation. It was in their self-interest to maintain such self-presentation.

Power orientation and nonviolence

While most of us think of power in terms of a physical or material sense, such as a knock-out in boxing or privileges based on financial status, it is the psychological nature of power that makes it so disturbing. Fear that emerges out of the opponent's power is devastating. If you subtract this psychological power from physical or material power, the impact of power appears relatively inconsequential.

In 1992, I invited Kenneth Boulding, peace activist, economist and ex-president of the American Association of Advancement of Science (AAAS), to deliver a keynote address at a conference on nonviolence. During our meeting and at the time of his lecture (Boulding, 1993), he emphasized that although power has three faces—threat power, economic power and integrative power—it is the integrative power that provides the alternate to violence because it grows out of good will and trust of the people (Box 4.1). Boulding lamented that psychologists have not paid much attention to it and that the success of nonviolence would depend on how we handle this type of power during the 21st century.

BOX 4.1 THREE FACES OF POWER

1. *Threat power*: Use of fear to control behavior, for example, "You do something I want or I'll do something you don't want." The Mongols, led by Genghis Khan, had a very clear policy: surrender or we would massacre the inhabitants. A number of regimes surrendered to him to avoid brutalities. The other response to his threat was to fight and show resistance until the end. In short, either we obey, as we do in paying our income taxes irrespective of our disagreeing with some of the tax laws, or we defy the law, as we do when driving above the stipulated speed limit.

BOX 4.1 (cont'd)

2. *Economic power*: It is based on the skills of production. The seller has the right to sell and the buyer has the right to buy. This power is related to threat power because historically, a lot of land grabbing involved threat power.
3. *Integrative power*: "This is the power of legitimacy, persuasion, loyalty, community, and so on. In a very real sense, power is a gift to the powerful by those over whom the power may be exercised, those who recognize that the power is legitimate. Threat power and economic power would be hard to exercise if they were not supported by integrative power, that is, if the former were not regarded as legitimate. King George had the illusion that he had the power to tax the American colonists, who then proceeded to withdraw legitimacy not only from the tax but from the monarch himself" (Boulding, 1993, p. 201).

Boulding (1993).

Power is generally defined in terms of our capacity to influence people. From time immemorial, pacifists have argued that power is used for the purpose of dominance and violence. Sharp (1973) believes that power may be viewed in two ways. First, the system of which an individual is a member is a recipient of power. In other words, power is concentrated in the hands of a few who control the members of the society at large. In the other way, power may be viewed as a hierarchical system dependent upon the good will of people. This notion is pluralistic and hence useful for the psychology of nonviolence.

Unlike Boulding and Sharp who viewed power from the viewpoint of community action, Rollo May (1972) offered five kinds of power that are based on individual orientation:

Exploitative power: It is characterized by the use of force and subjects people to abuse of all kinds, for example, slavery.
Manipulative power: A tendency to control others in various ways.
Competitive power: A tendency to remain ahead of others and keep the opponents down.
Achievement motivation: A strong desire to be successful, for example. It is similar to the concept advanced by McClelland (1961).
Integrative power: It is the blending of power with the others and is similar to Boulding's analysis.

While both Boulding and May believed that people use different types of power in various combinations, nonviolence, in particular, is characterized by integrative power. Elaborating on May's conceptualization of integrative power, Kool (1993) wrote,

> He related the essence of this power to Hegel's dialectic of thesis, antithesis, and synthesis. A corollary to this type of analysis is that if there is a body, there will be an anti-body, and growth will result from the attraction or repulsion of these two bodies into a new system. Thus, if a moral viewpoint is challenged by another moral viewpoint, the result will be a new synthesis, a new ethic embodying a higher moral principle. The notion of power in the minds of nonviolent individuals lies in their efforts to align themselves to the goodness of their community, a process which leads to self-cultivation and self-perfection. They are comfortable with criticism or even hatred because they tend to look beyond the existing social order and do not play by the conventional rules. In doing so, they never manipulate others because they do not promote their personal interests. (p. 16)

In traditional societies, the cleric usually hold a very powerful position. They demand unconditional respect for their organization. By adopting integrative power, the nonviolent individual acts like a saint who tends to develop a new synthesis to change the social order and often adheres to paradoxes, rather than maintaining the status quo and providing a uniform interpretation of religious books, as preferred by the cleric. The ethic of integrative power therefore makes the cleric uncomfortable. Hagberg (1984) analyzed several paradoxes of nonviolent individuals. For example:

- The more we know, the less we know
- Commitment means detachment
- Everything is interrelated; everything is separate
- Everything matters; nothing matters.

According to May (1972), the relationship between nonviolence and integrative power may be viewed in three ways. First, nonviolent individuals are ready to become aware of a problem. Second, they do not hesitate in accepting blame and responsibility (also see Baumgardner's study, 1990 reported in Chapter 3). And third, for them the community comes first, not their self-interest. Nonviolent individuals do not seek power, it comes to them as they proceed to seek social harmony and merge individual good with the social good. In doing so, they weaken the moral defenses of their opponents who abuse their power and use coercion. In short, both violent and nonviolent individuals use power, but the nature of their power is different.

Kool and Keyes (1990) examined the relationship between nonviolence and power. Power was measured through a very popular test, called the Mach Test (Christie, 1970). This test has been designed to study subjects' beliefs regarding the use of manipulation, deceit and flattery as interpersonal tactics and their belief concerning the moral qualities of other people. In terms of May's classification, it is similar to manipulative power (#2) as given above. The nonviolent tendencies were measured by Kool and Sen's NVT (Chapter 1). Tables 4.1 and 4.2 describe three items from the Mach scale and the correlation values between the NVT and the Mach subscales, respectively. Given the findings, it is clear

Table 4.1 Three items from the Mach scale and its correlation with the NVT

1. The best way to handle people is to tell them what they want to hear.
2. It is wise to flatter important people.
3. Once a decision has been made, it is best to keep changing it as new circumstances arise.

Table 4.2 Correlation values between the Mach Test and the NVT

The Mach Test	The NVT
Overall scores	–0.44
Subscales	
Deceit	–0.51
Flattery	–0.31
Cynicism	–0.43
Morality	–0.23
Mach tactics (DF)	–0.38
Mach Views	–0.42

All values significant at 0.05 or above levels.

that a typical Mach person takes a cynical view of life and when given an opportunity to choose between honesty and lying or between frankness and corner-cutting and manipulation, he or she will prefer the vicious, unkind and unethical route.

In Chapter 1, Kool's model of nonviolence was reported along with levels of aggression and moral concerns in a three-dimensional frame. The negative correlation between Mach scores and the NVT is clearly indicative of the nonviolent individual's rejection of Mach methods that promote self-enhancement through manipulation. Thus, instead of using flattery, deceit and other methods of manipulation, they share their rational choices with others to resolve a conflict. They share power with people and refrain from having a monopoly to enhance their self-interest.

At the heart of Gandhi's nonviolent movement in South Africa and India was a concept known as satyagraha, that is, seeking truth through love and ethical conduct and using harmony, sympathy, tolerance and self-suffering to build positive interpersonal relationship (Mayton, 2001). He kept on refining this concept as he indulged further to shape his nonviolent movement that lasted for several decades. Gandhi believed that the most difficult part in a nonviolent movement is transparency of character and maintaining "an inward gentleness and genuine desire to do the opponent good and wish him well. There must be no vilification of an opponent, but this does not mean there should not be truthful characterization of his acts. There should be no hostility to persons, but only to acts when they are subversive of morals or the good of society. There should be no intention to the harm-doer" (Iyer, 1983, p. 296).

In other words, adhering to nonviolence means no room for the Mach characteristics described earlier. In short, nonviolence involves sharing power with all, including one's adversary; else the resolution of conflicts will remain elusive.

Mutualism versus adversarialism: The vulnerability of being too psychological or sociological

In the above section, we chose to be very psychological as we moved along in our analysis of self-interest and power. However, the concept of nonviolence and aggression is empty without involving another person. To whom are we showing nonviolence? Against whom are we aggressing? Thus, focusing on the individual alone is not enough, as is typical in psychological research. In his thought provoking article, "How social an animal?" Daniel Batson (1990) argued that we are not selfish at all times, even though we might even communicate that we acted selfishly. We do care about others for their sake, not only for our own. Earlier, Gordon Allport (1968) echoed the same notion by stating that "the key problem of social psychology" (p. 1) is to understand the social nature of people. Groebel and Hinde (1989) contended that a major problem in the psychological analysis of violence and aggression is that psychologists tend to ignore the interaction between the perpetrator and the victim and confine themselves only to the psychological states of an individual.

In this section of the chapter, I will focus on some of the sociological issues that have psychological bearings in our understanding of self-interest and power. First and foremost, keep in mind that most conflicts involve some kind of an emotional outcome, not just a material impact. Should we accept this notion, we need to know how psychological processes shape with reference to the orientation of social groups.

In the context of violence and nonviolence, two expressions in a social system need to be examined: adversarialism and mutualism. The former is a mode of interaction based on competing tendencies and opposition of people to each other so as to maximize one's self-interest. It is best understood in a free market type of economic system in which each party is guided by its goals of procuring profits and amassing power. The central idea in this approach is that only violence is needed to curb violence and that success is possible when we oppose and look after our interest (individualism).

The other approach, called mutualism, is based on cooperation and caring rather than competition, and building compatibility rather than incompatibility. It is characterized by a tendency to connect and seek alternates to violence. According to Erikson (1969), it is about seeking support for, and nourishing each other.

Historically, philosophers have pointed out the existence of the above two modes of social expressions. Hobbes believed that there would always be conflict and war because the human being is born free but is subordinated by the society. In contrast, Buddha taught mutual respect, cooperation and total abstinence from violence. Given the above differences between adversarialism and mutualism, it is obvious that the former promotes individualism and the latter highlights collectivism. In adversarialism, there are many chances that escalation of tension may lead to hatred and destruction, what Freud called Thanatos, because the basic nature of competition is geared toward overcoming another individual to maximize one's gain. On the contrary, mutualism would serve as a powerful brake to inhibit genocide or other heinous acts of violence.

No social system, whether in the west or in the east, survives without a combination of both adversarialism and mutualism. We cannot be so selfish in competition that we deprive others of any existence nor do we adhere to unprecedented mutualism to give up everything in the name of cooperation and good will. "Most people", writes Barak (2003), "are neither compulsive adversaries nor compulsive mutualists. However, most people have not confronted that ambivalence toward people who are either close to or distant from themselves" (p. 282). For such people in particular, the orientation of society, adversarialistic or mutualistic, becomes significant to the extent that it offers a violent or nonviolent solution.

In the thought-provoking book, *Rambo and the Dalai Lama: The Compulsion to Win and Its Threat to Human Survival*, Fellman (1998) contended, "life is about the tension between adversarialism and mutuality. Both sets of forces are inevitable; the question is how they are expressed and in what degree of saliency" (p. 25). Unfortunately, argues Fellman, societies have been shaped to favor adversarialism over mutualism. Mutualism is ideal but the adversarialism is real or actual. The dominance of men over women, whether originating in biological prescriptions or in cultural moorings, the rich over poor, the able over the disabled, and so on, are manifestations of adversarialism that we have taken for granted in our daily lives, albeit the levels of resistance to such disparities vary from one society to another.

Focusing on the rituals that differentiate adversariality and mutuality, Fellman contended that such stylized expressions tend to signal cooperative or competitive and violent or nonviolent behavior. When rituals are adversarial, anger, fighting, or squabbles take place, but in mutuality, expressions of positive forms of behavior such as greetings, respect and humility will be offered. Fellman's classification of adversarial rituals is reported in Table 4.3.

The rituals of adversarialism involve several negative forms of behavior ranging from physical harm to verbal aggression. They bear resemblance to the various types of aggression presented by Buss and reported in Chapter 2. The reader may notice that the passive and indirect forms of aggressive behavior in Buss's classification are described as rituals of resistance of adversarial nature in Fellman's classification. They appear in many instances as fuzzy, bordering with mutuality and portray the same kind of ambiguity that we pointed out for the overlapping gray area between violence and nonviolence in Chapter 1.

For mutuality rituals, the social norms are not well defined. There is no set way to enhance cooperation and connectedness. Saying "Good morning"

Table 4.3 Fellman's description of adversarial rituals

a. Rituals of coercion
1. Ritual of killing, for example, war
2. Ritual of undermining, for example, abusing and insulting
3. Ritual of deprecation, for example, superiority versus inferiority
4. Rituals of denial, for example, mistrusting, blaming, and so on.

b. Rituals of resistance
1. Rituals of resistance based on adversity, for example, revolution, strikes, and so on
2. Rituals of adversity based on mutuality, for example, disobedience, demonstrations, and so on with the intent of least harm to the adversary.

may not mean anything, but just a passing courtesy. Writing "Yours sincerely" at the end of your letter simply does not make you sincere in the real sense, but staring at someone or not responding to "Good morning" are certainly considered negative forms of behavior. Laws do not tell us how to raise our children, but poor parenting is considered a crime. The boundaries of adversarialism are well defined by the law and well understood through social norms, but in the case of mutualism, there are no set limits. Are there any limits to compassion, sympathy and humanity? But the negative forms of behavior are distinctly classified to the degree of harm the perpetrator inflicts on the victim, for example, punishment is proportionate to the level of the crime. Thus, in the absence of clear-cut mutualistic rituals, even positive forms of behavior may sometimes appear adversarial. Precisely due to this reason, some forms of nonviolent behavior, such as sit-ins, protest marches, slogans, and so on are considered to be manipulative efforts hidden in the form of indirect, passive aggression.

In view of the fact that our society is geared toward adversariality, people generally orient themselves toward many negative forms of behavior. According to Barak (2003), "Consequently, a lot of people are more comfortable opposing than connecting, competing than caring, hating than loving, ridiculing than respecting, and so on. Recognizing ambivalences in ourselves and in our normative adversaries allows us to see the mutualism as we transcend the adversarialism" (p. 282). Not surprisingly, people often show extraordinary caring and love for strangers, much more than for their loved ones or vice versa as they

Table 4.4 Obstacles to peace

Cognitive	Affective	Social
Enemy imaging	Hostility	Us–them differentiation
Attribution biases	Distrust	Blaming
Rationalization	Denial	Self-fulfilling prophecy
Distortion	Macho pride	Excessive obedience

Source: Adapted from Wessells (1993).

begin to realize the norm of self-interest in the context of adversarialism or mutualism.

In the presence of adversarialism, obstacles to nonviolence are manifold. In his elaborate psychological analyses, Wessells (1993) presented three categories of obstacles: cognitive, affective and social (Table 4.4). The cognitive obstacles consist of schemata that contain organized framework of knowledge and expectations (see Chapter 3). For example, we have a schema of good guys and bad guys and of friendly and unfriendly countries. For years, the west believed that the Soviet Union was an evil empire, but not so now. Stereotypic distortion, enemy imaging, ideological rigidity and rationalization are some of the many cognitive factors that sustain adversarial relationships.

Among the affective obstacles, Wessells listed hostility, fear and distrust as significant affective processes that interact with cognitive processes. He contended that in the presence of fear and need for self-protection, even acceptance of war is considered a necessity. Citing one Gallup poll survey, Wessells remarked that during mid-1970s, approximately 52 percent Americans felt that America should maintain its power position even if it required waging a war. The third obstacle is rooted in the social factors including us–them, blind obedience, self-fulfilling prophecy, and so on. Thus, if a nation believes that the opponent has more dangerous weapons than what they have, they will collect intelligence and believe in the reports sustaining their belief about enemy power. For example, Wessells cited a CIA report during the 1950s that estimated that approximately 200 missiles are possessed by the Soviets, but, in fact, they had only four. The division between us and them is probably the most serious obstacle to the attainment of peace.

Moral exclusion: Us–them dichotomy

Morton Deutsch (1985) has written extensively on the issue of justice, and his concept, known as moral exclusion, refers to one's sense of moral community (see Chapter 3). Whom do we include in our moral community? Should we include those who have a different sense of fairness? The basic idea in moral exclusion is that when someone is undeserving, hurting him or her is not forbidden. Nagata (1993) analyzed how people of Japanese origin were interned in the mainland of America after the Japanese attacked Pearl Harbor. In contrast, Germans and Italians were not subjected to mass incarceration, although both Germany and Italy were also at war with America. According to Nagata, there were racial similarities of the Germans and Italians with the majority Caucasians, but the Japanese looked different. Pointing out further how Americans were guided by their self-interest, she exposed the hypocrisy that the people of Japanese origin were not incarcerated in Hawaii because the US army needed people for support services during the war.

The worst part of the moral exclusion of people of Japanese origin was that the action was supported by the Congress, the Supreme Court, and even by liberals such as the members of civic unions and leftist groups. Nagata argued that "exclusion was based upon ethnic heritage alone" (ibid., p. 87) owing to the colonial attitudes and long-standing racism. Pearl Harbor added fuel by making the people of Japanese origin an easy scapegoat.

Moral exclusion may occur within or outside the group. When it takes place within our own group, we can easily detect it and take remedial action. However, when it strikes the members outside our group, we may not take cognizance and therefore feel no remorse. According to Twenge and Baumeister (2005) exclusion contributes to aggression and decline in the level of prosocial behavior.

When we look at objects, we classify and categorize them, such as numbers, alphabets, and so on, but when we categorize human beings, such as they bear resemblance to us, we tend to carve people into categories of "us" or "them". As discussed in Chapter 3, categorization is a natural process as it provides economy to our cognitive processes. One such effect of categorization is that members of the out-group appear to be more homogeneous than those of our own group. Therefore, it was not surprising that all the members of Japanese origin were interned because of the prevailing stereotype at that time that "a Jap's a Jap". Research in social psychology clearly indicates that motivational factors have the power to enormously facilitate the categorization process (Sinclair & Kunda, 1999). If a white man is treated by a black doctor, the white man would remember him as a doctor, not a black man, provided the patient begins liking and respecting the black doctor. Otherwise, the racial categorization remains salient, that is, remembering the doctor as a black guy.

Moral exclusion is a very sensitive motivational process. We tend to exclude people against whom we are prejudiced and assign negative labels to them ever so easily. As a result, rational analysis is downsized and a lower level of thinking can be applied. In terms of prospect theory, Stage 1, in which automatic processing takes place and which is less rule-governed, becomes the dominant mode of cognition. In a study, Kool, Diaz, Brown, and Hama (2002) explored if levels of moral exclusion bear any relationship to nonviolence. We selected 12 items from Kool and Sen's NVT and asked the subjects to rate whether the answers to questions from the NVT were morally exclusive, inclusive or neutral. The results clearly indicated that those who scored high on nonviolence also scored high on moral inclusion and vice versa.

These results receive support from a study conducted by Cooney (1995) in which she reported that Kool and Sen's NVT scores (those scoring high on nonviolence) correlated negatively with the subjects' endorsement of moral exclusion, but were significantly and positively related to nondoctrinal religious attitudes, the latter being known to be inclusive in its belief system.

Positive nonviolence in positive psychology: Exploring human strengths in nonviolence

After the two forces in psychology, behaviorism and Gestalt, failed to provide a comprehensive view of human cognition and behavior, a third force in psychology, called humanistic psychology, developed with the contribution of Carl Rogers, Rollo May, Abraham Maslow and others. Even though different schools of psychology have virtually merged in one way or another, the reductionist epistemological traditions in psychology are continuing to dominate the growth of psychology. Unfortunately, this type of approach has no room for studying and understanding positive forms of behavior such as hope, optimism, resilience and well-being. Moreover, the growth of psychology has also become extremely problem-focused (or say, negative) in its search for applications of its theories and principles to everyday life. For example, Sheldon and King (2001) argued that the negative bias in psychology has taken an extreme form. Applying the example they mentioned in their article, if I look back on my career and feel that I am a better psychologist now than ever before, contemporary social psychologists would be quick to call me an individual living under a self-serving delusion or a temporal bias.

As a consequence, Seligman (1998, 2002), Myers (2000), Csikszentmihalyi (1990, 1997) and others felt that psychology should focus on what makes people happy and satisfied in their lives and how they can and do thrive with dignity and purpose. According to Alan Carr (2004), "As a scientific enterprise, positive psychology focuses on understanding and explaining happiness and subjective well-being and accurately predicting factors that influence such states" (p. 1).

Seligman (2002), a leading contributor, contended that there are three pillars of positive psychology. The first is positive subjective experience. It has three parts: past, present, and future.

1. The past consists of well-being and contentment
2. The present is focused on happiness
3. The future is optimism and hope.

The second pillar is built on positive individual traits such as intimacy, wisdom, integrity, aesthetic sense, and spirituality.

The third pillar is positive institutions including families, schools, and communities that promote positive character and sustain the positive subjective experience.

As mentioned earlier, absence of violence may mean nonviolence, but it is not the same as when we make efforts to promote peace. Military has the power to control violence, but it is a form of negative nonviolence only, for nonviolence also involves many positive forms of behavior such as empathy, forgiving and antipunitiveness. In this section of the chapter, I will now focus on positive nonviolence in the context of the above mentioned relatively newer growth in psychology, that is, positive psychology.

Self-actualization

Maslow (1954) presented a hierarchical motive system in which the first goal is to satisfy the basic needs of an individual, for example, physiological (hunger, thirst, and so on) and safety needs. As one grows, one seeks further congruence between one's experience and one's self-concept. Going through the middle order needs such as love and social needs, the self is enhanced further to bring about self-fulfillment. When one reaches the stage wherein one realizes the full expression of potentials, then one enters the stage of self-actualization. According to Maslow, the final goal of an individual is to attain self-actualization, but to reach there it is imperative that the basic needs be fulfilled.

A cardinal characteristic of self-actualized individuals is that they are guided by their internal principles. They are known for resisting outside pressures and are not guided by the reinforcement they receive from external rewards, but are intrinsically motivated to seek success for personal fulfillment. To investigate the relationship between nonviolence and self-actualization, we administered Shostrom's test of self-actualization and the NVT to college students. The results showed a significantly positive correlation between the two tests indicating that those who scored high on nonviolence were also high on self-actualization (Kool, 1994).

Do we really neglect basic needs such as safety and hunger as we proceed to higher level motives and finally to self-actualization? It is not so. Saul (1993) found that 65 percent of ballet dancers had physical injuries but they continued to satisfy their aesthetic needs. Our college students, to whom we administered the NVT and the self-actualization tests, were neither self-actualized nor were nonviolent in the ideal sense, but they shared the tendency to resist external pressures and appeared to be guided by their internal standards. As stated earlier in Chapter 3, self-control requires high levels of internalized standards, of the kind we find in self-actualized individuals like Gandhi, Mother Teresa, Tutu, Mandela, King and others. Orientation toward nonviolence is guided by the motive to self-actualize and by engaging in self-restraint.

Satyagraha and Tapasya

In our description of measures of nonviolence in Chapter 1, we referred to a nonviolence test for teenagers, the TNT, developed by Mayton and coworkers' (1998) at Lewis-Fort College, Idaho. Two subscales in this test are called satyagraha and tapasya and both bear significantly positive correlations with the NVT (Kool & Sen, 1984). According to Mayton and coworkers, the values of correlation between the NVT and their satyagraha and tapasya subscales were 0.39 and 0.34, respectively, and were statistically significant.

As reported earlier, satyagraha (holding on to the truth) is a Gandhian concept and a way of social and political action to bring about justice and fairness. According to Bondurant (1965), satyagraha involved the following:

- Engaging in non-cooperation to seek justice and fairness.
- Formation of local and higher level committees for discussion.
- Purification: humility, prayer and signing a pledge to remain nonviolent.
- Action: closing of shops (hartal), demonstrations through processions, contravention of selected laws, and so on.

According to Gandhi, no individual should indulge in *duragrah* or the persistence of wrongdoing—a concept opposite to satyagrah. He distinguished satyagraha from passive resistance which might contain some element of harassing the other party. In satyagraha, there is an emphasis on self-suffering to win the adversary. In the Gandhian view, this type of action is a normal activity in life and supporting this contention, Iyer (1983) wrote, "It is nothing unusual for a man to want to suffer for the sake of a high goal or an ennobling idea or for the sake of communal life" (p. 290). We believe that we have all indulged in some kind of satyagraha in our lives as we grew up in our families—brothers and sisters protesting and not eating for a just cause to seek cooperation and fairness from our parents or other loved ones. Most likely, such behavior in a modern textbook of social psychology will be labeled as self-handicapping, an analysis that would be grossly mistaken and considered to be flipping the positive view of nature onto its starkly dark side. The essence of satyagraha is the love of humanity, taking action based on truth and fairness, and *not* seeing the evil in "them", but knocking down the problem of seeing "us versus them". Satyagraha transcends from our motivation to follow universalism that makes us tolerant, appreciative and protective of all people and nature. It simply makes us morally inclusive (Kool & coworkers, 2002; Mayton, 2001).

Mayton, Diessner, and Granby (1996) administered Kool and Sen's NVT to 102 college students and correlated the obtained scores with those on Schwartz's Values Questionnaire. In terms of the value orientation of universalism, the two tests correlated significantly positive and the high and low scores on the nonviolence test also differed significantly in their levels of universalism, that is, those scoring high on universalism were oriented toward broadmindedness, social justice, unity with nature, a world at peace, and wisdom.

Let's now turn to tapasya, a word rooted in Hindu religion, meaning self-suffering or "the essential expression of truth and nonviolence" (Mayton & coworkers, 2002). Actually, the literal meaning of tapas (tapasya is the action form) in the Hindi language means burning, warm, or heat. Tapasya is like purifying gold in fire and testing virtue (real gold) emerging out of determination and indulgence. In doing so, we burn our negative feelings, attain penance, and indulge in self-purification. For sure, it was not an easy concept for Mayton and coworkers to translate meaningfully for the west, convert it into an objectively measurable form and retain it as a viable component in their test of nonviolence. More difficult was seeking the relationship of tapasya to the subscales of the TNT (see Chapter 1) and with the NVT, the correlation with the latter being 0.34 ($p < 0.01$). In another study, Konen and coworkers (1999) also recorded robust psychometric properties of the TNT with high reliability and validity on adolescents in the American samples.

Empathy and altruism

Empathy is undoubtedly a tendency that would characterize nonviolence and is an antithesis to violence. While sympathy is merely feeling for others, empathy is "understanding of the thoughts and feelings of others" (Betancourt, 2004,

p. 369). Simply stated, empathy is looking through the eyes of others. It is this human tendency that plays an important role in helping others (altruism). Sympathy, on the other hand, can dissipate without understanding the feelings of others. Since scenarios of violence and nonviolence involve understanding the other individual's intent and behavior, the role of empathy becomes salient in the analysis of nonviolence and aggression. Lack of empathy is related to some brain disorder. For example, research studies uniformly show that anti-social individuals with damage in their prefrontal brain lose the capacity to feel remorse and lack the ability to empathize (Blair & Charney, 2003).

Within the framework of motivation, two specific questions that are related to empathy are also relevant for nonviolence. First, are people genuinely altruistic, that is, do they genuinely promote the welfare of others? And second, even if they are not, is altruism a motivating tool for promoting nonviolence?

Before we answer the first question, we want to make it clear that the concept of empathy has many definitions and perspectives. For our purposes, empathy is viewed here as consisting of cognitive and emotional components. Whereas the cognitive component consists of perspective-taking, that is, the ability of an individual to imagine the feelings of others (perspective-taking), the emotional component is an empathetic concern, that is, realizing the joy or distress of the other individual and sharing such an emotional response.

To begin with the cognitive component, the ability of perspective-taking is needed to understand the feelings of others (Batson, 2002). Most arguably, the highest form of perspective taking of the intent of a wrongdoer is compassion, which is an attempt to understand the lack of understanding of the culprit. Having reached that stage, the victim is ready to voluntarily pardon him.

Remember the example we gave earlier in this chapter regarding the two-year old baby who hit you in the shopping mall. You empathized with it and even reciprocated warmly with compassion. If the baby fell down while hitting you, you might have even helped it in getting back to its feet. In short, you had empathetic concern for the baby, that is, the welfare of the baby was your utmost concern and you forgot how it stained your apparel.

What if you were thinking of your role as an adult and the desirability of behavior (without any sense of empathy) that accompanies such adulthood? In such a situation, you would be focusing on your own feelings, that is, you would be self-oriented, not other-oriented, even if you helped the baby based on your sense of social obligation. Many psychologists, borrowing from the hedonistic framework of psychology that contends that we indulge in pleasure-seeking behavior, believe that pursuing another person's welfare as a cardinal goal in life is pure fantasy. And even if we do care for others, it is only because such caring promotes our ego function. The above controversy in psychology is probably best addressed by Batson (1990, 2002) in his empathy–altruism hypothesis that states how an empathetic concern in an individual would lead to the altruistic motive for helping (Table 4.5). Our feelings are not the same when we are self-oriented as compared to when we are other-person oriented. For example, when we are self-oriented, our emotional response is linked to personal distress, whereas in case of other-oriented, it is linked to empathy. The reader may notice

Table 4.5 The empathy-altruism hypothesis

Feelings	Self-oriented	Other-oriented
Perception of help	Yes	Yes
Perspective taking	No	Yes
Emotional response	Personal distress	Empathy
Motivation to help	Egoistic	Altruistic
Target: Reducing distress	Own distress	Other's distress

Source: Adapted from Batson (1991).

that this has implications for power orientation as stated in Figure 1.2, May's work on integrative power in Chapter 3 and Boulding's analysis of power as stated earlier in this chapter.

Whereas severe doubts have been expressed regarding the purely unselfish motive in helping behavior, Batson has strongly argued against such a conclusion. Through his empirical research on genuineness of our concern for others, he has offered evidence that this type of motivation exists in us. Here is what Batson (1990) wrote in a very interesting article, "How social an animal? The human capacity for caring":

> Our lives would be decidedly awkward if we were looking out for others' concerns and not our own. It would be, as I believe one philosopher suggested, like a community in which everyone tried to do each other's washing. No one's washing would get done. I do not think we need to worry too much that our concern for others will override self-esteem to this degree. It seems more likely that we need to worry about protecting and nurturing the fragile flower of altruistic caring. Before we do this, however, we need to know the flower is there. Psychology, including social psychology, has assumed that it is not. I hope I have convinced you that it does exist or, at a minimum, that it is worth taking a look to see whether it exists. (American Psychologist, p. 345)

Let's examine two important issues raised in Batson's quote. First, is too much concern for others harmful for oneself? It surely is because it would make our own survival weak. From the evolutionary perspective, it makes sense too, because concern for others means diverting the resources to others that would have served our own interests. Owing to his immense concern for others, Gandhi could not provide enough to his wife and children. Leaving his lucrative earning as an attorney, he led the freedom struggle but maintained no bank account of his own, wore minimum clothes, and consumed the most frugal diet that one can imagine. As a consequence, his wife, Kasturba, and children complained to him for the hardships they faced (Howard, 1990). Many other prominent people such as Mother Teresa also endured unlimited hardships because of their concern for others.

Mark Davis (2004) strongly argued that most psychological theories view human nature in the context of self-interest, as stated in the beginning of this chapter. We know how to maximize our interest, but we are not oriented to look at others in a similar manner. Empathy offers an opportunity to an individual to see the other in a similar way and tends to reduce the gap between the self and the other. Thus, the boundaries between us versus them, in-group versus out-group, self versus other, and ego versus alter become blurred in the presence of empathy. The self-concept, in the presence of empathy, is enlarged as in the case of two romantic partners between whom the gap between me/not me reduces as their selves converge. As mentioned earlier, the interdependent selves in collectivist cultures are fueled by the empathetic responses of its members so as to nurture their sense of community.

The second question is: Do we have a genuine motive for altruistic caring? According to Mark Davis (2004), if we accept the fact that the empathy provides opportunity to reduce the gap between self and other, then this question is answered to some degree, even if not fully. Davis contended that there are at least five ways in which empathy influences attitudes and behavior:

1. Empathy may create emotional synchrony, for example, mimicry, facial expressions, and vocalizations, leading to the experience of similar emotions of joy or sorrow.
2. Empathy may create reactive emotions, for example empathetic concern leading to compassion or personal distress caused by the plight of the other.
3. Empathy may elevate the motivational state of the observer, for example, it may cause forgiving.
4. Empathy may cause reduction in the levels of aggression, a point in which we are interested here (Box 4.2). Once an individual has a perspective of the problem of the victim, empathy is likely to reduce harm to the target. Higher perspective-taking is positively related to lower hostility. Such an impact of empathy appears to be useful for facilitating negative nonviolence, that is, the absence of aggression.
5. Empathy may change the cognitive representation of the self and other and produce positive outcomes in interaction. This last outcome is particularly important in the context of positive nonviolence for the purpose of facilitating our efforts to build nonviolence. The role of empathy will be assessed in the following three ways:
    a. In this situation, the self expands, having overlapping features of the self and the other. The net gain, at a minimum, will be less prejudice, decreased stereotyping and better connections between self and the other.
    b. There will be increased perception of similarity, for example, even false assumptions of similarity between self and the other may promote satisfaction.
    c. With self-other merging, the other individual appears less threatening.

From the point of view of nonviolence and aggression, the above-mentioned role of empathy has important bearings. Davis contended that empathy contributes positively to social life in two ways. First, with its input, the relationships are maintained smoothly. And second, as a reparative function, empathy saves burning the bridges in a relationship. More than anything else, empathy "reduces the tendency to respond immediately and destructively to bad behavior" and "feeling empathetic concern for transgressors contributes strongly to a willingness to forgive, and with this a readiness to forgo retaliation and embrace reconciliation" (ibid., p. 38).

More specifically, we searched for empirical evidences showing a relationship between empathy and nonviolence and found that indeed a positive relationship does exist between the two tendencies. Mayton and coworkers (2002) reported that their TNT subscale on empathy and Kool and Sen's NVT bear a statistically significant correlation (0.42, $p < 0.01$), leading us to conclude that nonviolent and empathetic tendencies are related.

Does it mean that violent people do not empathize? In fact, they also empathize and hence the relationship of empathy with violence and nonviolence becomes very complicated. According to Baumeister (1999), if empathy can prevent violence, it can also fuel it. "To hurt someone", writes Baumiester, "you must know what that person's sensitivities and vulnerabilities are, without having compassion or pity for the person's suffering. That is perhaps most obvious in the emotional abuse of inmates or family members. Inmates can say the most hurtful things because they know the other person's areas of vulnerability. The empathetic bond to the other person becomes an instrument to facilitate cruelty" (p. 245).

Further, Baumeister cited an example of a father who, in order to punish his daughter, killed her favorite pet. It's undoubtedly a blatant abuse of an empathetic relationship. Thus, in the case of sadism, involvement of empathy becomes counterproductive. Therefore, as advised by Baumeister, psychologists

BOX 4.2 LESSON NUMBER ONE: "EMPATHIZE WITH YOUR ENEMY"

Blight and Lang (2004) in *Peace and Conflict: Journal of Peace Psychology* quote Ralph White and Robert McNamara:

> Empathy is the great corrective for all forms of war-promoting misperception . . . . It [means] simply understanding the thoughts and feelings of others . . . jumping in imagination into another person's skin, imagining how you might feel about what you saw. (Ralph White, *Fearful Warriors*, 1984, pp. 160–161)

Robert McNamara, former Secretary of Defense: "That's what I call empathy. We must try to put ourselves inside their skin and look us through their eyes, just to understand the thoughts that lie behind their decisions and their actions" (Morris, *The Fog of War*, 2003).

OUTCOME
SELF ⇔ OTHER ➔ EMPATHY + SYMPATHY ➔ NONVIOLENCE

should use this concept carefully in the context of nonviolence and violence. One way to resolve this issue is to examine the role of sympathy in addition to empathy. With sympathy present, the sadistic behavior of killing the pet by the father would not have been possible (see Box 4.2).

Forgiveness

The Webster dictionary defines forgiving as an excuse for a fault or offense (pardon). This act of forgiving might take place with or without empathy. Few would disagree that forgiving is not an important correlate of nonviolence. In fact, in our description of the factor structure of the NVT in Chapter 5, we pointed out that forgiveness emerged as an important component of nonviolence.

According to Thomas Hora (1983), an important aspect of forgiving is the desire not to blame the adversary. In addition, forgiving involves

a. A declaration that we are not aggrieved any further,
b. No more inducement of guilt to the transgressor, and
c. Personal response with no legal pardoning or no acknowledgment of weakness.

According to the Bible, "Nothing shall remain hidden . . . what shall not reveal." In order to deal with this situation, the best protection is to simply forgive, but it is not easy to reach that stage in our lives. According to a Chinese proverb, we cannot stop birds from flying over our head, but we can certainly stop them from making a nest above our head. In other words, we do not allow an adversary all he or she wants to do against us. To reach that stage in our life wherein we tolerate and pardon all evil acts, we need to be genuinely compassionate. Such a moral stage in our ordinary lives is more a fiction than a reality.

Fortunately, concepts such as love, that were once considered highly subjective and difficult to measure, have been defined, tested, verified and applied both in the laboratory and in the everyday situations (Sternberg, 1986). Measurement of forgiveness is a relatively new endeavor. Mullet, Houdbive, Laumonier, and Girard (1998), for example, have developed a test of forgiveness consisting of items on circumstances leading to forgiveness (Azar & Mullet, 2002):

a. *Social proximity*: Sample item, "It is easier to forgive a member of the family than somebody else."
b. *Severity of consequences*: Sample item, "I cannot forgive even if the consequences of the harm are minimal."
c. *Intent to harm*: Sample item, "I can truly forgive even if the offender did harm intentionally."
d. *Revenge*: Sample item, "I can truly forgive only if I have been able to take revenge over the offender."

e. *Cancellation of consequences*: Sample item, "I do not feel able to forgive even if the consequences of the harm have been cancelled."
f. *Apologies*: Sample item, "I do not feel able to forgive if the offender has not begged for forgiveness."
g. *Pressures from close others and religious authorities*: Sample item, "I do not feel able to forgive even if a religious person asked me to do so."
h. *Mood*: Sample item, "I forgive less easily when I feel bad."
i. *Personal philosophy and faith*: Sample item, "The way I consider the world brought me to always forgive."

A factor analysis of the data revealed that a general tendency to forgive was salient irrespective of situations that affected forgiveness. Azar and Mullet (2002) reported consistency in the scale properties across samples, for example, from France and Lebanon.

Another measure of forgiveness was developed by McCullough, Pargament, and Thoresen (2000). According to them, among the strong positive correlates of forgiving are moral development, age, agreeableness, and humility, whereas the negative correlates include narcissism and neuroticism. For our purposes, forgiving people show less criminality and greater readiness to repair the damage in the relationship. Both are useful for the maintenance and promotion of nonviolence (Carr, 2004). Physiological correlates of forgiving have also been identified in research studies. For instance, when subjects rehearsed non-forgiving responses, their blood pressure, skin conductance and heart rate increased significantly (Witvliet, Ludwig, & Vander Laan, 2001).

Positive emotions and positive nonviolence

With a view to free psychology from the prevailing negative bias, Sheldon and King (2001) strongly advocated that psychology needs to focus on positive feelings and emotions and how they help our mental resources and facilitate our functioning. In fact, research in this area is relatively new in psychology, but sociologists have long been advocating the usefulness of studying the social nature of our emotions (Mackie, Silver, & Smith, 2004). Leach and Tiedens (2004) argued that we need to study emotions for understanding social behavior. Unfortunately, psychologists have been too preoccupied with the private and internal states of an individual and they do not realize that not only are such states rarely private, but also that the cardinal feature of emotion is its responsive to the social scenario. For example, social situations trigger emotions in an individual and vice versa. Sometimes, it is even difficult to understand social relationships in the absence of emotions. With emotions present, we can construe the world, for example, with congruity in our emotions shared with others, our relationships tend to grow.

Whereas motivation is generic in nature, emotions are specific states. In the arena of positive emotions are love, joy, pride, contentment, and so on. If you are asked to work in a company (motivation to work to make a living), which type of work environment would you choose—the one that fosters joy, love, pride and other positive affects or the one that causes negative affect? We all know the answer to such a simple question. But in a situation demanding nonviolence (or should one opt for a nonviolent choice when facing an adversary armed with violent solution only) displaying nonviolence is not likely to trigger positive emotions. At a minimum, the scenario would be one of uncertainty of outcomes and a preparedness to endure pain. It is fair to say that given the context of our modern culture and its emphasis on the promotion of self-interests, we can expect a plethora of negative states associated with a nonviolent stance. For example, in a nonviolent movement, the participant knows before he/she joins the movement, and is well informed thereafter, that the road to justice is thorny—sit-ins, protest marches, fasting or hunger strike, to name a few—and such acts are demanding, requiring huge sacrifice and the bearing of insults, humiliation and threats. And yet, in the annals of human history we find from time immemorial, a large number of examples of individuals who resorted to nonviolence and succeeded with it as well. In our not too distant times, the efforts of nonviolent leaders such as King, Mandela and Gandhi were undoubtedly regarded as more virtuous than those who littered the pages of history with the red ink of blood.

In the framework of modern psychology that is preoccupied with hedonistic tendencies, the behavior of nonviolent individuals would be classified as sadist, compulsive, norm violating and many other such negative labels. Is this a fair description? How did we treat and describe Thoreau, the founding father of the modern civil disobedience movement in America, who was exiled from his county for his humane acts to save the blacks from the atrocities of their masters? What emotions did he live through during his struggle using a nonviolent method? We doubt whether our present simplistic psychology has much to offer to elaborate and understand the emotions of such people. Even in the scientific study of consumer behavior, with the manipulation of variables related to potential gains and losses, psychologists have not done well, mainly because they resort to the oversimplified classification of natural emotions (Richins, 1997). In fact, consumer behavior is very complex. For example, we buy an expensive car and enjoy it, but at the same time, paying for its monthly loan amount is certainly unpleasant. By participating in a nonviolent movement, that has no immediate reward but only hardships in sight, the gamut of emotions would be far more complex. Consider the following emotions described by Muste, a prominent nonviolent leader, at the occasion of the Lawrence, MA strike in the early 1920s for raising the wages of textile workers:

> That to permit ourselves to be provoked into violence would mean defeating ourselves, that our real power was in our solidarity and our capacity to endure self-suffering rather than give up the right to organize; that no one could 'weave wooden with machine guns'; that cheerfulness was better for morale than bitterness and that therefore we would smile as we passed the machine guns and the police on the way from the hall to the picket lines around the mill. (as quoted by Cooney and Michalowski, 1987, p. 64)

Notice how many contrasting emotional states Muste was referring to in his speech as he was preparing workers and comrades for a nonviolent action:

violence (compared to leading through nonviolence), self-suffering, cheerfulness, bitterness, smile (joy), and machine guns (fear). Among the many answers that positive psychology can offer, such as optimism, hope, and so on, we believe that any one emotion will not be useful in analyzing the affective states of nonviolent individuals. For sure, if we are looking at the affect, that not only includes emotions but also free-floating sensations, feelings or moods, we will be in a better position to delineate the emotions that personally become meaningful. For emotions *per se*, they need to fit in discrete categories, like joy, sorrow and so on, and are unlike affect that is long lasting and broader than emotions.

In the face of uncertainty of outcome, prospect theory would require the presence of a frame in which the cost of behavior is to be examined. Assuming that the cost is high, a negative frame would need to be viewed in a positive frame to believe that the pay offs would be higher in the long run. Optimism and hope may serve as catalysts in reframing the emotional impact and make it appear less severe. Once in a positive frame, psychological well-being is promoted (Carr, 2004).

But that is not all. In the face of a violent adversary or norm dictated by self-interests, a dedicated activist is likely to face positive emotions in the pursuit of his anticipated positive action. At the same time, he must be ready to absorb the adversarial circumstance that would normally generate negative affects. It is a mixed mode of operation in terms of positive and negative affects and a test of adaptability of the activist to remain motivated for the pursuit of his cause.

I believe that one psychological theory, "broaden-and-build theory of positive emotions" (BBT), proposed by Barbara Fredrickson (2002) is most relevant for our purposes. Expanding the traditional notion that positive emotions support well-being and momentarily guide behavior, she focused on the much larger role positive emotions can play in our lives. Such emotions may be of a transitory nature, but they tend to have a salutary effect in as much as they become relevant for individual growth and social facilitation. In her own words expressed in the *American Psychologist* (2001):

> This theory [BBT as abbreviated by the author] states that certain discrete positive emotions—including joy, interest, contentment, pride, and love—although phenomenologically distinct, all share the ability to broaden people's momentary thought-action repertoires and build their enduring personal resources to social and psychological resources. (Fredrickson, 2001, p. 219)

I doubt if any great nonviolent leader at any time in human history had appreciated the input of negative emotions. Anger, hatred, aggression, revenge, fear, retaliation and so on involve negativism and therefore are the antithesis to the nonviolent struggle. In addition, many leaders condemned loud expression of even positive emotions. Too much emotion of any type—positive or negative—might derail self-control and reason in an activist. In addition, louder celebrations may be perceived as offensive by an adversary under some circumstances while participating in a resolution of conflict.

Thus, perhaps contentment, more than love or joy, is an option in nonviolence for receiving optimum results; and so are cheerfulness and delight more important than euphoria and elation. In the context of Gandhi's ahimsa and satyagraha, the BBT applies very aptly. Through satyagraha, an effort is made to convert the adversary slowly and slightly as the circumstances permit, but without using coercion. It gives an opportunity to the practitioner of nonviolence to widen the array of his interaction with the opponent and in doing so, evaluate and build his or her personal resources to adapt to the adverse situation (Mayton, 2001).

Commenting on how positive emotions broaden our mental resources, such as attention, cognition and action, Fredrickson (2001) contended that under positive conditions, the subjects identified more things on cognitive tasks than under negative conditions in which fear and anger were induced. In addition, she also found that given the right frame, positive emotions tend to offset the effects caused by the negative emotions. Citing evidence from her research, she contended that the positive emotions are capable of assisting in recovery from cardiovascular imbalance caused by the negative emotions. In short, there are at least two ways in which positive emotions are useful: first, they broaden the mental capacities, and second, they undo the adverse effect of negative emotions. Children play for joy that leads to shared amusement and excitement, creates social bonds and attachment, and broadens social resources (ibid.). In other words, physical, intellectual and social resources are expanded with positive emotions and behavior becomes adaptive (Table 4.6).

Other contributions of positive psychology such as resilience, wisdom, and spiritualism will be discussed in Chapter 5 on the personality of nonviolent individuals. To sum up, it is contended here that if nonviolence is conceptualized as a positive form of human interaction, it should generate positive experiences, including positive emotion. Failing to achieve the substantive goals through nonviolence still provides the operator an opportunity to broaden his/her

Table 4.6 Positive versus negative emotions

Category	Positive	Negative
Mood	Good	Bad
Motivation	Approach	Avoid
Adaptive nature	Long-term benefit	Short-term benefit
Consequence of empathy	Good/supportive	Bad/hurting
Personal resources	Increase	Decrease
Cognitive	Expanded	Narrowed
Attentional	Expanded	Narrowed
Action	Positive	Negative
Physiological impact	Conserved	Depleted
Recovery following	Fast	Slow
Tuning	Yes	No
Building resilience	Helpful	Adverse
Social connections	Increase	Decrease
Prepare for life	Better	Worse

Source: Fredrickson (2001).

experiences and to build new resources to enhance his/her adaptive repertoire for further use of nonviolence or to judge its continued appropriateness in a conflict situation.

SUMMARY

Beneath the human capacity to adhere to nonviolence in the face of an adversarial situation must be the fuel of motivation to resolve a conflict. With the balance of society and our own survival tilted toward enhancing our self-interest, nonviolence, requiring a lot of giving up of not only our material but also mental resources, is not something easy to sustain. Research cited in this chapter on self-interest, moral exclusion, adversarialism and power point out in the same direction: we tend to look after our own interests only. Even empathy, a unique emotion that brings self and the other together, is viewed in the same hedonistic and ego-enhancing framework. Advances in the emerging area of positive psychology are promising for our understanding of nonviolent behavior, but evidence based on current psychological research is inadequate, though the available studies do provide a solid foundation for future research in this field.

SUGGESTED READINGS

Carr, A. (2004). *Positive psychology: The science of happiness and human strength.* Hove & New York: Bruner-Routledge.

Davis, M. H. (2004). Empathy: Negotiating the border between the self and other. In C. W. Leach & L. Z. Tiedens (Eds.), *Emotions in social life*. New York: Cambridge University Press.

Miller, D. T. (1999). The norm of self-interest. *American Psychologist, 54*(12), 1053–1060.

The Nonviolent Individuals: Who Are They Like?

OUTLINE

By and large, we live peaceful lives. Even the most violent among violent individuals is not violent all the time. Whether we view nonviolence in a narrow sense or consider it in a broader perspective, nonviolence is a highly normative process in our lives and that is the way we tend to take it in our interaction with others. Unless there is something unusual or life threatening, our lives are routinely shaped in peaceful ways—we park our car without anticipation of loss, take an evening walk without fear of being attacked, and so on. Conversely, a violent event disturbs the tranquility of our lives and becomes so salient that it overrides all the peaceful behavior that is going on in normal routine ways in communities all over the world. Thanks to the impact of technology, the episodes of violence travel around the globe within seconds, but nonviolence is quietly accepted, simply as a way of life. Off duty, even a ferocious general of an army is a loving father/mother and an adorable spouse. And so was Hitler, a vegetarian and a loving husband, in spite of the fact that his brutalities and genocide are unparalleled in the annals of history.

There are individuals who have had to work really hard, and for a significant amount of time, to make nonviolence conspicuous not only in their personal but also in their social lives. There is considerable injustice, abuse and exploitation in this world that is perpetrated by individuals, as in spousal abuse, or through organized gangs and mafia, or in the form of institutional abuse of power referred to as structural violence (Galtung, 1996). The individuals in such conditions may remain peaceful and manage their daily lives without any expression of violence. In a marital relationship, one spouse often tends to abuse the other throughout their marital life. Similarly, it is common among subjugated masses ruled by a bullying, tyrant leader or regime to accept their domination peacefully and continue to do so for centuries together. Genghis Khan, the cruel Mongol leader, had his ways of war and peace: to surrender and live peacefully under his regime or face slaughter upon resistance. In most cases in the annals of history, spouses have lived with admirable tolerance and the people in a nation have managed peacefully, or with uneasy calm, even with brutal and violent dictators.

To make this routine nonviolence appear more significant in a conflict situation, such nonviolent activities had to be, on many occasions, made exceptionally significant, giving a message to the adversary that there was an alternate to violence and to communicate the message of suffering. The means chosen for overcoming injustice were primarily nonviolent, though the same goal could also have been achieved through violent means. In doing so, means that caused no harm, or in some cases minimum harm, were adopted by the citizens. Who were those individuals who continued to prefer such nonviolent means? What drove them to adhere to nonviolence as a tool for accomplishing their mission? Are there any enduring personality characteristics that go along with such nonviolent individuals? Examining their life histories, do we find how their personal priorities, such as freedom of speech and travel, blended with their community needs, leading to the formation of a superordinate goal in their lives? This chapter is about addressing these and related issues regarding the characteristics of a nonviolent individual.

One bias that historians acknowledge in writing history is that the history written by intellectuals focuses more on intellectuals who made the history, ignoring many unsung heroes. According to Dellinger (1975), history is best depicted when it highlights the personal values of individuals and how they blended them into a social mission to oppose evils in the society. He further contended that the whole story of virtue and evil is about human development and social change as pursued through violent or nonviolent means.

The nonviolent heroes: A psychological perspective

Generally speaking, a hero is one who shows courage and risks his or her life for a noble cause. Plato's "just man" as described in his book, *Republic*, and Aristotle's man of practical wisdom could be considered classic examples of heroes and saints. In our modern era, there may be a Nelson Mandela to remove apartheid, a Mother Teresa engaged in social work or, if you like sport, "be like Michael Jordan". The central idea in heroism is that in addition to what people do by imitating the hero, there is an inner urge to be like him or her. However, every exemplar presents standards that are not easy for ordinary people to achieve and we, therefore, place them in a very special category, that, at the minimum, sets them apart in some form.

According to the guidelines of the Carnegie Hero Fund Commission, heroes perform voluntarily and without external pressures. In short, the two psychological attributes that interest us in heroism are empathy and risk taking. We have already discussed empathy in Chapter 4 and will therefore now focus on risk taking in terms of violating the norm of self-interest and organizing one's personal life to carve it for a social movement.

In terms of prospect theory, the cost of investing in a nonviolent behavior is likely to be high and therefore the scenario involves a negative frame. Then why do people continue to participate in such nonviolent activities? It is their heroism, a tendency to look beyond themselves, and as Batson (1991) argued, such people have motives that are purely altruistic. On many occasions, they do not have time to assess whether their own behavior could prove fatal for them. The CNN broke a story today, 11 January 2005, as I am writing this chapter, that a liquid container exploded in a bus in Brazil and the TV images showed how most of the passengers inside the bus were under flames. The people standing nearby rushed to break the window glasses of the bus and pulled the passengers out through the window openings, receiving in the rescue process, many injuries. There was plenty of risk, no time to think and no selfish motive. Having said this, let's view nonviolence. In a nonviolent scenario related to conflict resolution, there is likely to be no risk to the adversary, as he/she knows about the non-threatening demeanor of the victim; has a lot of time to plan for a solution to the problem; and the involvement of self-interest of parties is there only to the extent that injustice is removed.

Helpfulness and kindness are some of the very significant traits that correlate strongly with women. In fact, Gilligan's major objection to Kohlberg's work, as stated earlier in Chapter 3, was that women were ignored in the samples used for determining moral stages in Kohlberg's model of moral development. Empirical research also supports the contention that women express exceptionally high concern for others in their belief and action. According to Becker and Eagly (2004),

- Women donate their kidney at a higher rate than men.
- More women volunteered for the Peace Corps program than men.
- More female physicians worked for vulnerable populations in the "Doctors for the World" program.

Contrary to the above conclusion, from time immemorial, heroism is normally identified with masculinity. Upon critical examination of stereotypes that are involved in identifying heroes, males are mistakenly considered as forming the majority—at least this is the impression one gets from the statistics available from the Carnegie Hero Medal recipients involved in extremely dangerous acts (Becker & Eagly, 2004). In fact, among the recipients of the medal, less than 10 percent were women, a picture that is very misleading and goes a long way in confirming the stereotype that heroism is predominantly a masculine trait.

Heroism involves many behavioral domains that are not salient in everyday life or considered for awards. One good example is about those Germans who were involved in rescuing the people of Jewish origin from their Nazi predators. Oliner and Oliner (1988, 1995) reported that 86 percent rescuers gave care and compassion as the main reason for saving the lives of Jews by risking their own prosecution at the hands of the Nazi police. In this mission that involved a high personal risk combined with a sense of humanity, both men and women showed their heroism with great magnitude and there was nothing masculine only about it. Using the expression in Hebrew, both German men and women showed what is called as Chasidism, that is, those who act lovingly (Becker & Eagly, 2004). Sharon Shepela and coworkers (1999) called this behavior of Germans, protecting Jews at an enormous cost, "courageous resistance".

Both men and women are as heroic as the situation demands and the roles for which they are prepared. When issues of caring are involved, Dovidio and coworkers (1993) found that when requested to help, women, more than men, volunteered to fold clothes in a Laundromat. But conversely, more men than women were helpful in carrying the load. Such experimental studies show clearly that both men and women show gender-consistent behavior. Such gender-specific behavior shows its impact on the heroism of men and women. Since the Carnegie Awards are associated with physical strength, the higher numbers of men in comparison to women are, therefore, not surprising (Becker & Eagly, 2004).

The history of nonviolence in America also shows that both men and women fought for promoting nonviolence. In their book, *The Power of the People: Active Nonviolence in America*, Robert Cooney and Helen Michalowski (1987) reported a number of women who championed the cause of nonviolence by risking their lives and by facing personal humiliation and losing community privileges. A few such heroic women in the violent American society, who stood firm during the time when they were devoid of status and power are listed below.

Angelina and Sarah Grimke

Both these women belonged to the New England Non-Resistance Society. In 1848, they called the Seneca Falls Convention to address the problems of women who were prohibited from speaking publicly. In fact, their frustration had grown after American women were denied any speech at the World Anti-Slavery Convention in London in 1840. They dared to face the outrage of society, especially the clergy, for discussing women's rights publicly.

Jane Addams (1860–1935)

Known for her contribution to Hull House, a facility for helping the poor and the immigrants, and recipient of the Nobel Peace Prize, she engaged in a variety of social and political activities. One of the cardinal contributions she made was the realization that women, being more caring and nurturing, have a greater sense of responsibility and obligation than men and hence they should have adequate rights and roles to play in all spheres of life. As an activist, she opposed World War I and founded the Women's Peace Party in 1915. Later, she became the first President of the Women's International League for Peace and Freedom.

Emma Goldman (1869–1940)

An immigrant from Russia, Goldman was initially an advocate for violence on behalf of the oppressed. Very soon she realized the futility of violence and adhered to nonviolence. She resisted World War I by organizing the No-Conscription League. The government charged her for conspiracy, fined her $10,000 and deported her back to Russia.

Alice Paul (1885–1977)

A graduate of Swarthmore College and recipient of three law degrees, Paul firmly believed that the crisis in the world was not the creation of women as they had no say in the matters. She spearheaded the movement for women's rights and was instrumental in moving Congress to pass the Women's Suffrage Amendment. During her nonviolent agitation, she went on hunger strikes and was put into solitary confinement.

Jeannette Rankin (1880–1973)

Rankin was the first US Congresswoman who voted against war and, as a result, lost her seat in the next election. She said that she believed in her country but would not vote for war.

Dorothy Day (1897–1980)

A devout Catholic, Day was a champion of justice, peace and human rights. In 1917, she was a member of the suffrage team that picketed the White House.

She edited a newspaper and published several articles on peace and equality. Later in life, she opposed the Vietnam war.

Rosa Parks (1913–2005)

Known for changing the history of nonviolence in America by refusing to leave her seat in a bus in Montgomery, Alabama, Parks was a popular black activist. Her courage helped the black leaders to organize their movement effectively and the history of segregation changed altogether since then.

The purpose here in citing such brave American women should not be viewed narrowly. Women all over the world, for example, Nobel Laureate Aung San Suu Kyi of Burma, have shown courage in similar adverse circumstances and also deserve to be mentioned in the text. However, we leave this issue for historians to satiate the appetite of a reader who is looking for a global contribution of women in the field of nonviolence.

To sum up, the heroic acts of nonviolence involve the development of a sense of shared humanity and personal conviction. In the classification of Kohlberg's moral stages of development, heroism would be classified in the post-conventional operation stage in which individuals act in accordance to their conscience so as to transcend their personal values into social good. For Bandura, heroism would characterize self-efficacy of the individual that involves behavior consistent with one's belief to achieve the goal. Heroism, therefore, will mean personal fulfillment with a social mission targeted without violence.

Resiliency: The ordinary magic of nonviolent individuals

Research studies conducted by Kobasa (1979, 1982) showed that some individuals display extraordinary talent in adjusting to the adverse conditions in life. They show remarkable resiliency in adapting to life conditions. For them, stress is a challenge to mobilize additional resources to cope with a difficult situation in their lives.

Kobasa identified three core characteristics of such people:

1. *Challenge*: Considering that change is a natural process, such individuals show readiness to adjust and do not perceive it as a threat.
2. *Commitment*: Such people believe that what they are doing is important and useful.
3. *Control*: Believing in their inner strength, they guide their efforts and destiny.

The above three Cs of Kobasa compose the "Hardy Personality", a concept that embodies the resiliency of an individual. A key feature of resilient individuals is that they develop a strong sense of inner control that navigates their sense of meaning and action, orienting them toward nonviolent activism. They develop a strong belief that an alternate to violence is possible and that a pursuit of nonviolent methods will bring success sooner or later.

Studies on resilient children show that such children do not view adversity in negative ways and stop from moving toward their goal; instead, for them, it is considered positive and productive, providing an opportunity to test their strength (Garmezy, 1981). They have positive dispositions that they acquire, in most cases, from their role models early in life. Undertaking a difficult mission and responsibility is a joy for them.

Unfortunately, the inconsistency of relationship between the above-mentioned three Cs in Kobasa's work led to many questions including the central one: Is there a hardy personality? The core personality based on challenge, commitment and control did not emerge consistently in the factor-analytic studies and many scholars began to doubt the integrity of the concept of hardy personality (Kool & Agrawal, 2006).

Masten (2001) argued that the deficit-focused view of children growing in adverse conditions is not helpful in fully understanding resiliency and, in some cases, has been found to be misleading. Further, resiliency should not be considered as extraordinary because it is a common phenomenon reflected in everyone's adaptational system. In other words, resilience is an ordinary process that has been made to appear extraordinary. Therefore, resiliency does not require identification of a specific set of characteristics. It is the magic of an ordinary human being. According to Masten (2001),

> Resilience refers to a class of phenomenon characterized by good outcomes in spite of serious threats to adaptation or development. (p. 228)

According to Bonanno (2004), people have a remarkable capacity to return to normal functioning. Ozer, Best, Lipsey, and Weiss (2003) estimated that between 50 and 60 percent people in the USA are exposed to traumatic experiences, but relatively few among them (less than 10 percent) develop any significant amount of traumatic symptoms, commonly known as PTSD. Among those few who are traumatized, a large number are victims of personal threatening or violent events. For example, among those who witnessed the 9/11 attack in Manhattan, 7.5 percent developed PTSD but within six months, this number went down to less than 1 percent.

Resiliency is not something we are born with; it's learned through our tragic or tough experiences. It is a test of our positive approach to adverse conditions that we face during a critical period and how we come out of it stronger and brighter. Resiliency reflects one's personal journey that involves making connections, moving towards the goal, taking decisive action, self-discovery, positive view, keeping things in perspective, taking care of our own, and a belief that crisis is surmountable (Johnson, as reported by Murray, 2003, October).

There are two major approaches that have been pursued in resiliency research (Masten, 2001). First, the variable-focused approach involves analysis of the relationship between the degree of risk, outcome, and support (or, lack of support) from the environment. Factors that bear a relationship to resiliency are prosocial behavior, peer acceptance, and positive self-perception (Cicchetti, Rappaport, Sandler, & Weissberg, 2000). Second, there is the person-focused approach that studies resilience in terms of a holistic picture of an individual with a view to configure his/her adaptational characteristics. It has been generally observed that resilient children seek opportunities in a healthy context and look for positive consequences.

Seligman and Csikszentmihalyi (2000) strongly argued that human adaptation and development have not been viewed positively in psychological research and we are ignorant of our optimal functioning in the course of development. The new view of resilience that it is the magic of the ordinary helps us understand how we put our resources to work under different conditions and in what ways our competencies succeed in both supportive and adverse conditions. According to Masten (2001), this new perspective on resilience has rekindled positive psychology (refer to Chapter 4). With a focus on human competencies involved in adaptation and development, resilience has provided an impetus for positive psychology to search for the underlying phenomena of optimal functioning of human beings. To achieve optimal functioning, writes Murray (2003), we need to understand that:

- Resiliency is a personal experience, but it may involve others.
- Resiliency can be experienced by anyone; there is nothing extraordinary to it.
- Resiliency requires investing time and energy in small steps.

A few years ago, the American Psychological Association appointed a task force consisting of 15 psychologists to prepare a fact sheet regarding resilience (called Road to Resilience Campaign). It has also developed a website to help people understand resilience. For details the reader is referred to the following website and Box 5.1 (http://apahelpcenter/org/resilience/homecoming.html).

BOX 5.1 LESSON IN RESILIENCE: FIVE TIPS—THE AMERICAN PSYCHOLOGICAL ASSOCIATION: TIME FOR KIDS

1. Have friends and be a friend.
2. Believe in yourself.
3. Take charge of your behavior.
4. Be optimistic.
5. Set goals and achieve them.

Adapted from: Kersting (2004, October)

A survey of literature on nonviolent leaders clearly shows how such leaders faced various challenges in their lives under highly adverse conditions, but remained resolute and productive in their mission (Lynd, 1966; Rappaport, 1990). For example, Muste was a devout nonviolent leader in the USA who believed that human beings acquiesced too easily to evil forces and that we need not cooperate with the government if it is evil. He adhered to Gandhi's Satyagraha and popularized it in the American context. Peck, a leading figure in the nonviolent struggle in the USA, was against war and supported racial equality. During the freedom ride in 1961, when he accompanied a black to the bus terminal, he was attacked by a mob and had 53 stitches on his wounds. With similar multiple experiences, he became even more determined to carry on his nonviolent mission without any retaliation to his adversaries. The human history is glorified with such resilient individuals who adhered to nonviolence, albeit only a handful became famous and have been highlighted in our books.

Generativity

In offering his eight-stage theory of human development, Erikson (1965, 1968) disagreed with Freud's overemphasis on sex as the prime mover of behavior (see Chapter 2). For example, Freud's first stage of development is oral in which the child gets pleasure through sucking. Erikson examined the same behavior of the child but viewed it from the point of view of trust (or mistrust)—a relationship between the infant and the mother (Table 5.1). This is the first step in the development of the identity of the child that might accompany positive (for example, hope) or negative (for example, detachment) outcomes.

The next stage is autonomy versus shame in which the child learns to regulate its social behavior or face shame and self-doubt. Compared to Freud's anal stage in which pleasure is linked to the erogenous zone, Erikson focused on a child's sense of autonomy. For him, toilet training of the child was not simply a matter of biological pleasure, but a social situation in which it struggles to become assertive and successful.

A critical stage in an individual's development is the stage of identity and role diffusion. During this period, adolescents view themselves as having continuity with the past and learn to match their perception with other members of the

Table 5.1 Erikson's psychosocial model of development

Period	Feature	Positive	Negative
0–18 months	Trust vs. mistrust	Hope/trust	Detachment
18 months–3 years	Autonomy vs. shame	Will	Compulsion
3 years–6 years	Initiative vs. guilt	Purpose	Inhibition
7 years–11 years	Industry vs. inferiority	Competence	Inertia
12 years–20 years	Identity vs. role confusion	Fidelity	Confusion
21 years–34 years	Intimacy vs. isolation	Love	Exclusivity
34 years–60 years	Productivity vs. stagnation	Care	Rejection
60+ years	Integrity vs. despair	Wisdom	Despair

group. Those who remain confused not only fail to understand themselves but also the feedback they receive from others. Adolescence is typically characterized as the stage of identity versus role diffusion. During the late adolescence period, the teenagers may seek membership in different groups if the choice of a career is not resolved appropriately and this might affect their sense of continuity and confidence in their lives.

The formation of identity is a complex process and according to Marcia (1994), it may take one of the following four forms:

1. *Identity achievement*: Following exploration, identity is established.
2. *Identity moratorium*: Identity is kept on hold until a commitment is sought.
3. *Identity foreclosure*: An identity is formed without exploration.
4. *Identity diffusion*: Remain vulnerable to a sense of self and interpersonal relationship.

According to Erikson, as we enter adulthood, we begin to operate with a sense of mutuality and intimacy or remain, conversely, at a superficial and isolated level. This is followed by the stage of generativity in which individuals engage in work and relationships. In his book, *Gandhi's Truth*, Erikson (1969) presented an analysis of Gandhi's behavior explaining how he discovered his identity as a nonviolent leader through his experiments with the truth, satyagraha and ahimsa. In essence, Erikson argued that Gandhi was a practical psychologist who understood the capacity of human beings to change by demonstrating one's faith in nonviolence, continuous engagement with the adversary in moral and ethical ways, and, if necessary, through self-suffering, rather than retaliation.

Our identity does not wither away in life, but it may go through several transformations. Once an individual knows who he/she is, that is, discovers one's identity, one can engage in committing to others and building relationships. We cannot promote and guide generations without establishing our own identity. Therefore, transformation of our identity as we go along in our life is a natural process and the emergence of generativity (versus stagnation) stage takes place when the identity is meaningfully established with our own experiences as well as with those that we gain from others in the process of interaction. Generativity, in this sense, is a part of our identity.

Do adults develop a generativity script or "adult's plan" in their life to leave a legacy for the next generation? According to Erikson, the answer is in the affirmative. In his analysis of Gandhi's life, Erikson (1969) contended that when Gandhi left South Africa to return to his home country, India, he had the script of nonviolence ready to be tested to free the Indians from the British rule. The essence of generativity is founded on a core belief in a virtuous mission and in the case of Gandhi, it was bloodless war against the British rulers, with a just demand put in all humility. In one way or the other, all human beings, at their level of expansion of self and its influence, pass through this stage of generativity.

Generativity contributes to the development of agency and communion. By agency, we mean a product that is an expression of a self and its influence.

For example, writing a book, establishing a business or any endeavor that is an expression of self that embodies one's legacy is a part of generativity. This product might be highly agentic, narcissistic or intangible, but it nevertheless has the spirit of true reflection of one's influence on the next generation. Communion, the second process, consists of a gifting away of this product to the members of the community. Here the individual feels himself or herself to be a part of a larger system in which he or she is trying to create a sense of worth and meaning. McAdams (1988) considers this effort as equivalent to heroism as discussed above.

According to Kotre (1984) adults create a generativity script in many ways. First, biological generativity that consists of conceiving and nursing a baby. Second, parental generativity, consists of nurturing and disciplining the child. When we pass the trade and other technical skills to the next generation, it is called technical generativity. And finally, cultural generativity consists of preservation and renovation of one's culture. In a study, McAdams, Ruetzel, and Foley (1986) requested 50 midlife men and women to write stories about their dream or vision for the future. Analyses of the data showed that those who scored high on power and intimacy motivation, as assessed through the projective tests, were the ones who came up with the most generative plan for the future. In the case of a nonviolent individual like Gandhi, as Erikson (1968) argued, the generativity plan involved a mission that was not only savory for the Indians, but also for the adversaries, that is, for the British rulers. According to Erikson,

> His [Gandhi's] inclusion of his opponent in all his plans went so far that Kenneth Boulding could say recently that Gandhi had done more good to the British than the Indians. (p. 507)

Further, he wrote, "Gandhi thus emerges amidst the complexity of his personality and the confusion of his times as a man possessing that quality of supreme presence which can give to the finite moment a sense of infinite meaning, for it is tuned both to the 'inner voice' and to the historical actuality, that is, to the potentialities for a higher synthesis in other individuals or in the masses" (p. 510).

Studies on renowned personalities reveal that as their identity took a turn and became part of a larger identity, it tended to create a super identity consisting of a broader and richer generativity. One such way of preparing a larger script of generativity is to engage the adversary at a closer range. It is very commonly observed that nonviolent activists tend to challenge their opponent in proximity and without fear and retaliation. The invention of satyagraha by Gandhi was based on a motivation to transcend truth through nonviolent confrontation directly, without harm to anyone, and even to the extent of helping the opponent. Thus, generativity, in its positive form and nonviolent expression, is basically an expansion of one's self, immersed in the extended social self that is an embodiment of the human legacy in the form of a script of generativity.

Ripeness

In the description of resiliency and generativity, we focused on the strength of one's commitment and action through experiences earned during the life. In the context of nonviolence, however, it is significant that an individual is ready to negotiate and avoid any violence. We do not expect all individuals to remain nonviolent all the time, just as we do not expect them to be violent all the time. A conflict situation involves a condition in which an individual is supposed to cross the barrier and take a direction opting for violence or nonviolence. As we interact in a situation, develop a perception of a problem and find a solution, an important consideration is which trajectory would work: cooperation versus conflict, or violence versus nonviolence. In other words, what motivation do we have in dealing with the conflict—to inflict harm or negotiate through mutual understanding. Ripeness is a word that is used in the literature on conflict resolution to refer to that time when parties involved in a conflict are ready to induce a desired change.

Psychologists like Coleman (1997) and others (Pruitt & Olczak, 1995; Pruitt & Rubin, 1986) however use the concept of ripeness at the individual level in lieu of an interactive situational context. For them, ripeness is a motivation to reach an agreement and to affirm a commitment to change the normative process of conflict. It is a stage that is a product of one's experience and the situation in which he or she is placed. Thus, it is best understood and described in a social psychological model based on Lewin's field theory that explains behavior as a product of the interaction of psychological forces with those of influences of the environment. In the case of one's decision to stick to his or her viewpoint as opposed to the incompatible group decision (the situational forces), a freezing effect may occur, that is, the individual is unable to take a decision. However, with a deep sense of personal commitment, such dissonance can be reduced and an individual begins to behave according to his convictions.

Coleman (1997) cited an example of ripeness shown by a woman who was torn in conflict between her son and his stepfather. First, the stepfather and her son had differences of opinion, followed by emotional outbursts like name-calling, screaming and verbal threats. Finally, escalation of physical exchanges became a routine. The boy's mother was caught in between and the matter was referred to the police. Notwithstanding all the trouble that was a routine violent affair between stepfather and son, the mother struggled to keep her family together. Applying a MACBE model in which:

M= Motivation (A psychological phenomenon in a context: Conflict or its resolution)
A = Affect (inadequacies built over a period of time)
C = Cognition (misperception and misjudgment)
B = Behavior (miscommunication and hostility)
E = Environment (appropriate circumstance and timing)

Coleman (1997) analyzed the behavior of family members and the incompatibilities that generated conflict in the family. The mediation process helped them to lessen their blaming each other and also helped them develop an appreciation of appropriate social skills. The key element was development of trust between the parties that contributed toward ripeness. In short, ripeness is essentially a motivation that enables an individual to minimize conflict and seek opportunities to negotiate. Probably, the best example cited in the literature on ripeness is King Hussein, of Jordon, passing a psychological barrier during his meeting with Israel's Rabin in July 1994. The meeting resulted in a breakthrough to a long-lasting conflict between the two countries.

Psychology of wisdom

In Erikson's stages of development, the last stage is that of integrity (positive outcome) and despair (negative outcome). Following generativity, this stage is featured by an individual's commitment to life in a positive frame (development of wisdom) or a negative frame consisting of disgust caused by the failures. During this stage, one gets a sense of personal and interpersonal competence (or incompetence) and attempts to relate meaningfully with various aspects of life. In the psychological literature, this phenomenon is known as wisdom. It is the skill of an individual to be a good listener, advisor and evaluator to help not only himself or herself but also others. Sternberg (2000) distinguished two ways of understanding wisdom. One way through which we know about wisdom is through a layperson's description of wisdom (implicit mode). On the other hand, psychologists offer an explicit mode of wisdom that is determined by subjects' ratings of various concepts associated with wisdom and then delineating the concept by applying psychological scaling methods. Other explicit methods consist of describing the emergence of wisdom in the course of personality development, as we find in Erikson's stages of development.

Wisdom is about dealing with adversity. As we interact with others, situations involve conflicts of a wide variety. With wisdom, individuals solve dilemmas arising out of such conflicts, minimize their vulnerability and exhibit personal strength. Applying this concept to the understanding of nonviolence and violence would raise the following questions:

a. Is it wisdom to use violence when an issue can be resolved through nonviolent methods?
b. Is it wisdom to use nonviolence when it is failing (or likely to fail) to resolve a conflict?

The answer to the first question is simple. No rational human being would support violence when an issue can be resolved by nonviolent methods. On the other hand, the answer to the second question is not clear-cut, as it has no normative answer. When there are experiences about the failure of nonviolent methods, the norm of adopting peaceful methods to resolve a conflict becomes weaker and the proneness to violence increases. Upon observing the genocide perpetrated during the Nazi regime, even Gandhi volunteered to recruit soldiers for the British army, saying that between the two evils—British rule of India and

Hitler's senseless brutalities—the lesser of the two evils was acceptable to him. After a prolonged struggle, Nelson Mandela began to support violent means in addition to his initial faith in nonviolence, but it proved elusive and hurt the freedom struggle (Presbey, 2006).

With nonviolence as the salient norm of behavior of individuals in society, the answer to the second question will remain incomplete unless and until, with a sense of wisdom, one does not argue that violence will be used as a last resort because other prudent methods of nonviolence could not work. And this is exactly what most political leaders do to harness public opinion, giving the impression of acting with wisdom. Thus, wisdom involves personal strength in dealing with the dilemmas of life. Avoiding violence in the face of adversity is without any doubt an act of wisdom until the situation worsens to the extent that it becomes a threat to one's own survival. Such wisdom is the hallmark of the nonviolent personality.

Anasakti

Anasakti, an Indian concept based on the holy book, the *Bhagwad Gita*, is nonattachment to action. It refers to an individual's capacity to detach himself or herself from the consequences of the attainment of a goal. Unlike people in the west who tend to enjoy the consequences of their act, the concept of Anasakti teaches detachment not from their action domain, but from the consequences of goal attainment (Tewari, 2000). Essentially, it is a highly therapeutic concept, as most of our problems arise out of either failure in achieving our goal or due to the fear of losing the gains; for example, from the thought that someone may rob my expensive diamond ring or steal my expensive car.

Anasakti is a health-promoting concept in as much as it helps in maintaining emotional equipoise. It offers wisdom in balancing one's own life by avoiding adherence to extremes of life—excessive joy or sorrow. Success and failure are considered normal outcomes in life and Anasakti offers to deal with them in a dispassionate manner. This concept is relevant for the western psychologists who study behavior and its outcome. It is essentially a motivational concept as it involves analysis of satisfaction or dissatisfaction in the course of behavior. Two Indian psychologists, Pandey and Naidu (1992) have developed a measure of Anasakti and concluded from their research that:

a. Those who score high on Anasakti, score low on aggression.
b. Higher Anasakti is an indicator of better mental health.

It is emphasized that the concept of Anasakti is useful in differentiating our approach to nonviolence and violence when they are used as means to achieve a goal. Whereas most people separate means and ends to fulfill their desires, for example, "I am going to achieve my target with fair or foul means," Anasakti teaches selflessness and refraining from high levels of attachment to means and ends. For example, Gandhi was very thoughtful in his description of the relationship between means and ends when he wrote, "For me it is enough to know the means. Means and ends are convertible terms in my philosophy of life. We have control over the means but not over the end. I feel that our progress towards the goal will be in exact proportion to the purity of our means" (quoted by Iyer, 1983, p. 362). If the use of means becomes relentless for its own sake, as it often happens in war when soldiers begin senselessly killing for the sake of killing, violence exceeds the limits of human imagination. Therefore, it is important that the focus on means should never be undermined to contain violence. Anasakti, as a motivational force, regulates the unwanted and overenthusiastic use of means leading to violence.

According to Tewari (2000), there is an inherent danger in using concepts like Anasakti in the scientific domain of psychology, especially those with religious or ethnic implications. In its applied form also, intervention programs emerging out of such a religious connotation may also suffer. However, the positive motivational implications, argues Tewari, would be appreciated with greater scientific investigation and cross-cultural applications with a break away from its narrow ethnic orientation.

Components of the nonviolent personality

Research in the field of personality has drifted to such an extent in the last five decades that it is difficult to offer to the reader a compact description of the nature of personality. And yet, most psychologists believe that retaining the concept of personality is vital for the independent existence of psychology as a science. Notwithstanding the controversies that surround the definition of personality and its measurement, psychologists agree on describing personality in terms of consistency of behavior as demonstrated in some form of a cluster of traits—transitory or relatively stable. When leading contributors in the field of personality psychology such as Eysenck (1965) and Cattell (1965) began to describe personality in scientific ways using sophisticated statistical techniques, it heralded a leap in the growth of psychology.

The impact of the above approach did not last for a long time. Unfortunately, the situational and motivational effects that have an impact on the consistency of personality and the consequential changes that take place in behavior across the life span exposed the limits of such classical studies in personality. As a result, personality psychologists, realizing how variations in situational and motivational states change behavior, began to focus on the implicit nature of personality. To build your implicit view of personality, all you have to do is to build categories to describe people (Pervin & John, 2001). For example, in order to categorize extraverts, all we need is to have a prototypic description of extraverts with a list of features that describe their behavior. Similarly, to view nonviolent behavior, as per implicit theory, we need to compile prototypical behavior of nonviolent people and subsequently offer causal explanations supporting why people tend to behave as they do. By matching the content and organization of attributes compiled in the nonviolent category, the domain and extent of nonviolent behavior, with its causal analysis, would determine the implicit nature of nonviolent personality.

Based on the factor analysis method, seven components of the nonviolent personality were identified by Kool and Keyes (1990). See Chapter 1 for details:

1. Self-control including understanding and negotiation
2. Anti-punitiveness including compassion and forgiving
3. Forbearance including tolerance and judging the intentions of others
4. Equity of justice including equality of adjudicating justice
5. Self-defense
6. Constructive reform, and
7. Affective control including emotional control in the face of irritation.

In terms of popular research in the domain of personality—Goldberg's (1990) the BIG 5 and a personality measure developed by Costa and McCrae (1992)—the following factors constitute personality:

1. *Openness*: It refers to information-seeking and intellectual curiosity. A high scorer on this factor is curious, broadminded, imaginative and non-traditional.
2. *Conscientiousness*: Involving self-control, it refers to one's tendency to carry out the tasks in hand. High scorers are those who are reliable, disciplined and motivated.
3. *Agreeableness*: It refers to one's range from compassion to antagonism. High scorers tend to be those who are trusting and forgiving, helpful and straight-forward.
4. *Neuroticism*: This factor measures the emotional stability involving adjustment to distress, cravings and self-satisfaction. Low scorers tend to be calm, hardy, and relaxed.
5. *Extraversion*: It assesses one's interpersonal interaction and need for stimulation. High scorers are usually sociable, optimistic and fun-loving.

While there are no direct research studies linking specific components of BIG 5 with nonviolent behavior, there is some empirical support for nonviolence having a positive relationship with openness, conscientiousness and agreeableness factors. Nonviolent individuals are open in their communication, work hard to avoid conflicts and are forgiving to adjust with their adversary (Kool & Sen, 1984, 2005). Regarding neuroticism and extraversion factors, it is not easy to categorize nonviolent individuals as per research material currently available.

On violent behavior of nonviolent individuals and vice versa

Merely endorsing nonviolence as a way of life is not enough. In practice, all that we learn through our religious and spiritual training tends to contradict our behavior at various times in real life. We learn to show the other cheek when attacked, but in practice, we retaliate and remain unforgiving. Let us examine the behavior of nonviolent and violent individuals briefly and figure out what constituted their relatively nonviolent and/or violent behavior, albeit they are viewed nonviolent or violent in the historical context.

Gandhi

The great Indian leader, Gandhi, an apostle of peace and ahimsa (nonviolence), led the freedom struggle against the British rule during the first half of the 20th century. His commitment to nonviolence will always be remembered in the annals of history as a model for shaping his own behavior and that of an ideal community. He taught Indians to hate the British rule that was evil but love the British people (the enemy), and specifically instructed all those following his freedom movement not to harm British administrators or their family members. When an Indian mob became unruly and injured British administrators and their spouses and children and damaged their property, Gandhi went on a hunger strike unto death to condemn such acts. He broke his fast only after he was assured that the British brothers and sisters would never be ill-treated again.

Gandhi's famous "Dandi march" is said to have changed the course of humanity when he asked poor Indians to make their own salt by defying the British order, but at the same time, not to retaliate against the physical assaults inflicted on them by the British administrators. Those readers who have seen Lord Attenborough's film, *Gandhi*, would probably remember that this scene was an excellent example of two diametrically opposed ways of solving a conflict—violence versus nonviolence.

And yet, this Mahatma (the great soul), as affectionately called by the Indians, was ridiculed in the British media, portraying him as a mischief monger, a nuisance and a half-naked fakir (he wore minimum clothes because he wanted all the citizens in the world to have clothes before he got them). Many western journalists and laypersons believed that beneath his nonviolent movement was a hidden agenda to incite the Indian masses to hate the British people and to line them up for a mutiny against the British governance of India.

Like any other popular leader, Gandhi also faced considerable controversy regarding his philosophy and action. The following are a few examples of how he contradicted himself on nonviolence, albeit he offered justification for his own action in one way or the other:

a. Gandhi physically assaulted his wife, Kasturba, a few times and personally acknowledged his shameful behavior in his writings (Howard, 1990). On one occasion, when Kasturba refused to follow his instructions, he dragged her outside the home and shut the gate. Both Erikson (1969) and Gilligan (1982) criticized Gandhi for his violent behavior and failure to practice nonviolence in interpersonal relationship.
b. During the Boer war (1899–1902) and the British expedition against the Zulu (1906), Gandhi volunteered to serve the British Army (Steger, 2003).

c. In India, he volunteered to recruit soldiers for the British Army to support the opposition against Hitler's genocide. As stated earlier, Gandhi concluded that between the two evils, the British rule of India and the genocide in Germany, he would prefer the lesser of the two evils.

d. He believed that violence in some form would always be there. The only thing we could do is to minimize it. According to Iyer (1983), it was because violence "cannot be wholly avoided that Gandhi felt it necessary to use a negative word like ahimsa or nonviolence" (p. 206).

Hitler

What Gandhi did to his country as a patriot, Hitler did in no lesser ways to salvage Germany from its woes that had accumulated after World War I. However, the means he adopted for helping his country were vastly different. The former became a champion of humanity while the latter, with unprecedented display of genocide, was identified with evil on earth. Ironically, Hitler considered Jews and Bolsheviks as evil and organized the Einsatzgruppen (task forces) to track them down to achieve his mission (Lifton & Markusen, 1990). This was in sharp contrast to Gandhi's assertion to love the enemy, that is, the British people, but not the British occupation of India.

In 1943, an attempt was made by the Allied forces to prepare a psychological profile of Hitler. Henry Murray, who was at that time the Director of the Harvard Psychological Clinic, was assigned this task. In profiling the behavior of Hitler, he made two important predictions. First, he would commit suicide, which came out to be true. And second, Hitler suffered from "counteractive narcissism", a tendency triggered by real or imaginary insult or injury involving holding grudges, low tolerance for criticism, bullying, excessive demands for attention, tendency to belittle, and to take revenge. While such descriptions in psychoanalytic terminology are considered outdated in the modern literature in psychology, they offer the contrasting features of evil- and good-natured people.

There are segments of Hitler's behavior that would be appreciated by the nonviolent individuals. For example,

a. He would not eat until all others were served
b. He would offer a plate to even a lower level staff and be kind and nice
c. He was a loving and caring spouse
d. He was a vegetarian.

According to Baumeister (1999), many Germans did not believe even after Hitler's defeat, death and exposure of brutalities that he was a bad guy, because for them, he was a hero who had no choice but to lead the country in the ways that were available to him. Baumeister further argued that in judging evil, it is important to understand the aspect of affiliation. Not surprisingly, many people in Iraq still believe that Saddam Hussein was a good human being and, as an administrator of their country, he had to take actions, though harsh and brutal, that helped him to govern the country.

Leaving aside the issues of evil or good or the sides we take in judging personality, Gandhi offered a practical solution to emphasize the positive aspect of interaction. For him, freedom of India was unimportant if it was to be achieved through violence. He was a firm believer in the purity of the means that serve the ends. For Hitler, violence and nonviolence were means to an end, but for Gandhi, an end was important only to the extent that fair means were employed to attain the end.

Genghis Khan

Genghis Khan (1162–1227) was a brutal emperor who overran India, China, Persia, Afghanistan and Russia with ruthless bloodshed. He is said to have covered 11 to 12 million square miles during his raids, a record in the history of the world for conquering territory. However, in addition to his evil methods, he showed many virtues. For example,

a. He would treat all enemies nonviolently if they surrendered without resistance.
b. He was very tolerant of religious differences and even allowed his sons to marry Christian women.
c. He appointed a Jewish prime minister.
d. He donated money for the production of Taoist and Koranic books.
e. He is known as the first ruler to establish the International law.

In his book, *Genghis Khan and the Making of the Modern World*, Weatherford (2004) reported many humane and inhumane characteristics of this dreaded ruler. Again, the use of violence or nonviolence made him a combination of evil and good.

Ashoka

Ashoka, the legendary ancient king of India, aspired for a huge empire and any amount of killing was justified for his mission. His use of violent methods did not last long and after tasting enormous victories, he renounced violence and adopted Buddhism. It was an unprecedented transformation from a tyrant to a nonviolent, loving and caring king who began to spread the message of peace through his ambassadors in SouthEast Asia and the MiddleEast. With change in means from violence to nonviolence, there was a total transformation of behavior.

There are other nonviolent leaders whose personality profiles will be useful for understanding nonviolent personality. My intention here is to show how the use of violence and nonviolence as means differentiated personality patterns of legendary people. As is common in personality research, we face the same dilemma in identifying what constitutes a genuine nonviolent personality. Until such time, it is safe to interpret personality correlates of violent and nonviolent individuals in terms of cognitive, motivational and situational frameworks. That takes us back to our statement in Chapter 1 that given the choice between violence and nonviolence, the consistency in behavior, as reflected in the preference patterns of individuals, will be indicative of violent or nonviolent personality. The reader is welcome to consume this analysis following a trait approach or, as in fashion now, an implicit view of personality.

SUMMARY

This chapter deals with a description of the nonviolent personality based on choices one makes in terms of the selection of means—violent or nonviolent. Beginning with examples of heroism of nonviolent individuals, the chapter focused on how resilient people find nonviolence an effective tool to achieve their goals. In addition, concepts of ripeness, wisdom, and generativity were also described to show their relevance for understanding the personality of nonviolent individuals. Within an empirical context, an Indian concept, Anasakti (detachment) was also presented, but at the same time it was argued that such ethnic ideas are prone to be misunderstood if they are not properly scrutinized in a different, say Western, context.

SUGGESTED READINGS

Howard, R. W. (1990). Mohan K. Gandhi: Nonviolence, principles, and the chamberpots. In V. K. Kool (Ed.), *Perspectives on nonviolence.* New York: Springer-Verlag.

Iyer, R. (1983). *The moral and political thought of Mahatma Gandhi.* New York: Concord Grove Press.

Kool, V. K., & Keyes, C. M. L. (1990). Explorations in the nonviolent personality. In V. K. Kool (Ed.), *Perspectives on nonviolence.* New York: Springer-Verlag.

Mayton, D. M., Diessener, R., & Graby, C. D. (1996). Nonviolence and human values. *Peace and Conflict: Journal of Peace Psychology,* 2(3), 245–253.

Conflict Resolution

OUTLINE

OUTLINE (cont'd)

Why did you fight with your brother or sister? Why did your mother spank you when you were a child? Why does one person murder his neighbor? All three are examples of aggression and behind each of these is a conflict. Take any example of violence—whether at the international level, or the individual level, or the Palestinian situation or violence and aggression in the family—it is almost always due to some conflict. Is it possible to discuss aggression, violence or nonviolence without considering the role of conflicts in the escalation of aggression and violence? Dollard, Doob, Miller, Mowrer, and Sears (1939) were probably the ones to first realize the role of conflict and its corollary, frustration, in the genesis of aggression and advanced the now famous frustration-aggression hypothesis (reported in Chapter 2, along with its limitations). What is a conflict? Psychologists are of the view that conflicts involve situations in which there is an incompatibility of goals, needs or desires (Rahim, 1992). However, conflicts *per se* are neither good nor bad. It is how we view them and how we attempt to resolve them that make them good or bad. Aggression is an optional strategy and we, as human beings, have the ability to escalate or inhibit it. When you had a fight with your sibling, this fight was because you chose to fight. You could have compromised with your sibling or, you could have chosen to give in to whatever your sibling wanted.

As discussed in Chapter 1, conflicts place an individual at a choice point where one has the option to use violence or to negotiate through peaceful means. To the extent that one attempts to deal with conflicts by causing harm to the other person, one has taken recourse to aggression. The psychology of nonviolence is the study of behavior that is designed to inhibit aggression and to create optimum conditions for harmony in an otherwise adverse condition that may lead to delivery of harm to the adversary. Thus, our interest in this chapter is to try and elucidate how conflicts can be resolved through the use of nonviolent means and, also, to understand the extent to which such nonviolent conflict resolution strategies are effective in the context of real-world conflict.

In Chapter 4, a description of social traps was presented to show how good individuals feel when provided with immediate satisfaction. Our ancestors worked hard to make our lives easier: designed automobiles for our ease in mobility; guns for protection and hunting; atomic plants for electricity; and air conditioning to beat the heat. In return, what have we given to our environment, except for polluting it? Do we think of contributing to the enrichment of our environment even once a week? All we care about is our short-term gain and comfort. We are in a state in which we are using sliding reinforcers—stimuli that are rewarding in short spells but harmful with prolonged usage. We feel lazy to separate plastic, glass and paper while throwing away our garbage without realizing the harm we are doing to our recycling program and to our efforts for improving our environment. Such behavior is not pathological. Rather, it is rooted in our inability to foresee the consequences of our behavior. The above also holds true about immediate rewards in violence: our inability to understand the consequences of violence and the long-term benefits of nonviolence.

A conflict has generally been defined as any situation where there is an incompatibility of goals, needs or desires to which people may respond in a variety of ways. These responses could include any or all of the following: contentious behavior, insistence and coercion to have one's way, lack of concern for or intentional harm to the other person (Baron & Richardson, 1994). Although a variety of definitions of conflict are available, the following common elements of these definitions would help us understand the nature of conflict (Baron, 1990; Lawson & Shen, 1998):

- Conflicts involve opposing interests between parties such that the positive outcomes for one are equally matched by negative outcomes for the other, and are therefore zero-sum in nature.
- The parties must be aware of these opposing interests.
- Each party must believe (or act) that the other party is trying to thwart the interests of the other.
- Conflict is a process arising from past and current interactions and the context in which they took place.

All of the above characteristics can be fitted into the siblings' fighting example presented above. The two siblings felt that they had opposing interests; each felt that one was trying to thwart the other. The fight probably had antecedents in the past experiences of the siblings and they had probably developed scripts (see Chapter 3) for responding in this aggressive manner. This is nowhere more apparent than in the descriptions and examples provided by Bonta of certain

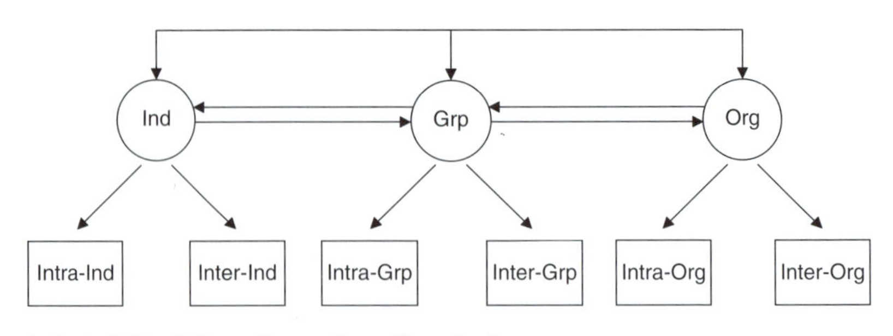

Figure 6.1 Levels of conflicts: Developing a taxonomy of conflicts

cultures where children are expected and taught to, and therefore, behave in ways that are truly nonviolent in nature (see Chapter 3).

Levels of conflicts

The incompatibility discussed above may occur at a variety of levels. It can occur in your own mind. It may also occur between two or more individuals, within a group or between two or more groups (Figure 6.1).

Intra-individual conflict

When we are undergoing conflict, we could be pushed or pulled in different directions, giving rise to different varieties of conflict, namely

- Approach–approach conflict,
- Approach–avoidance conflict, and
- Avoidance–avoidance conflict.

Thus, if you want to watch a particular program on TV and, at the same time, want to go to a party with your friends, there is an incompatibility of interests and you are being pulled in two directions. In other words, you are undergoing the approach–approach type of conflict. However, if you want to watch the program and at the same time are scared of horror scenes, you are being pushed toward and simultaneously being pulled away from the same TV program. You want to watch it and yet you don't. You are now in the state of approach–avoidance conflict. And lastly, you are in an avoidance–avoidance conflict situation when you get the feeling that you are between the devil and the deep blue sea: when you are being pulled away from both the TV program and the party, since you enjoy neither. In all three cases, one can see that it is the incompatibility of interests, needs or desires that is at the root of the conflict.

Inter-individual, inter-group and inter-organizational conflicts

There are times when the incompatibility is not within us. It may well be that you are feeling that someone else is trying to thwart your needs. As the names suggest, these types of conflict arise between two or more persons or groups. The consequences of these types of conflict are, however, different from those described above in the section on intra-individual conflicts, though the reason remains an incompatibility. Once again, we are placed in a choice position. We have at least five options. We can choose to use any of the following five styles of handling such conflicts, namely, avoiding, compromising, forcing, collaborating or accommodating. The particular style that we choose will depend on a large number of factors and have been discussed later in this chapter.

Conflicts can also be differentiated on the basis of their importance to, or their salience for, the individuals concerned. Conflicts may therefore be on a very superficial issue or may be on an issue as important as an existential one: centrality (dealing with issues related to one's sense of identity or self-esteem) and duration (that is, the length of time over which the conflict remains unresolved). More recently, Coleman (2003) has differentiated conflicts on the basis of the nature of the issues involved. Conflicts may, therefore, be distributive, integrative, inefficient, non-negotiable or intractable.

Distributive conflicts involve an issue over a quantity that is divisible, but of a zero-sum nature. One is thinking of a fixed pie, within which, if one party takes a larger share, the other is left with a smaller piece. At its extreme, it is that type of conflict in which one party may retain everything, leaving nothing for the other party (zero-sum). Thus when we have a conflict over the division of a sum of money, what one gets depends on what the other gets. If A gets more, B will get less. If A takes the whole sum, B gets nothing. We can, however, change this negative frame into a positive one. We can start thinking of what to do so that neither of us suffers. One such solution could be that I say, "I take the whole amount this time but you may take the full amount the next time." When the conflict is such that a solution of the above type is possible, we describe it as an integrative conflict. Thus, there can be win-win solutions to such conflicts. There are other conflicts which are extremely complex and difficult. For example, conflicts may become non-negotiable. The conflict between Gandhi and the British over the independence of India was non-negotiable as far as Gandhi was concerned. Another example is that of an intractable conflict in which the parties do not concede and the conflict tends to prolong; for example, the case of Ireland or the India–Pakistan dispute.

However, no matter how conflicts are categorized, it should be clear that it is our perceptions that make a conflict seem distributive or integrative, non-negotiable or intractable. No conflict, *per se*, is distributive, integrative, inefficient, non-negotiable or intractable; it is our evaluations that make them so (Rubin, Pruitt, & Kim, 1994). Our need for social identity is so strong (refer to SIT in Chapter 3), that in-group–out-group formation takes place at the slightest pretext. This is the reason why Hitler could convince fellow Germans to incarcerate the Jews: by making the Jews appear not only different from the Germans, but also a potential danger to the purity of the race. In other words, Hitler was attempting to make a case for a non-negotiable conflict. When we have a conflict with people for whom we have a negative schema, the only possible solutions appear to be distributive. You change the schema and the script becomes different. Start thinking of how this individual had helped you in the past, that is, reframe the negative schema into a positive one, and you would begin to look for more integrative options. The same conflict has now become an integrative one. When some Germans failed to develop the schema sought by Hitler, and continued to see these Jewish people as human as they themselves were, they rushed to rescue them, often at the cost of their own lives. Chapter 3 described the Amish way of forgiveness: their schemas and, therefore, their scripts are totally different from those employed by the modern materialistic world. Get locked into the shackles of self-interest and the conflict grows intractable. In other words, it is the color of the lens with which you view the conflict that decides its appearance.

The development of conflicts

Another important aspect regarding conflict is that it is not a static entity. Rather, as Pondy (1967) puts it, it is dynamic and passes through several stages. Figure 6.2 shows the stages of the development of conflict.

The stage is set for a conflict by any situation inherently characterized by a scarcity of resources. When there is enough for all concerned, there is hardly any reason for a conflict to develop. However, when the situation is such that each individual is striving to take as much as he can from these scarce resources, people start perceiving that others are there to thwart their interests. This has, therefore, been called the latent stage, where, though, there is a potential for the development of conflict, it is not inevitable.

It is only when we start to feel the pinch and when we perceive a scarcity, that the conflict moves to the second stage, that is, the perceived stage. We must, of course, remember that this perception may be based on a subjective analysis of resources and may vary widely when we compare it to the objective reality. In this regard, Gandhi's remarks are often quoted: "there is enough for every man's need, but not for every man's greed." This perception, coupled with the

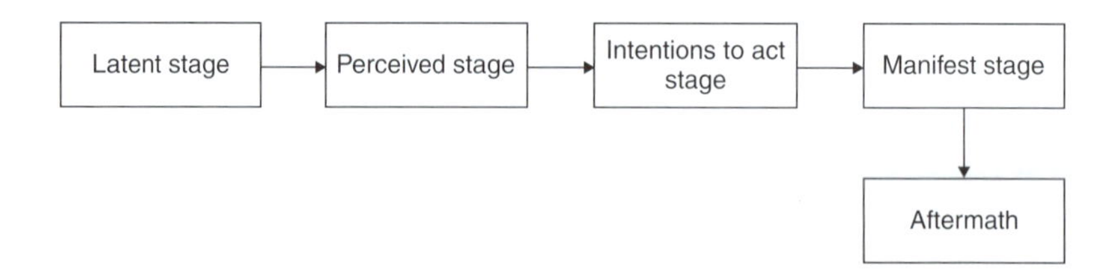

Figure 6.2 Stages of conflict development

idea that there are others who are competing for the same "scarce" resources, leads the conflict to the third stage, the intention to act stage. Both parties are now sure that the other is trying to thwart its goal fulfillment and thus they must do something to stop the other. Research has shown that the intended action depends on the conjoint function of two factors: our concern for self and our concern for others. Using a 2 × 2 classification with high and low concerns for self and for others, there are four possible ways of action (Figure 6.3), each leading to particular outcomes for each of the concerned individuals. This analysis of the stages of the development of a conflict seems well aligned to Sherif's realistic conflict theory (based on the series of studies described later in the section of the Robbers Cave experiments) which also stated that conflicts arise out of a real conflict of interests and can be resolved only by developing a common goal.

Will awareness of possible outcomes affect the resolution of the conflict? To understand this scenario, the matrix below describes the possible consequences (Figure 6.3). Given this condition, the relationship between our decided course of action and its result is bi-directional: with the action not only deciding the result, but also, more importantly, the awareness of the outcomes having a possible effect on our decision. It is only after the parties have decided whether they will take some action and also what action they will take, that we come to the fourth stage, that of the manifest stage. This is the stage when the conflict comes out into the open and now everyone may know that there is a conflict of interests between the two parties. Of course, if both parties decide to use avoidance as their strategy for handling the conflict, then no one may get to

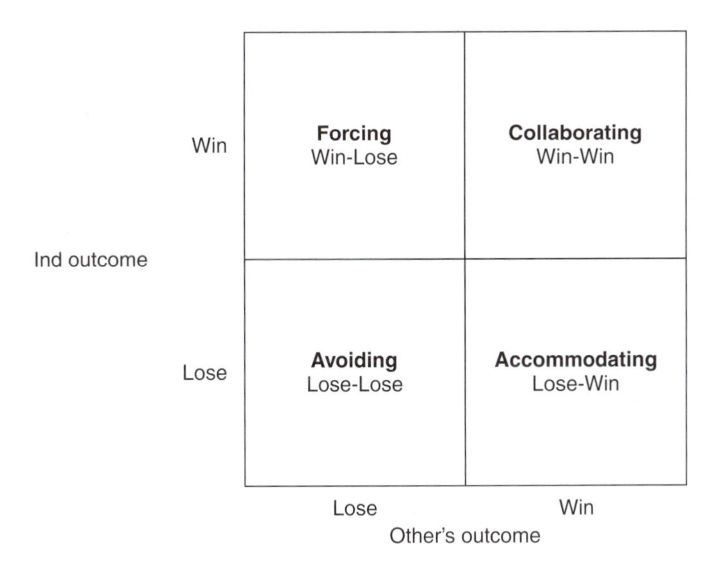

Figure 6.3 Possible ways of handling conflict and their consequences

know about it. The actions that are undertaken lead to different outcomes or aftermath, or the final stage. This last stage is important in its own right. It makes us aware of the fact that conflicts may sometimes only seemingly be resolved. This aftermath is a direct consequence of the strategy used by the opponents. Whether one uses forcing, accommodating or avoiding as the way in which to "end" the conflict, one party will always feel that it has lost in the bargain. For the time being, violence or aggression may cease, but a cold war is simmering inside, leading to consequences that can be extremely deadly.

The five-stage process expanded on above also provides an insight into the history behind a conflict. This knowledge of the process comes in handy when we try to control or resolve conflicts. It becomes exceedingly clear that conflict management at the earlier stages of perception and intention to act would reduce the emotions and cognitions from becoming deep-seated, thereby making the conflict non-recalcitrant or tractable and stopping it from proceeding to the intractable point or to what has also been called protracted conflict.

Protracted conflicts

Definition of intractable protracted conflicts

Since the early work of Morton Deutsch (1962) using the Prisoners Dilemma Game and that of Sherif, Harvey, White, Hood, and Sherif (1961) at the Robbers Cave, we have come a long way in our understanding of the dynamics of conflicts. Today, it is not just simulated situations and field experiments that provide insights into the nature of conflicts and their resolution. Rather, our knowledge has been considerably advanced by real life conflicts such as marital conflicts, workplace conflict, communal disharmony and even international conflict. Social scientists are now trying to understand what drives and fuels such situations and what causes them to become protracted and intractable.

Protracted literally means long drawn out; intractable refers to something that refuses to change. What is a protracted intractable conflict? These are conflicts that have raged for years or even centuries and appear to be inherently irreconcilable. Their intransigence makes them catastrophic and traumatic for all concerned. They are intense in nature and are over issues that refuse to lend themselves to traditional negotiation strategies. They often deal with personal and group identities and are often also rooted in power disparities and perceived injustice. There are many examples of protracted conflicts in our recent history. To name just a few, we have the India-Pakistan conflict over Kashmir, the Israeli-Palestinian hostilities, the tension and violence that have prevailed in Northern Ireland, the situation in Bosnia-Herzegovina, that in Somalia, Burundi and Rwanda.

Coleman (2000) defines such conflicts as "recalcitrant, intense, deadlocked and extremely difficult to resolve." But why have these conflicts become intractable? What conditions have made them so? Are there basic differences between conflicts that are tractable and can be resolved, and those that are intractable and refuse resolution despite the best efforts of various mediators? No matter what the issue over which the conflict had occurred, there seem to be certain basic features that distinguish protracted intractable conflicts from conflicts that are not so. Coleman stated that the retractable conflicts differ from tractable ones on five aspects. These are context, issues, relationships, processes and outcomes. Let us try to understand each of these.

1. *Context*: Intractable conflicts seem to be rooted in a history of domination and perceived injustice. They occur in situations where there has been a long-perceived imbalance of power and ethnocentricism. In fact, this power disparity has become the accepted norm and has been further legitimized and strengthened by myths that have been handed down over succeeding generations. Group dominance, bias and conflict become institutionalized, often leading to structural victimization and structural violence in terms of basic human rights such as safety and dignity. Such victimization can also be rooted in an important group membership, such as race or gender (Deutsch, 2003). The importance of the context is further clarified from the ways in which intractable conflicts most often surface or even resurface at times of change and anarchy.
2. *Issues*: Intractable conflicts generally involve issues related to basic human needs, central values and principles or other symbolic issues and, as such, they do not lend themselves to traditional methods of bargaining and negotiation. In other words, the issues are non-negotiable. When a Sikh from India is forbidden to wear his traditional headgear (the Pagri), one that is mandated by his religion, it is not a point over which one can bargain.
3. *Relationships*: Conflicts become intractable because the social structure has become such that there remains hardly any scope for friendly inter-group contact. This mutual exclusiveness also damages, and sometimes even destroys, the faith and the trust that is so important for any peaceful solution of the conflict. As the conflict escalates, the in-group–out-group feeling tends to get even further polarized leading to the formation of collective identities (Druckman, 2001). Every individual is seen as a Palestinian or as an Israeli; after the 9/11 incidents, Americans were extremely concerned about the identity of people they interacted with: Muslim or non-Muslim. Coupled with this is the complex intra-group dynamics, with cross-nation conflict often serving to distract locals from the more pressing problems at home. This fact has been cited for the India-Pakistan conflict (Rushdie, 2002), for the Israeli-Palestinian conflict (Friedman, 2002), and even for the war by the US on Iraq (Krugman, 2002).
4. *Processes*: Intractable conflicts are fuelled by intense emotions and a variety of cognitive processes that may be seen even in tractable conflicts but at a less intense level. A suitable example is the role of humiliation in Somalia, Burundi and Rwanda (Lindner, 2001). Dysfunctional cognitive processes could include heightened stereotyping, ethnocentricism and selective perception, leading to moral disengagement or even moral exclusion (Opotow, 2001).

5. *Outcomes*: Results of an intractable conflict are, more often than not, trauma. This trauma may be felt by both—those who are the perpetrators of the heinous acts in the form of guilt and those who are at the receiving end. We see such events being marked by the loss of loved ones, hunger and disease, rape and violence, and isolation and meaninglessness. The end result of such trauma is general dysfunction not only at the individual level, but also with respect to governmental functioning (Parakrama, 2001).

Not only are the above-mentioned five factors complex, but they are also nested in equally complex psychological, social, political, and cultural systems. It is the sum total of these interactions that creates the intractable, often mercurial and irascible nature of the conflicts. Today, they pose a serious challenge to both individuals and nations across the globe. In recent years, researchers have attempted to probe into the factors, antecedents and correlates of intractable conflicts. The researches are diverse and have been undertaken by a variety of perspectives. According to Coleman (2004), these perspectives are:

- *Realism*: Strategies for deterrence and force; activism for social justice relations.
- *Pathology*: Targeting trauma/malignant processes.
- *Postmodernism*: Context-based approach, called constructivism (refer to Chapter 7).
- *Systems*: Managing chaos.
- *Human relations*: Cultivating tolerance and reconciliation.

Some early studies on conflicts

While conflicts have been witnessed all through the history of mankind some have been effectively resolved, and others have escalated over the years. However, their scientific study is of more recent origin. Some of the most interesting insights have been provided by simulated situations ingeniously devised by various researchers. Some of them have been detailed below.

Simulations of conflicts and their resolution probably started as way back as in 1940 with the work of Mary Kay Follett (1940). One of the situations presented by Follett was that of two sisters fighting over a single orange, both wanting it, though, for different reasons. While a competitive approach produced more animosity between them and also led to retaliatory moves dividing their attention from the main issue, a conciliation with each deciding to make do with less than to none at all (that is by each taking half the orange) solved the conflict in a very amicable manner. Once they had decided to split the orange, they also decided that since one wanted the orange for its juice and the other for the peel to make a fruit cake, both their interests could be met by taking even half the orange each. Each of the sisters could then take what they wanted from their own half as also what they needed from the half they had given to the other. Thus, what seems to be a very obvious solution could not be had unless they decided to cooperate with each other.

The Prisoners Dilemma Game (PDG)

Imagine that you and an accomplice have been charged for a crime. Imagine also that the District Attorney has just so much evidence that he can charge only one of you with a serious sentence. Further, you are not permitted to communicate with each other, even though the sentence that each of you receives depends on not only what you do or say but also on what your accomplice does and says. What are the options in front of you? You can decide to keep quiet or inform against your partner. Your partner also has these two options. This brings to the fore a 2 × 2 matrix with the following outcomes: if you decide to keep quiet but your partner informs on you, you will get a heavy sentence and he will go free. The opposite would be the result if he decides to keep quiet but you decide to inform against him. So, you can either maximize your gains, in which the other loses, or be altruistic and attempt to save your partner. The risks associated with the latter are, however, very high, because if he is not guided by such altruistic motives, you will lose. The two of you are therefore caught in what has been called a zero-sum game, where the sum of your gains and the other person's loss amounts to zero. Of course, the situation can also arise where both of you decide to inform against each other, leading to both of you getting a moderate sentence. But how can both of you help each other? This would happen when both of you decide to keep quiet. This would produce a non-zero solution, wherein the loss of one is not equal to the gain of the other. A large number of simulated trials with a variety of samples have shown that people soon learn that cooperating with each other, that is, both remaining quiet, leads to the maximum gain for both the players, while competing with each other does not produce such large gains. The same has also been replicated in the laboratory with different payoff matrices, again clarifying that cooperation is a much better strategy than competition.

In the laboratory version of the game, two people, A and B, are asked to choose between one of two alternatives X and Y. Thus, their choices would result in a 2 × 2 matrix, that is, XX, XY, YX and YY. If both opted for the same gain, that is, both opt for Y, they would be locked in a competitive situation such that one could win only if the other lost, that is, only if the other decides not to confess. However, should they decide to cooperate, that is select option X, they could both win, though with smaller amounts (Figure 6.4).

The Acme-Bolt Trucking Game

A variation of the Prisoners Dilemma Game is the Acme-Bolts Trucking Game that won the American Psychological Association Advancement of Science Award. Both these games have been used widely in research and practice and have helped to delineate the factors and consequences of cooperation and competition.

		Prisoner A	
		X:No confession Cooperation/ B	Y:Confession Defect on B
Prisoner B	X:No confession Cooperation/ A	Both get small penalty	A goes free B gets 10 years
	Y:Confession Defect on A	A gets 10 years B goes free	Both get 5 years

Figure 6.4 Prisoner's dilemma: Payoffs in a 2×2 matrix

The Acme-Bolts Trucking Game was developed by Morton Deutsch (1962). He presented a simulated situation involving two transport companies whose profit depended on the length of the route taken by them. There were two routes, one shorter than the other, but with one hitch. The shorter route was wide enough to accommodate only one vehicle at a time. As a result, if one party chose to take the shorter route, the other would have by necessity to take the longer route. So, if one party stood to gain, it would be the other party's loss, and therefore it becomes a zero-sum game. Experimenters have created power disparity conditions by giving one party sole power over the gates of the shorter route. Yet, the use of the shorter route solely by one company did not produce as much gain as when the two companies were able to cooperate and enter into a mutually benefiting agreement. The reason was that power disparity creates retaliation by the other, gradually leading to the two being locked in a situation of negating the other's move rather than on actually maximizing their profit.

The Robbers Cave Study

Perhaps the most intriguing was the field study undertaken by Sherif and his colleagues (1961) based on a personal life experience of the principal investigator. Popularly referred to as the Robbers Cave study because of its geographical location near the park with the same name, it attempted to understand how two groups absolutely unknown to each other, and therefore neutral, can very easily be made to develop into adversaries, and, even more importantly, how the adversarial relationship can be reversed, causing the two groups to become extremely friendly. The study was conducted on twenty-two 11- and 12-year old boys who had signed up for a summer camp. They were divided into two groups randomly and brought in separate buses and kept in camps at a distance of one and a half miles apart, so that they did not even know of the existence of the other group. Each group was asked to give itself a name, the names finally decided upon by the boys themselves, being the "Eagles" and the "Rattlers". What was surprising was how this very simple act of giving oneself a name influenced the identity of the group, reminiscent of the SIT described in Chapter 3. Oblivious to the presence of the other group, each group engaged in common camping activities and, in the process, developing the traditionally seen team spirit and group feeling. Each of the two groups became well knit in a short span of one week. It was then that one of the groups was found in the baseball diamond of the other group. One could easily see the kind of negative feelings and behavior with which this act was greeted. This was also the first time that each group realized that they were not the only campers in the area. Though there was only minimal contact between the two groups, one could see the clear "in-group" and "out-group" formation. During the second week, the camp instructors arranged a series of competitions between the Eagles and the Rattlers. With it being possible for only one group to emerge as the winner, intergroup rivalry soon heightened. Typical behavior thereafter was open hostility and aggression that increased with every competition, reaching a peak after the end of the second week.

The researchers wanted to study the other side of the coin too. If the two groups consisting of boys who did not even know each other and were unaware of the existence of the other group could start manifesting intergroup hostility, would certain other activities also lead to the dissipation of this enmity? During the third week of the camp, the investigators arranged to have the two groups meet regularly. The researchers found that, contrary to the popular theory, namely the contact theory of conflict resolution, merely meeting each other did not have any effect on the perception of the other group as a rival. Rather, these meetings only escalated the negative feelings. However, when these boys were made to face common hurdles, which neither could remove singly, they cooperated and were able to overcome the obstacle. One such instance was when a water crunch was created and the boys were told that at least 25 people were needed to locate the leak and plug it. Another was when they wanted to rent a movie that was too expensive for either group to manage singly. Forced to work together for a common goal (that is, a superordinate goal) was a major impetus for cooperation and one that could not be achieved through mere intergroup contact. Once the two groups were able to successfully get rid of hurdles because of cooperating with each other, hard feelings between the Eagles and the Rattlers decreased. So much so, that it was no longer the Eagles or the Rattlers but "we" and the camp ended with the boys riding home together in the same bus.

A number of issues were clarified through the observations made by Sherif and his associates. First, in line with the SIT, group identity is an important factor for the development of the in-group feeling. It has generally been proposed that it is competition over scarce resources that leads to conflicts and hostility. The Robbers Cave study however proved that even before there could be any competition, and even though the boys had no felt scarcity, the mere development of an in-group feeling led to an out-group feeling too. Moreover, this out-group feeling was marked with the same degree of hostility and prejudice that one sees in conflict situations. Intergroup tension and conflict preceded the competitive activities, or in other words, it was the development of the in-group feeling *per se* that led to negative feelings toward the out-group. So, rather than competition or an incompatibility of goals inducing conflict, as would be predicted by the realistic conflict theory, it was what Tajfel (1969) and others have referred to as social categorization, as discussed earlier in Chapter 3. Secondly, engaging in competitive activities in which only one group could emerge winner went a long way in escalating the hostility between the groups. Moreover, each group spent more time and energy in hurting the other group and in stopping it from winning than in working toward its own success. Thirdly, mere face-to-face contact, or even engaging in activities that did not require cooperation, failed to bring about any change in the relationship; rather it increased the hostile feelings. Fourthly, when faced by a common threat, one that could be tackled only by cooperation, the groups could come together and work together. And, last but not the least, it was the successful cooperation that reduced the intergroup hostility and led to the development of a new all-inclusive sense of identity.

Gaertner and coworkers (2000) reanalyzed the findings of this study. Using three concepts from the social categorization perspective, the authors offered a few tangible conclusions. The three concepts used by them are: decategorization, recategorization and mutual differentiation. While decategorization refers to the undermining of group identities in the face of personal contact and the evaluation of individuals not in terms of their social identity (that is, as Eagle or Rattler), but as individuals, recategorization refers to the formation of the supergroups after working on mutual goals. Mutual differentiation explains how intergroup cooperation is increased and hostility reduced when the erstwhile opponents realize that they have complementary skills through the use of which they can reach goals not possible singly. Thus, if a task is divided such that it capitalizes on the strengths of each party and mutual interdependence is stressed upon, there is a greater chance of amicable relations in the future than when the task is equally divided between the two parties.

Gaertner and coworkers drew upon a large body of research to show how these three concepts drawn from Tajfel's work are embodied not only in the Robbers Cave study but have also been replicated in a variety of situations involving intergroup behavior. The research also helps us to conclude that all three phenomena are important and are salient for resolving intergroup conflict. For example, Bettencourt, Brewer, Croak, and Miller (1992) concluded that contact that permitted more personalized interactions led to more positive attitudes not only toward people from the out-group actually present there but also toward other out-group members seen on video. Similarly, interventions focused on creating a more inclusive in-group identity were highly successful (Gaertner, Dovidio, Anastasio, Bachman, & Rust, 1993). The effects of mutual differentiation are brought to the fore through an ingenious study by Brown and Wade (1987), in which students worked on a magazine article. The contact experience had a greater positive effect when the two groups were given different roles than when they were given the same role. Obviously, what mattered was whether each group felt that it could reach its goal only when both worked together.

Are findings such as the above limited to the analysis of interpersonal conflict or, even more narrowly, to laboratory simulations under highly controlled conditions? Do they offer any insights for communal hostility or for hostility between nations? To test the same in real life situations, Blake and Mouton (1962), famous for their managerial grid approach to leadership styles, recreated the essential features of the Robbers Cave study with over 1000 executives in 150 different groups. Each group engaged in intra-group activity, followed by competitive activities and ending with common obstacles being thrust upon them. The findings closely replicated those from the Sherif study showing that the processes seen among teenagers could be generalized for adults too.

While the results of the study on executives closely paralleled those obtained by Sherif, there are other examples to the contrary. Maoz (2000) described a study in which Jews and Palestinians were involved in a coexistence project. The setting was of a third party intervention in an actual ethno-national conflict. The difference was that conditions replicating the Robbers Cave study were not created but they actually existed. Maoz presented the case of a series of structured encounters between Jewish and Palestinian teachers in Israel between the years 1990 and 1993. The third party consisted of implementers and facilitators of the program and the whole idea was based on Allport's contact hypothesis and also the findings of the Robbers Cave study. Thus, it was felt that when these two groups would be brought into contact and forced to work on a superordinate goal, positive intergroup attitudes would be fostered. The work plan was divided into seven stages, but surprisingly only six of the 15 teams got beyond the third stage. Only 59 of the 136 teachers that participated completed it. Of the six teams that did get through the entire program, only two actually implemented it in class. When the level of satisfaction derived from the course was measured, 60–75 percent of the teachers from both groups felt that they had gained considerably in terms of understanding teachers from the other group better and in getting the perspective of the other group regarding the conflict. However, as far as the academic goals were concerned (for which the program had ostensibly been derived), there was less satisfaction. What were the reasons? An analysis by the author revealed that groups did not behave like the groups of children at Robbers Cave. The situation was far from the one involving conflict between the two groups. In fact, there soon formed a number of subgroups and coalitions each with their hidden agendas, and each wielding differing levels of power. Thus, whereas in planned groups, many of the above factors could be controlled, in the natural setting, both intra- and intergroup dynamics got translated to the new situation that did not allow meaningful contact to take place.

What is even more striking is the marked similarity in the attributions made by each of the two parties in conflict. They often seem to be a mirror image of the other, with each attributing virtues to oneself and vices to the other (Myers, 1999). This has been clarified in a variety of international events. For example, in the classic study by Bronfenbrenner (1961), ordinary citizens of Russia were found to voice exactly the same misperceptions about Americans as the latter were expressing for the Russians. These mirror image perceptions were found to persist even till the 1980s (Jervis, 1985; Tobin & Eagles, 1992). Mirror image perceptions fuelled the arms race, with both nations claiming that they would prefer to disarm but the actions of the other nation were compelling them to arm themselves (Plous, 1993). Negative mirror image perceptions can also be seen to be behind the Arab-Israeli conflict (White, 1977), the Catholic-Protestant hostility in Northern Ireland (Hunter, Stringer, & Watson, 1991) and the Muslim-Hindu conflict in Bangladesh (Islam & Hewstone, 1993).

All of the above studies have important implications for our understanding of nonviolent behavior. Whether it is in the PDG, the Acme-Bolt Trucking Game, or the boys in the Robbers Cave Experiment, people, who would normally not indulge in aggression, have been seen to become competitive if not aggressive. The role of the context in which they had been placed seems to be the deciding factor. The studies also implicate that teaching people to be cooperative is possible and the risk of aggression might be reduced.

Cognitions: The drivers of conflict

Why is it that some conflicts escalate rather than be resolved at an early stage? It is partly due to the twin processes of emotions and cognitions. The Robbers Cave Experiment, reported earlier, provided enough data to show how such processes had undergone changes and also altered the dynamics of the situation. In addition, the re-analysis by Gaertner and coworkers (2000) provided further insights to the understanding of escalation and the control of prejudices.

If conflicts are leveraged by subjective views rather than by objective reality, it is but natural that we will be guided by feelings and thoughts. Since conflicts involve social interaction, either directly or through a third party (as in arbitration), it is but inevitable that concepts from social cognition be considered in the analysis. Social cognitive theory provides a cogent analysis of why people start perceiving an incompatibility of interests. It also enables us to understand why some people choose a cooperative intention to act, while others choose the confronting stance.

Attribution

As discussed earlier in Chapter 3, we generally tend to explain the negative behavior of others as being caused by personal dispositions while our own negative behavior is caused by situations beyond our control (self-serving bias). It is important to remember that such an attribution is only for the explanation of negative behavior. For positive behavior the opposite holds true, for example: "We are moral but you are deterred". In situations of conflict, one must remember that we are thinking of why our opponent is behaving in a negative manner, attempting to thwart our needs and interests. Studies show that when we attribute the thwarting as being due to internal factors, such as "this person really wants to hurt us", it produces greater negativity and aggression toward the other party. The situation is complicated by its ambiguity. If we had had enough information we would not have made mistakes in our attributions. It is only because there is a communication gap that faulty attribution is occurring. Ambiguous situations also tend to activate certain stable internal characteristics, one of them being the hostile attribution bias. Individuals who are high on the hostile attribution bias tend to perceive ambiguous behavior of others as intentional and therefore become even more negative toward them (Dodge, Murphy, & Buchsbaum, 1984). In fact, the attribution bias poses special challenges in the mediation process (Ng & Ang, 1999).

Stereotyping

Stereotypes are cognitive frameworks consisting of knowledge and beliefs about specific social groups (Baron, 1997). In other words, stereotyping leads to generalizations that make the person engaging in stereotypes perceive all members of a group as possessing certain traits. How do stereotypes operate during conflicts? It has already been explained that conflicts tend to raise negative attributions regarding the opponent. As negative attributions increase, it leads to an increased perception of the other party as an out-group.

In-group–out-group categorizations serve an important heuristic purpose for our cognitive processes. Information relevant to an active stereotype is processed more quickly than unrelated information. Also, stereotypes cause persons to pay greater attention to information consistent with the stereotype, so much so, that information inconsistent to the stereotype may be actively refuted. All of these processes reduce cognitive effort for person perception, since people are simply judged by their membership group and not as individuals. Further, in-group–out-group classification leads to stereotypical thinking that lead to formation and sustenance of prejudices (ibid.). The end result is the attribution of more negative intentions to our opponent than the situation warrants and greater difficulty in arriving at an amicable solution. Even when one attempts to suppress stereotypes, it often produces a "rebound" effect, such that stereotypic thinking actually increases (Macrae, Milne, & Bodenhausen, 1994). In this context, violence and not nonviolence, toward the adversary is an expected outcome.

Cognitive effort

Do conflicts arise over trivial issues? In most cases, they do not and, if they do, our life becomes very miserable. It happens only when we begin to perceive a triviality as important in our interaction. And how do we generally react to important situations? We are usually not in a hurry to resolve them, lest we get hurt, and therefore tend to exert maximum cognitive effort so as to arrive at the best solution. There are studies (for example, Wilson & Schooler, 1991) that show that issues over which we think too much make us even more entangled as we go along. The reason is that the more we think about something and the greater the extent to which we analyze an issue, the more the confusion that arises. Thus, even in conflicts, the more we try to analyze why our opponent is behaving in the way he/she does, the more confused we become, making us less able to think with clarity and putting us into mental ruts, extricating ourselves from which becomes difficult.

Lateral thinking

For any conflict to be resolved in an effective manner, lateral thinking seems to offer the key. Lateral thinking involves the consideration of a large number of options along with the creative generation of ideas, allowing one's imagination to explore all aspects of the problem and types of solutions. Fisher, Ury, and Patton (1991) call this skill "creating options for mutual gain" Some aspects of lateral thinking with reference to conflict resolution are as follows:

- Separating the act of inventing them from evaluating them.
- Broadening the choice of answers rather than looking for a single answer.
- Searching for mutual gain rather than trying to maximize one's own gain.
- Inventing ways to make the final decision easier.

While the first can generally be attained through the use of brainstorming techniques, the second often requires looking at the conflict from a variety of perspectives. This can be achieved by having people from different disciplines look at the problem or by even having people who are not party to the conflict to take a look at it. The role of third party mediators of the type used by Kelman (described later in this chapter) is an important by-product of such thinking. They are often able to see the trees while the actual parties to the conflict get lost in the forest. The third aspect reflects on the possibility of achieving win-win solutions. The last aspect enables greater effectiveness for the solution by making it easier for people to say "yes" to the suggested solution. It is on these aspects that Fisher and Ury have based the concept of principled negotiation, detailed later in this chapter.

Conflicts, affects, and emotions

Our cognitions are often determined by our moods and emotions. Happy moods produce a positive flow (Fredrickson, 2001) leading to positive thoughts and unhappy moods create negative thoughts (for example, depressive thoughts are dysfunctional (Beck, 1999). When our judgments are guided not just by rationality, but also by our mood at that time, it is referred to as the mood-congruent judgment effect.

Mood also affects our creativity, with people tending to be less creative under negative mood conditions (see Chapter 4). Since the finding of amicable solutions to conflicts involves the search for creative options, negative affect would naturally reduce the chances of effective conflict resolution. Moods also have an effect on stereotypical thinking. We generally suppose that, when a person is in a happy mood, he will indulge less in stereotypical thinking. However, this is not supported by research findings, which in fact show the opposite, that happy moods increase such biases. The reason is that, when we are in a happy frame of mind, we have the tendency to maintain that positive flow and would not want to engage in any activity that would cause the reduction of the ongoing happiness. As a result, we tend to avoid analytical thinking, look for shortcuts, and, as discussed above, stereotypes provide just this type of shortcut.

While moods affect our cognitions, the opposite is also true. When we have positive expectancies we generally react with positive feelings. Providing positive information regarding an individual creates a positive expectancy and we are more likely to like that individual. We may react positively to an apology for seemingly provocative behavior but the opposite may be true if we interpret a positive event such as praise as pure flattery.

If such mild mood states have important implications for the ways in which we think, one can just visualize the effects of heightened emotional conditions. According to Zillman (1988, also refer to Chapter 2) emotions produce cognitive deficits, leading to a reduced ability to think rationally, with a greater reliance on cognitive heuristics such as stereotypical thinking. The use of cognitive heuristics is also enhanced by time pressure (De Dreu, 2003). Recent studies on the role of emotions in conflict resolution clarify the role of emotional intelligence (basically it's our ability to judge and manage emotions) even in the intentions to act in conflict situations. Thus, Jordon and Troth (2002) show how people with high emotional intelligence preferred to seek collaborative solutions when confronted with conflict. Emotions have also been found to affect the cognitive processes involved in reconciliation (Burlingame-Lee, 2004), and in the reduction of prejudices (Dovidio et al., 2004), while Farnham (2004) is of the view that both reason and emotion have their own particular contribution to the resolution of conflicts.

The implications of the above work in the context of nonviolence are quite complicated. On the one hand, we know that nonviolence requires our ability to seek a peaceful solution of a conflict that might be distorted owing to negative mood swings. On the other hand, it is also true that positive moods contribute to creativity. Irrespective of the facilitating or inhibiting effects of mood, nonviolence, as viewed by its practitioners like Gandhi and others, is best presented as a rational rather than as an emotional engagement in the form of a behavioral outcome.

Information processing, discussed in Chapter 3, can also be used to obtain a cost-benefit analysis for any reconciliation, with the assumption that reconciliation is undermined if it is viewed as a costly, novel and irrevocable concession. That people engage in a cost–benefit analysis is also proposed and empirically validated by Louis, Taylor, and Neil (2004). Yet, people have been found to be ready to forgive and forget even in what appears a very costly situation. This reasoning can be drawn from the assumptions of evolutionary psychology: that those emotions that have adaptive value and are necessary for a lasting social order have been retained through the ages and guide our behavior even under non-optimal conditions.

Overcoming cognitive barriers

Negative attributions can be reduced by not allowing people to jump to conclusions concerning negative intentions of their adversaries. While it may be slightly more difficult with people who are high on the hostile attribution bias, two strategies are often helpful. These are: avoiding insincerity and providing people in conflict with explanations for the behavior of the opponent (Baron, 1997). The reason is that we tend to jump to conclusions when we lack complete information. We often attribute negative intent because we do not know the real reason for the other person's behavior. Very often it is found that there are sufficiently valid reasons for a certain stand taken by the opponent. Learning about this reason reduces negative attribution.

Similarly, encouraging individuals to think carefully when dealing with others can reduce stereotypes. The emphasis should be on the individual's unique personal characteristics and not on his membership of a certain group. Since it has also been seen that positive moods tend to enhance stereotypic thinking, an effort can be made to keep the mood of the negotiators more neutral. In order to reduce the tendency to exert too much cognitive effort while thinking of the conflict, participants should be encouraged to consider a wide range of alternatives but not to dwell upon them excessively (Wilson & Schooler, 1991).

The detrimental effects of strong emotions can be countered by reminding the participants that many of the actions of the opponent are not intentional but due to circumstances far beyond his/her control. This has been found to reduce the degree of anger associated with the opposite party (Zillman, 1993). Baron (1984) also suggested that, if individuals are exposed to emotions that are incompatible with anger, the degree of anger is reduced. This can be done by giving the participants a small gift or by even introducing humor into the situation.

In terms of the facilitation of nonviolent ways of conflict resolution, what this means is that while we are attempting to help the conflicting parties see madness in their use of violence (that is, helping them to become more rational), we are also trying to create positive mood states. So, rather than a suppression of emotions, I see nonviolent conflict resolution more as a function of managed and controlled emotions, or as a function of emotional intelligence.

Fisher and coworkers (1991) also recommend certain steps for dealing with heightened emotions in the conflict resolution process. These are:

1. Recognizing and understanding not only your own emotions but also those of each of the other persons involved.
2. Acknowledging your emotions as being legitimate and then making them explicit. Hiding or suppressing them will only cause you to burst out later.
3. It is important to allow the other side to let off steam. Remember that nothing is achieved in a fit of emotion. Once they have let off the steam, they will be able to think more rationally.
4. It is also important that you do not react to emotional outbursts from the other side.

The above also seem to be in line with the aspects of emotional intelligence and that is probably why people who are high on emotional intelligence are more effective negotiators.

The role of need for closure and the self-concept

While considerable emphasis has been laid on the situational variables behind non-hostile and win-win solutions, there appear to be certain stable individual differences in people's responses to conflict. There is research to show that the stance taken by people in a conflict situation depends on their understanding of the situation. Specifically, cooperation is more likely when the conflict is seen in a relatively complex way, that is, as a mixed motive situation in which the respective goals of the two parties are only partially incompatible. In contrast to the above, confrontation and coercion are more likely to happen when there is a simplistic conceptualization of the conflict, wherein one's own position is seen as indisputable and there is no attempt at understanding or appreciating the other's view (Golec, 2002; Reykowski, 2002).

The question that now arises is why some people are able to form a complex understanding of the conflict situations while others form only a simplistic one. This seems at least partially related to the individual's personal need for closure or the tendency to avoid ambiguity. The higher one is on this tendency, the quicker one wants to get out of the conflict situation and a return to stability. It is this urgency that makes the individual resort to coercion or confrontation, since the more aggressive one is, the quicker one can supposedly end the conflict (Kruglanski, Bar-Tal, & Klar, 1993). The high need for closure makes people avoid ambiguity, contributes to a lack of openness to new experiences and orients people toward a preference for decisiveness. All of the above have important implications for the nature of information processing that takes place in a conflict situation. With a greater use of cognitive heuristics and stereotyped thinking, both lead to more hostile solutions (Golec & Frederico, 2004).

Another factor that can influence one's responses to a conflict is the self and even the extended self. It has long been understood that a conflict over deeply held values and beliefs tends to threaten the core self and makes people defensive with hostility as the end result (Carver & Scheier, 1981; Ellemers, Spears, & Doosje, 2002; Exline, Baumeister, Bushman, Campbell, & Finkel, 2004). A recent study by De Dreu and van Knippenberg (2005) reveals how even the extended self becomes implicated in the conflict process. According to them, the extended self does not simply include material objects that one prizes but also non-material items such as arguments and attitude positions of an individual. Once an argument is made public and attitudes are explicitly stated, the self tends to take ownership over them and feels threatened to the same extent as when deeply held values and beliefs are opposed. As with all threats to the ego, the individual gets extremely defensive and there is a natural tendency to protect these attitudes and arguments through greater use of self-enhancement techniques and more hostile moves. More importantly, the analysis by De Dreu and van Knippenberg (ibid.) shows that such self-enhancement tendencies are negatively moderated by the motivation to process information more thoroughly. Thus, those individuals who generally tend to process information more thoroughly would tend to use less of self-enhancement. At the same time it has also been found that those who have a more stable and secure self-concept would also tend to use self-enhancement to a lesser degree.

How does the person react to the conflict in such situations? A term that has often been used is posturing. This is the tendency to present further arguments to defend one's original argument. We could probably also understand this effect in the light of another well-known social phenomenon known as the escalation of commitment. So, rather than being open to novel ways of solving the conflict, people who are high on the need for closure or those who feel that their extended self is being threatened would spend their time and energy in proving their point. As a result, amicable solutions become very difficult, as pointed out by Golec and Frederico (2004).

We will now focus on some of the ways in which real life conflicts are generally resolved. One of the foremost of these is negotiation.

Traditional negotiation

A common way to end a conflict is through negotiation. A negotiation involves the coming together of the two parties in conflict to arrive at some sort of an agreement that will end the conflict. While a number of definitions have been given, the common elements are that there must be two parties, and each party must be clear regarding its interests and what it hopes to accomplish through the process of negotiation. Each party must also be convinced that the negotiation will offer some relief and has to agree to follow the line of action resulting from the negotiation. Traditionally, negotiation is distributive in nature, with the focus being on self-interest and maximizing one's gains. One also sees a certain amount of defensiveness and a highly guarded approach, stemming out of the lack of trust for the other party. Conflicts, when resolved through traditional negotiation strategies, can adopt either a hard approach or a soft approach. The core features of the latter include a certain amount of flexibility and a tendency to maintain an agreeable relationship with the other party. Hard negotiation is, however, based on a tough, adversarial stand, using the power of one's personality and getting compliance from the opponent (Johnson, 1993). Each has its advantages and disadvantages and is more appropriate when used in certain circumstances than in others (ibid.). Despite the relative uses and advantages, it is clear that traditional negotiation is distributive in nature and does not produce optimal results. It is because of this that other and more effective ways of negotiation have been worked upon. No matter how well you bargained, no matter what you gained, you always tend to focus on what you lost (Kahneman & Tversky's ideas, discussed in earlier chapters). The feeling of dissatisfaction always remains paramount.

Principled or integrative negotiation: Toward a nonviolent approach to conflict resolution

Though it is probably events and people in the last half a century who have drawn attention to nonviolent conflict resolution (for example, Gandhi in India, Martin

Luther King in the US, Nelson Mandela in Africa), there have been known examples of such nonviolent conflict resolution all through history. The saga of unknown heroes in our own families, neighborhoods and smaller communities does not get space even in the local media, but nevertheless they do contribute to the mainstream existence of peaceful living.

Integrative negotiation

Traditional negotiation attempts to resolve conflicts through distribution of the fixed resources over which the differences had arisen, and hence leads to win-lose solutions. Integrative negotiation, in contrast, attempts to create win-win solutions by expanding the pie. Consider the classic conflict resolution case posed by Mary Follett (1940): "two men are quarrelling in the library. One wants the window open; the other wants it closed. The two argue about how much to leave the window open with no solution arising that satisfies them both." Finally, the librarian arrives and asks one of them why he wants the window open. "To get some fresh air," he replies. She asks the other man why he wants the window closed. He replies, "To avoid the draft." The question then becomes one of how they can bring in fresh air but avoid the draft. The solution is "to open a window in the next room" a simple enough solution but which neither could see because they were so involved in defending their own stand. They were not trying to understand the needs of the other person and were not able to separate their stand from their needs. Their inability to search for the alternatives had been the obstacle to resolving the conflict. While the example given above seems simple, many of even the so-called serious conflicts escalate due to the same problems. They can be as easily resolved as the one mentioned above. In short, on many occasions it is our lack of knowledge regarding alternatives available to resolve conflicts that cause violence. The reader would recall the example in Chapter 1 regarding the response of students to the items to the Nonviolence Test (Kool & Sen, 1984, 2005)—the students simply did not know any alternative to violence although a category for endorsing nonviolence was made available to them.

One of the first scientific analyses of integrative negotiation was the Harvard Negotiation Project, on the basis of which Fisher and Ury (1981) proposed some important guidelines. According to them, if negotiators focus on the following four aspects, integrative negotiation, also known as principled negotiation, can take place.

Separate people from the problem

It has already been noted that ego threats and ownership are very easily assumed in any conflict, causing an unnecessary focus on "I" and "we" and "you" or "they" rather than on finding an amicable solution to the problem. It is therefore advocated that there should be a conscious effort to shift the focus from the people in conflict to the issue over which there is a conflict. By separating the issue from the people, anxiety due to perceived threat to the ego is reduced and attributions become more tuned to reality, stereotypical thinking decreases, the end result being that greater attention is given to solving the problem than to defending one's stand.

Focus on interests, not on positions

In most cases, the conflict gets escalated because of both parties sticking to their own positions and not being ready to take the opponent's perspective. For integrative negotiation to take place, it is important that both parties be able to focus on the interests of everyone concerned. In other words, they should be looking for a solution and be open to solutions that would be in the best interest of everyone.

Search for options

Conflict resolution often comes to a stalemate, or leads to unsatisfactory compromises being made because the opponents are unable to think of ways other than the one already suggested by each. However, if one is to create win-win solutions, one has to be able to engage in out-of-the-box or lateral thinking. This type of creative problem-solving can be enhanced through techniques such as brainstorming, the Delphi technique, the Nominal Group technique, the Devil's Advocate or even general group discussion. Each of the above has been known to have its own advantages and disadvantages, and thus the choice of a particular technique would be contingent on a whole host of person and situational factors.

Develop objective criteria for evaluating the result of the negotiation

Many a negotiation leads to hard feelings because the negotiators judge its results on the basis of subjectively derived indices. In order to find a solution that would satisfy both parties, and be the best possible one under the circumstances, there should be an effort to establish some objective criteria for evaluating the result of the negotiation, both in terms of the substantive issue and in terms of the harmonious relationship between the two parties.

The use of the above-mentioned four approaches are likely to change the stance of an adversarial relationship to one of problem-solving. In fact, it has often been said that

> the principled skills go beyond hard versus soft and change the game to negotiate on the basis of merits. For example, in soft bargaining, the participants are friends, in hard bargaining they are adversaries, but in the principled approach they are problem solvers. (Luthans, 1995, p. 291)

Another difference is that while both hard and soft bargaining are related to the amount of trust or distrust one has for one's opponent, integrative negotiation proceeds independent of trust. This facet of trust becomes all the more crucial when one considers that many an attempt at conflict resolution falls through because of an inherent dilemma regarding trust building between adversaries: parties are not able to enter into the peace process without a certain amount of mutual trust and at the same time, they cannot build trust without entering the peace process. Taking the Palestinian issue as an example, Herbert Kelman (2005), of Harvard University, has shown how this dilemma can be resolved through a process of gradual trust building through successive approximations based on mutual responsiveness and reciprocity. According to Kelman (1995), his approach has brought about at least three changes. First, it has led to the formation of a group of people who are now in positions of influence and can act as opinion leaders. Second, the trust building process of the workshops has filtered down to the community level. And third, the workshops have helped to create a more harmonious and healthy political climate for further steps to take place. Similar work has been undertaken by Ronald Fisher in the Cyprus region to help in the peacemaking process among the Greek and Turkish Cypriots (Fisher, 1994).

An approach similar to that based on the Harvard Negotiation Project is the Conflict Resolution Model (CRM) (Littlefield, Love, Peck, & Wertheim, 1993; Wertheim, Love, Littlefield, & Peck, 1992). In general, there are four characteristics of this model:

1. *Developing expectations about win-win solutions*: This is necessary because people are generally of the view that negotiation always leads to a win for one party accompanied by a loss for the other. Conflict resolution training therefore teaches people to adopt a cooperative attitude.
2. *Identifying the interests of each party*: Another common pitfall is the non-awareness of the exact position of the opponent. It is this that creates suspicion and faulty attribution regarding the motives of the other party. The authors of the CRM model suggest that clear communication between the adversaries would enlighten each party to the other's viewpoint. A critical feature is active listening, which tends to create greater empathy and thereby enhances the chances of cooperation.
3. *Brainstorming for the generation of options*: The options generated should address the interests of both parties and should work at constructive problem solving. Special instructions during the brainstorming period that encourage quantity, variety and deferment of judgment have been seen to generate better options than when participants brainstorm with no specific instructions (Buyer, 1988).
4. *Combining options into win-win solutions*: This stage attempts to combine options into an integrative solution that is geared to the interests of both the parties. The model also incorporates the concept of BATNA (Best Alternative to a Negotiated Agreement).

The similarities between the two models described above can be readily perceived. Both models have been empirically tested and it has been generally concluded that training in the above produces significant changes in the degree to which mutually satisfying agreements are reached (Ryan, 1990). Most of the empirical work on negotiation has been on distributive negotiation (Bazerman,

Curhan, Moore, & Valley, 2000), the main reason being the lack of conceptual clarity of integrative negotiation. Johnson and Johnson (2003) have posited that this shortcoming can be overcome by using the social interdependence theory, emanating from the seminal work of Morton Deutsch (1949) and later expanded upon by Johnson and Johnson (1989). The basic premise of the theory is that the ways in which interdependence between the adversaries is structured determines the nature of the interpersonal interaction, which, in turn, decides the outcome of the interaction.

Johnson and Johnson (2003) delineate six steps that would enable amicable conflict resolution based on the principles of integrative negotiation. The first two steps are based on defining the exact nature of the conflict through open communication between the negotiators. The third step involves describing the reasons underlying the needs and interests of the negotiators, with better solutions being reached when both parties make descriptive rather than evaluative statements. The fourth step is that of perspective taking and attempts at trying to understand why the other person is thinking the way he/she is. The fifth step is engaging in deriving creative options that would maximize the joint gain. And the sixth and final stage is deciding which option to adopt. The efficacy of training in the use of these steps is clarified by a meta-analysis reported by Johnson and Johnson (ibid.). It has also been seen that even if only one party is trained in the use of the above process, the chances of creating a win-win solution are increased (Davidson & Versluys, 2000). It has generally been understood that for positive results, both parties must engage in integrative negotiation. This has been clarified by the matrix of negotiated outcomes presented in Figure 6.5.

As shown in the matrix, the most satisfying solutions are reached when both parties engage in integrative negotiation. The position changes when one party is striving hard to arrive at a win-win solution while the other is adamantly pursuing its own private gains. There is, however, empirical evidence to show that even when one party is trained to engage in integrative negotiation, the final outcome is more positive, with trained–trained dyads of course being the best, but trained–untrained dyads being better than untrained–untrained dyads (ibid.; Feeney & Davidson, 1996; Johnson, Johnson, & Dudley, 1992). The degree to which agreement is delayed and information is processed more thoroughly decides the nature of the opening move (De Dreu & Carnevale, 2003).

It must however be borne in mind that the degree to which integrative negotiation is reached is also a function of person variables, with more cooperative, prosocial individuals engaging in more problem-solving behavior, demonstrating less contentious behavior and achieving higher joint outcomes than those who have more egoistic motives (De Dreu, Weingart, & Kwon, 2000).

It is clear that integrative negotiation is more likely to take place under certain conditions than in others. These antecedents can be classed under individual, group and situational variables. Under the first, would-be variables such as the effect of alcohol, that has been seen to produce greater aggression among negotiators (Schweitzer & Gomberg, 2001), and motivation (Beersma & De Dreu, 2002). Group factors include the ways in which each party perceives the

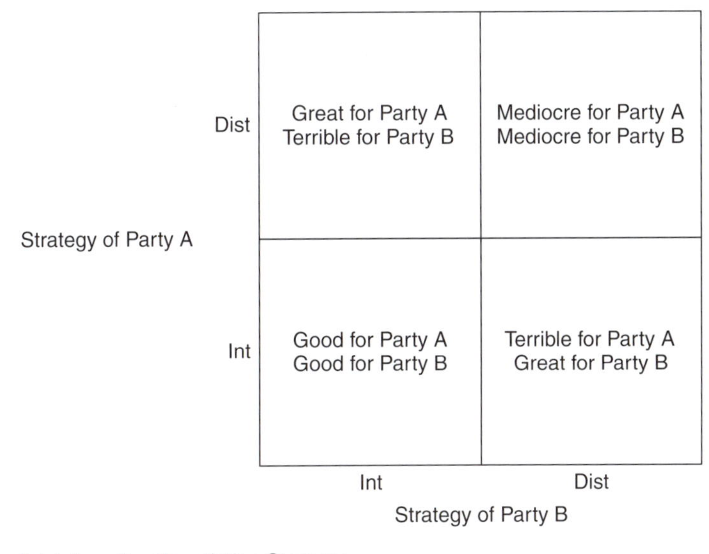

Figure 6.5 Matrix of negotiated outcomes

other. Thus, when one party has a negative perception of the other party it may lead to a decrease in the amount of cooperation indulged in. Another factor is logrolling. This is the initial concession made by one party on issues that are not so important. This sets the stage for cooperation and then the party is able to bargain favorably on more important issues (Moran & Ritov, 2002). People with greater goal clarity, higher learning values and more group discussion were found to arrive at more integrative solutions than people who were not so (Bereby-Meyer, Moran, & Unger-Aviram, 2004).

A comprehensive model for integrative negotiation, based on features gleaned from various models and empirical research is presented below. As the Figure 6.6 shows when integrative negotiation rests on the solid foundation of positive attitudes, appropriate behavior and adequate information, optimal results can be obtained. The figure also clarifies the nature of attitudes that facilitate integrative negotiation; what can be considered appropriate behavior and what is meant by adequate information (it generally refers to what are the options (BATNA) of the two parties).

GRIT: Graduated and Reciprocated Initiatives in Tension Reduction

It has often been seen that efforts at integrative negotiation are perceived as weakness and the initiator of such negotiation is then exploited. It was to overcome this limitation seen and felt in real life conciliatory processes that Osgood (1962, 1980) suggested the above strategy. The very name of the

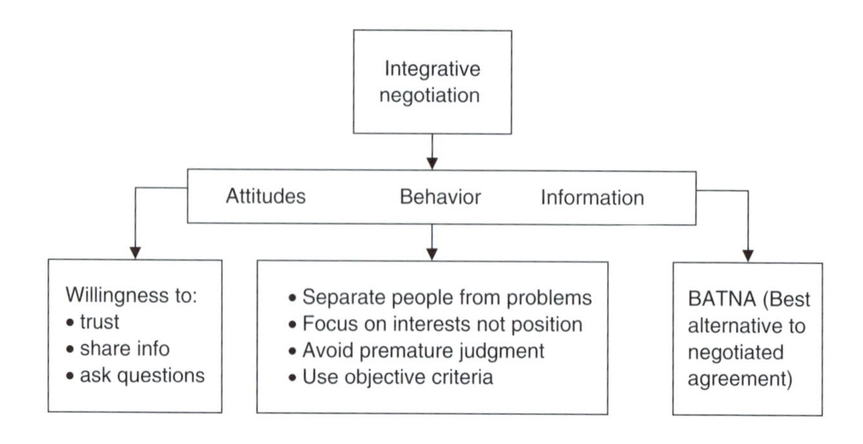

Figure 6.6 Comprehensive model for integrated negotiation

strategy is telling: it shows that the opponent is not weak, he is not scared, rather, he has grit. As the name suggests, the initiative starts by one party taking some de-escalatory steps and then inviting the opponent to take similar steps. While GRIT is conciliatory, it is certainly not tantamount to surrender and the initiator maintains retaliatory capability. In case, the opponent takes some step that goes to escalate the tension, the initiator also responds by retaliating but the retaliatory step is milder than would be the case if normal retaliation were to take place. The objective is that the conflict should in no case be re-escalated. The essence of GRIT is what Deutsch (1993) termed "firm, fair and friendly". You have to be firm in resisting exploitation, fair in holding on to one's moral principles and friendly by being cooperative.

GRIT has been tested in the laboratory and in real life practice. The laboratory studies have clarified that even at games such as the Prisoners Dilemma discussed earlier, cooperation does breed cooperation and repeated conciliatory efforts do boost trust (Linskold, 1978). Outside the laboratory, GRIT-like strategies have been tried for the diffusion of international conflict, and have been found to be effective. When the USA and Russia were facing each other in the Berlin crisis of the 1960s, the pulling back of American tanks one by one was reciprocated by Russia following suit. The most significant effort is, of course, what has come to be known as the Kennedy experiment (Etzioni, 1967). On June 10, President Kennedy set the stage for a series of steps that can be likened to GRIT. He said that "Our problems are man-made...and can be solved by man", and announced the first conciliatory step. The stopping of all nuclear tests by the USA led five days later to an announcement by the Russians that they were halting production of strategic bombers.

The role of forgiveness

The Oxford Dictionary defines "forgiveness" as "pardon" (see also the section on "forgiving" in Chapter 4). While history stands witness to the role of forgiveness in extraordinary situations as well as in close personal relationships, there are also casual day-to-day social relationships in which forgiveness can play an important role. Based on several studies conducted by Bono (2005), it could be safely concluded that forgiveness might solve social conflict. Bono's work shows how forgiveness and apologies could lead to leniency toward the wrongdoer. Long and Brecke (2003) in their book, *War and Reconciliation: Reason and Emotion in Conflict Resolution*, examine a large number of both intra- and inter-state conflicts to show how important forgiveness is in the reconciliation process. Using the forgiveness model of reconciliation, they have attempted to delineate the underlying factors, including the role of truth telling, a redefinition of social identities, partial justice for the perpetrators of the wrong, and a call for new peaceful relationship between the erstwhile opponents. Ohbuchi and Takada (2001), too, elaborate on how certain conflicts are extremely tenacious and seem to gradually become intractable. In such cases, forgiveness does seem to be a way out. Various cognitive, motivational and situational factors are called into play. These include a re-appraisal of the situation, feelings of empathy and guilt, need for relationship maintenance, and group coherence. Another type of conflict that often escalates to intractable levels is an identity conflict. These, unlike conflicts over material quantities, do not lend themselves to any sort of negotiation, because they normally involve non-negotiable issues. In such cases, the only end to the conflict seems to be through reconciliation via the process of forgiveness (Auerbach, 2005). Yet, forgiveness forms only a necessary cognition and is not a sufficient condition for reconciliation. This is probably best exemplified by the Israeli-German case of identity conflict, as discussed earlier, where even though forgiveness did feature, an optimal solution could not be found.

Whether forgiveness will be granted to the party that apologizes also depends on the timing of the apology. Apologies that come in later in the crisis period are more effective than when it is tendered soon after the relationship turns sour. This could be because the victims have then had time to express how they have been wronged and have therefore a better chance of being understood (Frantz & Bennigson, 2005). Thus, there obviously seems to be a "right" time to tender an apology. This "right" time has often been termed as "ripeness" by social scientists.

The role of ripeness

Many a time, people, nations or groups have spent years, if not decades, in conflict, with relationships so strained that it is at the proverbial edge of the sword, the delicate balance which needs but the slightest of nudges to start its cruelty. And then, the day comes, when the first ray of hope breaks this armor. The parties seem ready to forgive and forget, they are ready for a new lease of life, one that is not tainted by hostility. It is, as if a psychological barrier has been removed, the time has become "ripe" for conflict resolution (refer to Chapter 4 for additional information). This could not have come about without the two parties feeling the need for conflict resolution. Kriesberg (1991) defines this as ripeness. Other conceptualizations of the same genre include a "readiness to negotiate" (Deutsch, 1992), " a decision to get to the table" (Zartman & Aurik, 1991), "the motivation to escape conflict" (Pruitt & Olczak, 1995) and the "motivation to reach agreement" (Pruitt & Rubin, 1986).

Coleman (1997) has analyzed how various motivational, affective, cognitive and behavioral components actually cause the conflict to be viewed as a normative condition that the parties may become defensive about and thereby not be ready for its dissolution. Using Lewin's concepts of Force Field Analysis and the three-stage change process of unfreezing, moving, and refreezing, one can understand how a condition can be made ripe for conflict resolution. In other words, it is necessary to either reduce the forces against change (that is, those forces that make the parties resist conflict resolution) or increase the forces for the change (that is, those forces that make the parties feel that conflict resolution will produce positive gains for them). Simultaneously, it would be necessary to unfreeze the individuals from their present feelings and cognitions regarding their adversary, and to move them to a new and more positive perception. Both research and practice has been cited by Coleman (ibid.) to show how workshops along the above-mentioned lines have effectively created changes in perception of parties, nations or people who were content to stay with the conflict and go in for a resolution. Kelman and his colleagues (Kelman, 1990, 1999; Rouhana & Kelman, 1994) have conducted workshops of this type described in an earlier section and have been able to create changes in the Israeli-Palestinian conflict.

Role of culture

Neither conflict nor its resolution occurs in a vacuum. Rather, within the Lewinian concept of psychological field, one salient feature that plays an important role is culture. In an earlier chapter, we have focused on how culture and its artifacts determine the level of aggression or nonviolence. Stories, legends and myths, toys and games, and, socializing practices shape both directly and indirectly the degree to which conflicts are permitted, with whom they are natural, the ways in which they should be resolved, and the role of significant others in the resolution of the conflict. Thus, in some cultures, the cleric may play the role of the mediator, in others it may be a locally elected leader, in still others it may be someone who has inherited that role through birth in a certain family.

The role of culture may also be understood in terms of social identity theory (SIT) (Worchel, 2005). Whom do we identify with? Social identity theory proposes one factor as similarity, and this could also be cultural similarity. Thus, one reason for the perception of certain groups as in-group but others as out-group is what is dictated by the local culture: we normally identify with people whom we consider similar to ourselves. So people belonging to the same culture are considered similar while others are considered dissimilar and therefore not part of the in-group. It has already been pointed out that in-group–out-group formation goes a long way in setting the stage for a conflict. In almost every culture, there are some groups that have been considered as adversaries or out-groups for generations and that perception has become the accepted norm. It is considered natural to be in conflict with them, and people do not normally try to resolve such conflicts. In other words, it has become part of the culture that is handed down through the generations and exacerbated by stories, legends, myths and even history, causing the in-group versus out-group feeling to become deeply entrenched. Further, the history, the myths and the legends also supply the ways in which the conflict can be resolved.

Worchel (ibid.) has outlined how peaceful coexistence can be achieved even between groups culturally perceived as protagonists. Three conditions seem to be necessary. These are:

1. Cognitions, that is an acceptance of the fact that even such protagonist out-groups have as much a right to exist as the other group;
2. Emotions, that is the lowering of fear and suspicion of the out-group; and
3. Behavior or a willingness to engage in cooperative interaction with the out-group.

Thus, intergroup contact and interaction need to be consciously increased and the emphasis should be laid on preventive rather than resolution aspects. The issue of security also needs to be addressed. This can be achieved by increasing the internal security of the group so that they do not feel threatened by the fear of attacks from the out-group. Also relevant is the idea that people often fail to realize that there is great diversity even in their own group, feeling that, though they are homogenous, it is the out-group that has characteristics different from them.

Let's draw on research and practice in the realm of education to point out the efficacy of this last issue for creating greater acceptance of diversity. For the past 50 years or so, the field of special education has been advocating that if we are ready to accept wide individual differences within the so-called normal group, why cannot physically or mentally challenged people be also perceived as lying along the same continua? Why must we propose one set of psychological principles for the non-challenged students and another for the challenged? A unified approach has shown its effect and today we do not speak of the psychology of the mentally retarded and the psychology of the visually handicapped. Rather, all students are considered as having the same psychology, differing only in degree. Today, intergroup contacts between various categories of challenged and non-challenged children through mainstreamed, integrated and cross-integrated education have helped people to understand that these challenged children have as much a right to existence and that they are no threat to the others. As a result, stereotypical thinking, faulty attributions, and negative affect have been greatly reduced in these integrated settings. If this can be done in the educational setting, we should also be able to achieve the same to promote peaceful coexistence among culturally dissimilar groups and nations, as suggested by Worchel (ibid.).

Role of cultural values

Recent analyses of culture have found the framework provided by Hofstede (see Chapter 3) to be immensely useful. His analysis is based on five values by which almost all cultures of the world may be differentiated. These dimensions are power distance, individualism versus collectivism, masculinity, uncertainty avoidance and the orientation to time. While the dimensions were isolated in a study that included over 100,000 executives from IBM from over 50 countries, they have been found to be applicable not only to the understanding of business relationships but also for international relationships. The example of former Yugoslavia, an area fraught with hostility and conflict, clarifies how the Hofstede dimensions provide insights over and above those provided by other perspectives (Soeters, 1996). Hofstede's analysis of Yugoslavia reveals the following: that it has high power distance, extremely high collectivism and high uncertainty avoidance. When we try to understand the nature of the inter-group dynamics in former Yugoslavia, it is this combination that leads to the way in which conflicts are handled. For one, the high collectivism will not permit the existence of minority groups and they are therefore forcefully suppressed or forced to dissolve in the mainstream culture. Secondly, since all the groups are embedded within this same culture, they would have the same values and would therefore all react to conflict in the same way. In other words, their intentions to act in the face of conflict would be the same, and would thus only escalate the level of the hostility and thereby violence. When this combination of high collectivism and high uncertainty avoidance is coupled with high power distance, it allows the growth of elite groups and gives them considerable power. This seems to explain why elite groups appear to thrive in Yugoslavia.

In fact, Hofstede has pointed out that the above combination of collectivism, uncertainty avoidance and power distance is a "violent" culture combination and examples can also be gleaned from other countries. Thus, Turkey and Greece also share this violent combination and their history is marked with hostility and violence toward each other. Other examples are that of Iran, the Gulf countries and many African nations.

The introduction of Hofstede's theory to the area of peace and conflict has a two-fold implication. While not undermining the role played by other perspectives, it does add to the understanding of why hostilities are calmed down very easily in some parts of the world but not in others. Secondly, it is not just business that is undergoing globalization today. International policing and cross border policing are becoming increasingly cost effective and necessary. As such armed personnel, too, need to be trained on cultural differences as much as their business counterparts, the role of these and other dimensions are important and need to be tested in the area of negotiations.

When negotiations are to be carried out between parties from two differing cultures, the pattern becomes very different than when both are from the same culture. Generally, people from collectivist cultures are found to be more prone to integrative negotiation than those from individualistic cultures. However, when one party from a collectivistic culture, say Japan, faces another from an individualistic culture, say the US, the position becomes very different, with the Japanese becoming extremely distributive. In a study on negotiation between people from two basically different cultures, China and the Netherlands, it was concluded that culture determined the nature of the emotions felt, which, in turn, affected the ways a negotiation was perceived by the participants (Ulijn, Rutkowski, Kumar, & Zhu, 2005).

Kimmel (1994) compared the response characteristics of Germans, Japanese and Americans to the issues relating to conflict resolution. It was noted that there were huge differences among them ranging from style of talking to conflict tolerance. For example, whereas Germans adopted a serious style of talking, the Americans and the Japanese were informal and formal, respectively. They differed on valued traits as well: The Germans valuing knowledge, the Japanese graciousness, and the Americans competence. Other differences are listed in Table 6.1.

That culture determines the ways in which individuals choose to respond has been clarified in a meta-analysis, revealing that over and above the main effect of culture, the role of culture is mediated by gender and organizational role (Holt & Devore, 2005). While people from individualistic cultures predominantly choose forcing as a preferred style, those from collective cultures prefer the withdrawing, compromising and problem-solving style. Yet even in individualistic and collective cultures, there are important gender differences, with more females preferring the compromising style even in individualistic cultures. Gender differences have also been seen to exert independent effects with females preferring the compromising style regardless of culture (Hoffman, 2005). So great can be the role of cultural sensitivity, that Kimmel (2000) has warned against such cultural insensitivity. Cultural differences can also be seen in the ways adopted for conflict resolution. Wessells (2001) pointed out how spiritual beliefs and practices are at the core of conflict resolution in Angola. Wessells and Monteiro (2001) present a very interesting account of how former child soldiers who have killed in combat are not allowed to reenter the community because they are seen as being haunted by the spirits of the people they killed. Reconciliation of these children takes place only when a faith healer performs certain rituals.

Table 6.1 The cultural perspective in conflict resolution

	Germans	**Japanese**	**Americans**
Purpose	Ascertain truths	Good relations	Solve problems
Target	Conversion	Consensus	Compromise
Before meeting	Examine issues	Build support	Brainstorming
After meeting	Taking positions	Consensus	Evaluation/outcomes
Style of talking	Serious	Formal	Informal
Valued traits	Knowledge	Graciousness	Competence
Conflict tolerance	High	Low	Medium

Source: Adapted from Kimmel (1994).

School-based programs for the control of aggression and conflict resolution

This is perhaps stated most eloquently in an article titled "Why we must teach peace", by a Washington Post columnist, McCarthy (cf. Girard & Koch, 1996). Founder of the Center for Teaching Peace and a teacher for high school student programs on conflict resolution, McCarthy explained the need for teaching conflict resolution in schools. He said: "Studying peace through nonviolence is as much about getting bombs out of our hearts as it is about getting them out of the Pentagon budget. Every problem we have, every conflict, whether among our family or friends, or among governments, will be addressed either through violent force or nonviolent force. No third option exists. I teach my classes because I believe in nonviolent force—the force of justice, the force of love, the force of sharing wealth, the force of ideas, the force of organized resistance to corrupt power" (p. 6). Why is it that it is difficult to resolve conflicts through negotiation or compromise? According to McCarthy, "We don't know because we weren't taught" or as he puts it, the result of such academic neglect is "peace illiteracy . . . a land awash in violence" (p. 8).

Mary Parker Follett (1940) advocated not only the integrative approach to conflict resolution but also stressed that schools should have courses geared to making students understand conflicts and how they can be effectively resolved. Kreidler (1984., cf. Girard & Koch, 1996) too, believed that school-based conflict resolution programs can be very successful in reducing the degree of violence and in the creation of cultures of peace.

The peaceable classroom

In order to build a peaceable classroom, Kreidler (ibid.) specified five aspects. These are cooperation, communication, tolerance, positive emotional expression and conflict resolution. A similar concept of peaceable classroom has been expanded on by Bodine, Crawford, and Schrumpf (1994., cf. Girard & Koch, 1996). According to them, a peaceable school should have two goals. First, it would enable the school to become a more friendly and productive place to learn, and secondly, it would help students to learn skills that will help them to become better citizens in their adult lives. In other words, a comprehensive school-based program would focus on all the members of the school and not just the students. It would also, by necessity, focus on a change in the school culture and values.

Considerable emphasis has been laid on promoting cultures of peace in schools. According to Malley, Beck, and Adorno (2001), schools today must take on functions over and above that of mere teaching of academic knowledge. Developing a sense of community and helping the students grow into responsible citizens should also be part of the school curriculum. To this end the authors have described a framework that can be used. A paradigmatic shift is required, focusing on the following points:

1. Emphasizing the primacy of human relationships as the medium of learning.
2. Cultivating context that bring out the best of human qualities.
3. Creating communities that emphasize the holistic development of the children.
4. Emphasizing cooperation rather than competition.
5. Valuing individual differences.

In case the above is not feasible, since it requires major changes in the values and goals of the school, there are other strategies that can be used even in the present school setup. Mattaini (2001) describes the Peace Power! Project that consists of concrete practical tools that are flexible enough, so that they can be incorporated even within the existing setup. Other programs include the Responding in Peaceful and Positive Ways (RIPP, Farrell, Mayer, Sullivan, & Kung, 2003), GREAT (Guiding Response Expectations for Adolescents for Today and Tomorrow, Meyer, Allison, Reese, & Gay, 2004), EHV (Kulaksi, Soglu, & Dilmac, 2003), and the Heritage Project (Thompson, Murray, Harris, & Annan, 2003). One such program, using what the proponents have called behavioral journalism (McAlister, Ama, Barroso, Peters, & Kelder, 2000) was used in two schools in Texas (for details, see Kool & Agrawal, 2006).

No matter which program is adopted, each of them opens a new avenue for counselors in schools. This is because the situations are complex and require considerable adaptation on the part of the children, the teachers and even the parents (Gerstein & Moeschberger, 2003). Programs have therefore also been developed to teach counselors how to be successful in this new endeavor (Moeschberger & Ordonz, 2003).

A meta-analysis of school-based conflict resolution training programs

A meta-analysis of 16 studies was undertaken by Johnson and Johnson (2003) to study the impact of the peace education program. The students for all these 16 programs were drawn from eight different schools and included children from the kindergarten to the ninth grade. The explicit purpose of the meta-analysis was to test the effect of the presence or absence of a training program entitled "Teaching students to be peacemakers" (Johnson & Johnson, 1995). The program is a 12-year spiral program with each successive year introducing the child to more sophisticated conflict resolution techniques of negotiation and mediation. Not only are the students taught the essential steps of effective negotiation and mediation but they also learned the correct sequence of the steps.

The findings of this meta-analysis are extremely insightful and provide ample data to demonstrate the effectiveness of such a program. First, the authors were able to gather information on the types of conflicts seen in the children, with the difference between rural and urban children being highlighted. Very few conflicts occurred over academic work, and almost none over values and beliefs. There was an overwhelming difference between the urban and the rural children in terms of the amount of violence seen. While 89 percent of the urban children reported conflicts with verbal and physical violence involved, only 38 percent of their rural counterparts did so. This is a clear indication of what urban life is doing to our children. Another interesting aspect was how these children were resolving their conflicts before their training. The findings reveal that they were rarely managed constructively; no untrained student used problem-solving negotiation, and very few indicated that they would be willing to give up their mutually incompatible goals in lieu of amicable interpersonal relationships.

After their training, the students manifested greater knowledge on various aspects. One important finding across studies was that 90 percent of the students accurately recalled 100 percent of the integrative negotiation steps and more than 75 percent could recall the correct sequence of the steps even a year later. Some of their other gains were that they had greater knowledge regarding the following:

1. In describing what they want.
2. In describing how they feel.
3. In describing their interests.
4. In taking perspective of their opponent.
5. In creating options to maximize mutual gains, and
6. In deciding which alternative to adopt.

It was also clear that the number of integrative solutions reached was higher among the trained students. The students remembered the procedures and were able to use them in a variety of situations including the playground, the lunchroom, the school bus, and at home. Parents went so far as to vouch for the fact that these children were using the strategies taught to them with friends, neighbors and siblings and with even pets. Trained students exerted greater effort to resolve the conflict and their attitude toward conflict became more positive than that of the untrained students. There were important implications to this change in attitude. The students not only learned the procedures and the skills required to execute the procedures but also evinced a keen desire to use them in their day-to-day lives.

The practical significance of such a training procedure is very clear. It has been seen that a large majority of school students, the world over, report that they face a variety of conflicts, both at school and at home (Benbenishty, Zeira, & Astor, 2000). As a result, they often tend to feel unsafe or fearful. Given such a scenario, the school becomes an important testing ground for integrative negotiation procedures. The results also clarify that there is a significant transfer of training effect and the children were using not only the actual steps but also in the same sequence as had been taught to them. It led to the children having a changed perception of conflicts and the ways to resolve them. It is highly likely that once children get used to implementing integrative negotiation strategies as children, they would probably continue to use them in their adult lives too.

Cooperative learning and peer tutoring

Think for a minute on a typical school scenario. Is it not totally competitive? Every student seems to be vying for the first rank or attempting to please the teacher so as to get some brownie points. So pervasive is this feeling of competition that when a teacher asks a question in class, students try to out-shout the others so as to be the only one to give the "correct" answer. Even while one student is giving an answer, there will be others out to prove that this student is wrong. Even in the sports field, one sees competition at its height. Though the motto of the Olympic games is participation, and not just winning that is of prime importance, sportsmen and women strive hard to get medals and awards, often by resorting to unfair means. The last few games have seen a massive rise in the number of sportspersons testing positive for drugs. Not only do we see people trying to reach the top through drugs, but we also see the use of negative competition tactics such as trying to prove that while our team is drug-free, there are others that are resorting to steroids. Once again, faulty attributions are at work: if "I" win a gold medal, "I" deserve it, but if "You" win a gold medal, you have increased your strength and stamina through steroids.

How does one expect students to manifest cooperative behavior when rewards at school are competitively determined? It was to remedy the above and decrease the prejudices at school that Aronson and his colleagues (for example, Aronson & Osherow, 1980; Aronson & Patnoe, 1997) devised the Jigsaw technique of teaching and learning. Learning in a typical Jigsaw technique entails dividing the entire lesson in such a way that each child learns one part and is responsible for teaching that part to the rest of the class. Thus, the final effect is like a jigsaw puzzle where once the parts are fitted in, a whole results. The complete lesson can be mastered only if each child is able to, not only learn his section, but also to effectively teach the others. In this way, cooperation amongst the peers forms the essence of the technique and has thus also been referred to as cooperative learning or peer tutoring. The result is highly gratifying, especially in classrooms with racially diverse students. Now, suppose you were trying to teach a lesson on Japan. Instead of teaching the lesson yourself, you, as a teacher, could assign parts of a chapter on Japan to children in racially and academically diverse groups of five to six children each. Thus, six children from a racially diverse group could be assigned different parts of Japan, say the geography, the history, the culture, the foods, and so on. Each child would be told to master his part and then teach the others. As a result, each child is not only forced to learn and teach but also to listen to the others. Similar experiments were conducted by Johnson and Johnson and others (2003). The results were clear: there were multiple advantages—academic as well as non-academic. The lesson was learnt, confidence increased, communication skills got enhanced, and self-esteem was heightened. More importantly, prejudice was found to decrease to a greater extent than that achieved by simple desegregation or contact without a superordinate goal.

Desegregation

Why do we hold certain stereotypes? If one looks back, it is clear that most stereotypes have lack of contact as their foundation. Asians tend to develop a stereotype of Americans, but so do Americans regarding Asians, because the two have often remained segregated from each other. But once an Asian develops a close friendship with an American he/she soon learns that the latter is also guided by the same motives and the same emotions. A few more cross-nationality friendships, often due to forced contact or through serendipity, and our stereotypical views of others undergo a change and we start thinking of people from other nations or communities as humans first and an American or an Asian only secondarily (Deutsch & Collins, 1951).

When the same was advocated for schools in the US following the historic Supreme Court decision in 1954, it was however found that racial prejudices showed only a minimal decrease. The question is: Why does desegregation work in some situations but not in all? The answer lies again in the nature of the contact.

Why does desegregation sometimes fail to deliver the goods? One of the reasons is that, even though the children from diverse communities and backgrounds have been brought together, they are still in a disparate power situation, with the children from the majority community receiving more attention from the teachers. Since those who come from a higher socio-economic group tend to have greater access to better nutrition and are therefore more healthy, tend to have more money and can therefore afford better clothes, and over the generations are found to show fewer genetic disorders, and tend to be more attractive. Another factor is that in many cases, the majority of the teachers also belong to the same majority community. Greater attention from the teachers leads to the self-fulfilling prophecy of these children doing better in class, and therefore tending to occupy a more privileged position (that is, the Pygmalion Effect). It is these same children who tend to outperform the others often only because of the extra attention they have received and hence get a larger share of the rewards. What is the end result? The children from the majority community are perceived to be better than those from other communities and the purpose of the desegregation is totally defeated. In contrast, the peer tutoring technique offers contact on the basis of equal status and it is this equal status contact and working toward a common goal that reduces the intergroup prejudice.

Conflict resolution versus conflict management

As far as organizational psychology and industrial relations (IR) are concerned, we have come a long way in our understanding regarding conflicts. At one time, they were thought to be an evil that had to be routed. Thus, each time a conflict developed, there were efforts to resolve it, at least on the surface, though the ways in which they were resolved (coercion, by the more powerful party and accommodation or avoidance by the less powerful party) often did not lead to optimal results. Moreover, attempts were made to create conditions such that conflicts could be prevented. Then IR professionals gradually came to realize that despite their best efforts they were unable to eradicate conflicts from the organization. Soon it dawned upon them that conflicts are an inevitable part of the organization, in fact of any group; you can control them but you cannot eliminate them. This led to a plethora of techniques being designed to "manage" conflicts including arbitration, negotiation, conciliation, and so on. This was the period when different types of negotiation were researched upon and every effort was made to get people to go into integrative negotiation. Though the conflict was resolved, it was hardly ever in the true sense of the word. Many a time, it would be simmering within, only waiting to be sparked off by some minor happening. In other words, a lack of open, manifest conflict does not mean that people are in total agreement with each other or with the management, or that union–management relations are perfect. These are all examples of a "passive organization" and sometimes such passive organizations are a bigger threat to the organization than an open conflict.

Why do people refrain from open conflict despite acknowledging that all is not going according to their wishes? Two recent events help us to understand the dynamics. When the giant Enron bypassed all rules of corporate governance and engaged in massive book cooking, not one out of its large workforce of managers and even lawyers said even a word. Did they not know about it? They certainly did, as casual conversations with the employees revealed. Another instance is that of the Italian dairy giant, Parmalet. When the company was charged for fraudulent practices, knowing employees often joked about its problems much before the fraud was discovered. These are just two examples. In almost every organization, many wrongdoings are glossed over by knowing employees. Whistle blowing does not take place. The reason is apparently the perceived high cost of entering into a conflict with the authorities. It is simpler to remain involved in one's real work than to get involved in a controversy, unless we are directly affected by the consequences of the happenings. Such passivity is definitely detrimental for the organization. Had the employees of Enron spoken against the corporate malpractices both financial loss and loss of image could have been prevented. People seem to have the right values but refrain from acting on them. The phenomenon has been likened to the famous bystander effect noted by Latane and Darley in the Kitty Genovese case, and it seems to be guided by people defining their roles very narrowly (see Chapter 7 for more details).

Another reason for a lack of conflict is high group cohesiveness. Two of the most commonly seen effects of cohesiveness are groupthink (permeability of divergent views reduced) and the risky shift (group decision being more risky than the individual). Both seem to be propelled by the same factors: a premature closure or consensus building without due thought to the consequences generally caused by a perceived invulnerability of the group. The Bay of Pigs fiasco is a real-life example of how perceived invulnerability produces a tunnel vision and seems to close one's ears to any note of dissent. Even though many senators had urged President Kennedy not to attack Cuba, the US did and we are all aware of the aftermath.

In view of the above, the current attitude toward conflicts in groups and in organizations is one of conflict management and not of conflict resolution. The modern approach is based on the premise that while conflicts could prove to be detrimental for the organization, a total lack of conflict is equally detrimental. It is also based on the findings that conflicts have both dysfunctional and functional aspects. While the dysfunctional aspect is the increase in hostility and negative affect and cognitions, there are important functional aspects that include creative thinking and deep analysis of the solutions to problems. These also help to optimize group cohesiveness by keeping the group from falling into the ditch of groupthink and risky shift. Conflict management entails a two-pronged approach: a conjoint effort at reducing the dysfunctional aspects of conflicts balanced by the stimulation of functional conflict.

What is functional conflict and how can it be enhanced?

Functional conflict refers to the idea that there is a certain level of conflict that is necessary for the effective decision-making in a group. When there is extremely high group cohesiveness, it produces poor decision-making. Therefore techniques should be used that would help to reduce either the cohesiveness or the degree of consensus in the group. Given below is a summary of the techniques that can be used. In order to allow comparisons, the conflict resolution strategies have also been given.

Conflict Management

Conflict resolution	**Conflict stimulation**
Problem solving	Communication
Superordinate goals	Bringing in outsiders
Expansion of resources	Restructuring
Avoidance	Appointing a devil's
Authoritative command	Advocate
Changing attitudes	
Changing structural variables	

Alternate Dispute Resolution (ADR)

In today's era of democracy, it has been accepted that employees should be able to express their dissatisfaction, whether it be over a minor irritant with their superior or a serious problem regarding working conditions or terms and conditions of work. This has normally been formalized through grievance redressal systems and there are generally laws relating to this effect. Every organization today is governed by certain rules and government provisions such as the Factories Act and other employee welfare acts make it mandatory for the organization to have certain formal procedures whereby conflicts may be resolved and employee demands met. Even the International Labor Organization has not only defined what grievances are but has also delineated certain procedures for dealing with them. The grievance procedure is one of the important means available to the employee to reach solutions to their conflicts. Such formal grievance handling procedures are however expensive and also time-consuming. Moreover, the decision reached is often far from satisfying to both the employee/s and the management.

The economic cost in following formal conflict management procedures is over and above the high cost of litigation. In addition, there are other less tangible costs. One is the manpower turnover cost. Another is that of the large amount of time spent in reaching agreements. It is because of the above that more and more companies are resorting to informal conflict resolution techniques or to what has been termed Alternative Dispute Resolution (ADR). ADR refers to any means of settling disputes outside of court, including a wide spectrum of processes that employ communication skills of creative thinking to develop voluntary solutions acceptable to those concerned in the dispute. The focus is thus on the expressions: "voluntary", "communication" and "creative". While we see the latter two as being at the base of all types of integrative negotiation, the hallmark of ADR is that it is voluntary. Generally ADR has been seen to be consisting of five basic approaches. These are negotiation, conciliation, mediation, fact-finding and arbitration. The burgeoning cost of litigation and the time delays are causing more and more companies to experiment and actually adopt ADR techniques of conflict resolution. Thus, the growing use of ADR by the US corporations has been reviewed (Lipsky & Seeber, 1998), while Pruitt (2000) discusses the main criteria against which the benefits of ADR have been evaluated. Courts too are supporting ADR as an effective way of reducing the backlog of cases pending settlement (Suskind, Babbitt, & Segal, 1993). In many states of the US, it is becoming mandatory to use ADR methods for certain types of cases. Thus the state of Arizona makes it compulsory to use arbitration for cases under $50,000.

The most common methods of ADR are negotiation, mediation, neutral evaluation, mini and private judgment, summary jury trials, the settlement conference and arbitration. Of the above, the two most commonly used are arbitration and mediation. Arbitration is a simplified trial, with either both sides agreeing upon a neutral third party arbitrator, or each party selecting one arbitrator who, in turn, chooses a third so as to comprise a panel for the resolution of conflict. Arbitration hearings normally last only a few hours and the opinions are not on public record. Thirty five states of the US have adopted the Uniform Arbitration Act as state law.

Mediation is an even less formal alternative to litigation. Mediators are trained in negotiation and they bring opposing parties together and attempt to work out a settlement or agreement that both parties accept or reject. Thus, the mediator does not take decisions. Rather, he helps to develop workable and effective solutions for both the parties. Some mediators are attorneys, but others are trained in mediating. They help the two parties reach an amicable solution to the conflict without resorting to expensive legal procedures.

An important aspect of the use of ADR is the idea that since there are no legalities involved, the decision may not be binding to the parties. This however is not true, because even before entering into an ADR procedure, the two parties can come to an agreement that the decision will be binding on both. Seeing the popularity of ADR methods, there are resources that can help locate an ADR expert. Normally the yellow pages of the telephone directory carry such a listing. The ADR expert helps in not only deciding whether a case should be resolved through ADR or not, but also helps to decide on the best ADR method for settling a particular case, that is, how to go about it, and in the actual implementation of the ADR procedure.

Restorative Justice (RJ)

Justice is not merely about retribution and punishment. In fact, a large number of people have started to feel that the present systems of conflict resolution, especially the legal systems, are far too retributive in nature. As a result, people who have committed one crime are forced into committing other crimes, because even after they have served their sentence they are not accepted by the society at large. The high rate of recidivism (that is, people who are repeated offenders) provides support for this idea. It is to prevent such recidivism or turning one-time criminals into hard-core ones, that there is a special system wherein juveniles are not clubbed with adult criminals. Not only is there a different procedure for passing judgments on them, they are also segregated from adult criminals by putting them into reform schools and not into the traditional jail. However, the gains made through such approaches are not enough and have caused people to think of what else to do. One such concept is that of restorative justice.

Restorative justice is an attempt to restore balance within the community after offences have been committed. It is used as an alternative to imprisonment and the emphasis is on developing a balance between the offender and the victim. A three-pronged effort is made that includes in the process, the offender, the victim and the community of which both are residents. Restorative justice aims at providing the victim an opportunity to confront the offender in order to understand why the crime had been committed.

There are mediation processes between the offender and the victim and information is also supplied to the victim and his/her supporters so as to educate them and the community at large. Sentencing in the courts of England and Wales have also changed with the times and they have started focusing on restorative justice principles (Rafferty, 2002), while several experiments have been started in Canada (Roach, 2000; Wilson, Huculek, & McWhinnie, 2002). It is hoped that when prisoners are helped to claim responsibility for the crimes they have committed, they will be less prone to commit such crimes in future. Another noteworthy model is what has come to be known as the Afikpo Nigeria model (Elechi, 1999). The South African Truth and Reconciliation Commissions have also made successful efforts to transform prisons (Allan & Allan, 2000). Some of the recommendations of these Commissions are especially noteworthy and set examples of new directions for prison management (see Chapter 7 for more information). Some of these recommendations are:

- Prison officers should receive human rights training so that they are able to show more humane treatment toward the prisoners.
- Prison staff should be trained in prison law and conflict resolution, and emphasis should be laid on the ethics of prisoner treatment.
- Prison staff should receive training in creative and humane ways of motivating prisoners to regain their human dignity and to cooperate with the rehabilitation process in prisons.
- The commissions also lay out recommendations for prisoners:
  - They should receive skills training.
  - They should receive training in recognizing their basic needs.
  - They should be given training in human rights and nonviolent conflict resolution techniques.
  - They should have access to literacy classes.
  - There should be counselors in every prison.

From the above, it can be seen that the focus is on human rights and on the fact that prisoners are human too. While conflicts need to be resolved and justice should be given to all, efforts should also be made to restore the self-esteem of the offenders and the victims so that they may once again be brought into the mainstream society.

Why do many conflicts remain unresolved? One major reason is our understanding of a conflict and our avoidance of the understanding and recognition of our personal role in the conflict, its escalation and its resolution. Why do we avoid self-assessment in a conflict situation? It is often because it becomes intimidating to face the negative feelings toward ourselves. It often becomes painful to analyze the stages through which the conflict developed. This fear can be reduced and our willingness to face the conflict increases by emphasis of the following three facts:

1. That conflict is a natural part of an interaction and that we all experience conflict
2. That one can choose the way in which one wants to respond to the conflict
3. That conflict can be beneficial.

In terms of the last, it is becoming increasingly clear that as conflicts are successfully resolved, problems get solved, communication is improved, cultural and group differences are better understood. In a seminal publication, *The Handbook of Conflict Resolution*, Deutsch and Coleman (2000) advocate that researchers and practitioners both have an important role to play in our understanding and management of conflicts. While they stress that both basic research and its applications are important, they lay greater emphasis on the theory-to-practice pathway. Thus, basic research would be able to isolate the methods of nonviolent conflict resolution while practice would enable more and more people to get training and education regarding its benefits and implementation.

Recently, Peter Coleman (2004) argued that dominant ideologies might influence the outcomes in conflict resolution. In particular, he was referring to the ways in which superiority and high moral grounding of certain members in a group might influence the decision-making even with "unspoken assumptions". Also, over a period of time, media coverage and mainstream socialization tend to shape the reality of a conflict leading to false information to be mistakenly accepted as truth (ibid., p. 219). Gergen (2001) has been highlighting this issue for a long time in his writings on social constructivism. Social constructivism means that the context makes an idea interdependent such that as the context changes, so does the implications of an idea. What we thought of homosexuals centuries ago is vastly different from how we view them today. Further, giving the example of language, Gergen argued that language in the mind of the child is subject to cultural process as it learns it in a context. For Gergen (ibid.), "An effective empiricism requires a posture of culturally, ethically, and potentially informed pragmatism" (p. 808). He further wrote, "In effect, a theory itself is a form of practice" (p. 811). Given this problem regarding the polarization of the two parties in conflict situations, military decisions are often contaminated so to make the adversary look "really" bad to justify a war (Roblyer, 2005). Therefore, Morton Deutsch (2005) emphasized that misjudgments need to be reduced to prepare the parties for a resolution of conflict and it is possible by (1) checking the reliability and validity of information, (2) bringing outsiders in to see the nature of the problem, (3) considering counter arguments, (4) focusing on feedback, especially from others, and (5) combining 1 through 4 to assess one's position. Following his advice, CR undoubtedly requires a lot of quality experience and skills of an expert to operate effectively in a conflict situation.

SUMMARY

The essence of nonviolence is conflict resolution (CR). No matter what society or community we live in, there are bound to be differences, disputes, or incompatibilities. This chapter begins with the taxonomy of conflicts involving individuals, groups and organizations and proceeds to analyze the stages of conflict development. A summary of the early work on CR was also provided, including the classic work of Deutsch and Sheriff, and how their work has shaped the growth of contemporary research on CR.

This chapter also dealt with the role of attribution, stereotyping, self-concept, effort and other cognitive factors in making judgments to resolve conflicts. The role of forgiving, ripeness, and culture in CR was also presented with special reference to negotiations. Citing examples from school- and industry-based programs, the significance of CR was highlighted. For example, it was argued that if children learn

CR at early stage it would be helpful to them in resolving conflicts later in life. At the end of the chapter, Alternative Dispute Resolution (ADR) and Restorative Justice (RJ) were discussed, as these have been found useful in handling the conflicts.

SUGGESTED READINGS

Coleman, P. T. (2004). Paradigmatic framing of protracted, intractable conflict: Towards the development of a meta-framework—II. *Peace and Conflict: Journal of Peace Psychology, 10*(3), 197–236.

Deutsch, M. (1993, June). Constructive conflict resolution for the world today. Lifetime Award address, Annual Meeting of the International Association of Conflict Management, Hegenhoef, Belgium

Deutsch, M., & Coleman, P. T. (2000). *Handbook of conflict resolution*. San Francisco: Jossey-Bass.

Kimmel, P. R. (1994). Cultural perspectives on international negotiation. *Journal of Social Issues, 50*(1), 179–196.

Lumsden, M., & Wolpe, R. (1996). Evolution of conflict solving workshop: An introduction to social psychological approaches to conflict resolution. *Peace and Conflict: Journal of Peace Psychology, 2*(1), 37–67.

7 The Role of Psychology of Nonviolence in the 21st Century

Four levels of operation: Theory building, applications, applicability and applied
On examining the dimensions of relationship: Psychology of/in/and nonviolence
- Psychology of nonviolence
- Psychology in nonviolence
- Psychology and nonviolence

Approaching the levels of nonviolence
The culture of nonviolence and peace
Terrorism
Insights from classic researches in psychology
- Zimbardo's Prison Experiment
- The perils of obedience
- The uninvolved bystander
- Deindividuation and its effects

Need for an interdisciplinary approach
Structural violence and adversarialism
Some practical considerations
Summary
Suggested readings

Before 1988, the American Psychological Association, the apex body of psychologists, did not have a division of peace psychology. Issues concerning peace were handled, among many other issues, by the Psychologists for Social Responsibility (PsySR). In other words, a formal, concerted effort in the field of psychology of nonviolence is a relatively new phenomenon, albeit many isolated efforts were made in the past to focus on the issues of war and peace, as stated in Chapter 1. The chronology of peace psychology is neither strong nor is it elaborate (see Jacobs, 1989; MacNair, 2003).

Both Kenneth Boulding and Elise Boulding have made a great contribution to peace issues, the former more specifically in the domain of economics and the latter in sociology, but both represent a broad spectrum of social sciences. During the mid-1980s, I came in contact with Kenneth Boulding who lamented that within the social and behavioral sciences, psychology was making the poorest contribution to issues concerning peace. Upon his encouragement, I organized a symposium on nonviolence in Wisconsin in 1988 and the proceedings of this symposium resulted in the publication of a book, *Perspectives on Nonviolence* (Kool, 1990) in which, among others, Boulding (1990) also contributed a chapter, "The role of organized nonviolence in achieving stable peace". In the proceedings of a later symposium, Boulding (1993) again published a chapter, "Nonviolence in the 21st century", in which he pointed out the relevance of the emergence of integrative power, already discussed in Chapters 1 and 4 of this book.

In 2001, Christie, Wagner and Winter edited a book, *Peace, Conflict and Violence: Peace Psychology for the 21st Century*, in which several psychologists offered their perspectives on peace issues including culture of peace, peace education, Gandhi's satyagraha, and others. In his review, Feshbach (2001), of the University of California, Los Angeles, mentioned that this book covered a wide variety of topics, but lacked coherence. According to him, this book contains a "potpourri of articles" and several articles do not even centrally relate to issues of peace. It is obvious that when many researchers, having different backgrounds and long-term sustained research experience, make an effort to contribute to a publication, it is not easy for the editors to glue them together. I believe that the book offers a valuable piece of information to those who are interested in this subject.

Four levels of operation: Theory building, applications, applicability and applied

Seeking insights from the above developments in the field, I will focus narrowly on some specific contributions that psychology has to offer for issues concerning nonviolence. Given the range of basic and applied research, the role of psychology in the study of nonviolence may be analyzed in four domains (Kool & Agrawal, 2006; Oskamp & Schultz, 1998).

1. Theory building
2. Application
3. Applicability
4. Applied

In Chapter 1, we paid a lot of attention to issues that broaden or limit our efforts in developing a theory of the psychology of nonviolence. A number of psychological methods for testing nonviolence were described along with the features of nonviolence, for example, refusal to harm others and building harmony. On the other hand, a description of violence also accompanied them to draw the contrasting features. For example, Hitler believed that a program of eugenics was useful and a few German scientists also endorsed his ideas concerning purity of race, albeit with scientific fallacy. We can always use, misuse and abuse a theory.

The issue of applications deals with the ability of the researcher to develop a program, to investigate its benefit to the community, and, finally, to demonstrate them tangibly. Hitler firmly believed that a program of eugenics could be put into action and its benefits would be useful for the Germans. Samples of the behavior of Jews were highlighted in the media to demonstrate the justification for launching the killings.

Applicability of basic research, a sensitive area, is often neglected by the researchers, for it involves investigating the desirability of a program and its acceptance by the community. Hitler believed in the desirability of his program of eugenics, but the world did not. The question of applicability that lies between basic research and in its applied form is very crucial in psychological science and represents the dispute between the activists/practitioners and the pure researchers. In his recent book, *Judging nonviolence: The dispute between realists and idealists*, Steger (2003) has raised several issues that question the applicability of basic research and how they cause division among the members of the academic community because of differences in their value orientation.

Life is considered sacred and killing anyone is an act of violence. However, both euthanasia and abortion are unquestionably the most debated issues in the American society. Both Democrats and Republications look at the demography of their voters in the constituency before making any decision on such controversy. On the other hand, in many countries in Europe such issues have been resolved without much political heat. For example, the issue of euthanasia has been resolved in Holland. In short, issues concerning applicability refer to the preferences and values of the members of a community (Boxes 7.1 and 7.2).

BOX 7.1 THE APPLICABILITY ISSUE: EUTHANASIA

Take the issue of euthanasia. A patient who is not only terminally ill but also suffering from unbearable pain and finds that there is no point in prolonging life requests for medical assistance in ending his life. This patient wants to decide the future of his life, but the society does not grant him this right. If a physician assists him, as Dr Kovorkian of Michigan did, he will be charged with the murder of his patient. In this example, we find that the issue is our knowledge that the patient cannot be cured. The applicable aspect of the problem is concerned with our ability to develop an intervention program such that patients can die without any additional suffering to what they have already had. And finally, the applied nature of the intervention consists of a positive demonstration that such assisted suicide is possible. One issue that remains important is that of applicability, that is, the desirability of an intervention program and its acceptance. Given the religious concerns about sanctity of life and other legal issues that vary from one culture or society to another, the

BOX 7.1 (cont'd)

issue of euthanasia has become very complicated. While it has been resolved in Holland, it is hotly debated within the USA and the individual states differ in their approach to dealing with this issue.
Kool and Agrawal (2006)

BOX 7.2 TWO EXAMPLES OF ISSUES CONCERNING THE FOUR-TIERED APPROACH

Consumer behavior: Advertising and the pathological behavior of consumers

- *Basic research*: Advertising of goods results in increase in consumer spending.
- *Applicable*: Consumer goods are allowed to be advertised.
- *Applied*: Social psychologists must demonstrate the impact of advertising; for example, how intense advertising is resulting in pathological consumer behavior of living beyond their means in the Third World countries. Are there virtues in altruistic marketing, that is, teaching consumers the use, abuse and misuse of advertised products?
- *Applicability*: Should the advertisers warn consumers about their consumption habits as in case of cigarettes?

Should we depend on a child's testimony in a criminal case?

- *Basic research*: Children under 10 are very suggestible and their testimony cannot be considered reliable.
- *Applicable*: Not applicable: Laws prohibit their testimony as supportive evidence.
- *Applied*: Social psychologists must define the limits of the use of children's testimony based on basic research; for example, with good practice children improve their accuracy levels (Roper & Shewan, 2002).
- *Applicability*: Lawyers may cause emotional damage to children in cross-examination. Children can offer some clue as to the nature of the crime. The issue of applicability is not easy to resolve.

Kool and Agrawal (2006).

It is expected that the issue of applicability will be no less debatable in the 21st century than in the past centuries. In Chapter 1, we had mentioned several forms of nonviolent action. Whether in the USA or India or South Africa, the choice for nonviolent action has never been easily made, bearing in mind the merits and limits of the available techniques. The debate between opting for a principled form of nonviolence versus using nonviolence as a technique (without adherence to nonviolence as a life style) was mentioned in Chapter 1. Citing examples from the approaches adopted by Gandhi, King, Neibuhr and others, Steger (2003) contended that the debate between realists and idealists was centered over many issues of applicability of nonviolence and there are no simple answers to this debate.

The applied aspect deals with the positive results that a nonviolent action plan yields. If a sustained form of nonviolent action succeeds and brings harmony between the two adversaries, it represents the applied domain. In Chapter 6 on conflict resolution, several examples were cited regarding the applied nature of research on nonviolence.

On examining the dimensions of relationship: Psychology of/in/and nonviolence

Positioning with any or all of the above-said four contributions of psychology in the domain of nonviolence is not enough, for we need to demonstrate how the relevance of psychology can be demonstrated and enhanced. For this purpose, relating psychology to nonviolence may bear three approaches:

1. Psychology *of* nonviolence,
2. Psychology *in* nonviolence, and
3. Psychology *and* nonviolence.

Psychology of nonviolence

It is a scenario that develops when psychological principles can be applied to the study of nonviolence. By and large, this has been the major thrust in this book, as we had explored how cognitive, motivational, affective and personality attributes help our understanding of nonviolence.

Psychology in nonviolence

Perspectives on nonviolence are complex and interdisciplinary, and far exceed the limited focus on human behavior that psychology has to offer. Thus, when scholars study nonviolence in its holistic way, the role of psychology becomes supportive and ties up with the evidences from other disciplines that also study nonviolence. A typical example will be that of an authoritarian personality that emerges in a social and political context, and the personality needs of aggression and cynicism are sustained by the prejudices that authoritarian individuals harbor (Adorno, Frenkel-Brunswik, Levenson, & Sanford, 1950).

Psychology and nonviolence

Given that nonviolence and psychology are independent fields of study, we bring them together only when we need one to explain the other. For example, when

BOX 7.3 THE SEVILLE STATEMENT ON VIOLENCE

All five statements begin with, "*It is scientifically incorrect* to say"

1. War is inherited.
2. Violent behavior is genetically programmed.
3. In the course of evolution, aggressive behavior received preference.
4. We possess a "violent brain" equipped with animal ancestry.
5. War is the result of instinct.

"The same species who invented war is capable of inventing peace. The responsibility lies with each of us."

we are engaged in peace building in a community, we seek the help of psychology to demonstrate how enhancing cooperative behavior leads to promotion of a culture of peace (Johnson & Johnson, 2000).

Whether we study *Psychology of Nonviolence*, *Psychology in Nonviolence*, or *Psychology and Nonviolence*, a common denominator among all the above-said approaches is eliminating the myths that distort the relationship between nonviolence and psychology. Called concientization, it is the fundamental requirement of any course of study (Lykes, 1999). For example, the most significant and vital issue concerning the myths is the belief that war is inherent in human nature. The Seville Statement on Violence, drafted in Seville, Spain, by 20 scholars from 12 countries, and with multidisciplinary backgrounds, was debated during the United Nations International Year of Peace, 1986, and was later adopted by the UNESCO. The Seville Statement on Violence was published in the *American Psychologist* in 1994. A summary of this statement is reported in Box 7.3. However, Gerald Beroldi (1994) was critical of the Seville Statement and believed that the UNESCO resolution was more a public propaganda than any real scientific announcement. Rebutting Beroldi's contention, Scott and Ginsburg (1994) promptly defended the Seville Statement. They posited:

> "There were no political litmus tests applied to any of us, and regardless of our academic disciplines or political orientations, we could not conclude, on the basis of the evidence we had researched, that the most critical answers were to be found solely in biology." And they continued, "insofar as the Seville Statement calls attention to the most pressing behavioral problems of our society—violence and war—and addresses these in terms of the nature of human nature, it shifts the emphasis from biology to psychology." (p. 849)

BOX 7.4 THE TIGER TEMPLE OF THAILAND

In a Buddhist temple in Thailand, called Wat Pa Luangta Bua Yanasampanno Forest Monastery (Tiger Temple), the tigers live with other inmates and roam freely. They rest and sleep wherever they like. When they see a herd of cattle, they often get excited, but following instructions from their monk trainers, they resist the temptation to attack other animals to hunt for a meal outside the temple. Like any other pet, they live nonaggressively in the temple, and if there is any instinct of aggression that exists, it is not in operation even among ferocious animals like the tigers. This 12-acre facility is a new home for raising and protecting the tigers from extinction.

For more information, visit webmaster@tigertemple.com

I would like to add further: If violent species like tigers can be tamed at the Tiger Temple in Thailand (Box 7.4), controlling human aggression should also be possible.

The Seville Statement on Violence is one of the many controversies that make it harder to understand where violence begins and nonviolence ends. It reminds us of the gray area between violence and nonviolence that we mentioned in Chapter 1. The misuse of scientific theories, according to Scott and Ginsburg, has created a dichotomy between the scientists "that not only served Hitler's objectives but is still espoused by various groups and fueling inter- and intrasocietal conflicts today" (p. 849).

Approaching the levels of nonviolence

Although I mentioned in several pages of this book that nonviolence is not simply the flip side of violence, yet the discussion in this book tends to drift in the direction of a comparison of violence and nonviolence. Believing that both are characteristic of human nature, comparing them is useful, albeit it does not help in a complete understanding of nonviolence. To comprehend nonviolence fully in an individual as well as in a social context, we need to rely on what Galtung (1969) called the level of actors. Borrowing from his work, Anderson (2004) suggested that the interconnectedness of micro (individual) to macro (community/international) levels of peace is a valid and robust way for understanding the spectrum of behavior that ranges from personal to international levels. He offered the following sequence that bridges behavior from the individual to the international level:

MICRO =>personal <=> interpersonal <=> social and intercultural <=> local and civic <=> national and domestic <=> international (<= vice versa) MACRO

A microlevel approach to the study of nonviolent behavior consists of an analysis of the cognitive, affective and motivational characteristics of an individual, which is a major focus in this book. However, deciphering nonviolence and peace issues is not easy, as pointed out by Anderson (ibid.):

> No one would disagree that war and killing are examples of violence. The debate is over where to draw the line between violence and other forms of behavior. For example, is telling the child "no" an example of violence? Is disciplining children violence? (pp. 107–108)

Aggression involves a target and if this target is an individual, then some antecedent should characterize the interaction between the two (Geen, 1990). Similarly, nonviolence involves tolerance, self-control and forgiving, and other characteristics that we show within our family and to our near and dear ones as a daily routine. However, as we move away from personal levels in Anderson's analysis, that is, from micro to macro, the understanding of nonviolence and its behavioral attributes pose problems. We deal with the wrongdoings of our family members with compassion, but not with those of outsiders. In cases of capital punishment, the family of the victim would demand the death penalty, but the killer's family makes a plea for mercy and forgiving.

The relevance of psychological concepts such as "us and them" and moral exclusion, as discussed elsewhere in this book, are critical in building nonviolent communities. In line with Bandura's contention, do we disengage ourselves morally as we begin to move from micro- to macro-levels? In a broad sense, with the broken families and loosening of social bonds, sustaining and predicting the future of nonviolence will be an uphill task. Moral disengagement, as we find, is a reality over and above our moral background and idealized self that supposedly develops in us. As stated earlier, moral responsiveness is not only poorly practiced but is also very inadequately studied by the psychologists. Expanding the level of behavioral analysis from the individual to the social level, therefore, is not an easy proposition.

The culture of nonviolence and peace

In Chapter 3, I described several cultures that have been identified as "nonviolent cultures". In essence, Bonta (1997) posits that such cultures tend to raise their children in a cooperative environment, and even if they are prepared to be competitive, they remain sensitive to the needs of other children. Among the Inuits, the ambiguities of social relationship with members of the tribe are processed carefully to avoid any disturbance to peace in the community. When a child is teased, "Why don't you kill your younger brother?", the child answers, "No", because he knows what the society expects.

The issues concerning peace have recently been taken very seriously by the United Nations. The UN adopted the year 2000 as the year of "Culture of Peace" (Schwebel, 1998). In 2001, a conference on Assessing Cultures of Peace was organized by the Clark University to highlight the parameters of a peaceful society and human existence (Anderson, 2004).

The Director of Unit for the International Year for the Culture of Peace, UNESCO, David Adams (2000) reported that as we enter the new millennium, a "global movement for a culture of peace" would be our priority. The body recommended eight steps in promoting a culture of peace:

1. Culture of peace through education
2. Sustainable economic and social development
3. Respect for all human rights
4. Equality between women and men
5. Democratic participation
6. Understanding tolerance and solidarity
7. Free flow of information
8. International peace and peacekeeping

An appeal was made to every individual in the world and to the participating 23 million teachers to promote the culture of peace. Within the schools around the globe, the following should be promoted in each classroom

1. Respect for life
2. Rejection of violence
3. Sharing with others
4. Listening to understand
5. Preserving the planet
6. Rediscovering solidarity

BOX 7.5 A SIMPLE BUT SMART WAY TO DEMONSTRATE NONVIOLENCE

I received a very weird request from a speaker during a symposium that I was conducting in 1992 at SUNY, Utica, NY. He wanted two bins full of garbage during the coffee break. With the help of my colleagues I provided him the garbage. When we re-entered the lecture hall to begin the proceedings after the coffee interval, the entire place was found littered with filth. I was grinding my teeth owing to this foolish behavior of the senior professor, but he was smiling and this demeanor appeared disgusting to me. He then started picking up the litter and putting it back in the bin. Two participants got up for help, four more, six more, and the help kept pouring in. Within minutes, the entire lecture hall was clean again.

The professor walked to the podium and said that if only a few of us joined hands and raised the level of community action, we could solve many problems without violence and conflict.

I remember Professor Ted Herman, of Colgate University, NY, for demonstrating a community action so spontaneously and in such a simple way.

Kool (1993).

Table 7.1 Indicators of peace

	Violence		Harmony	
Context	Objective	Subjective	Objective	Subjective
Global	Death rate	Viewpoints	Agreements	Viewpoints
Cultural	Death/injury	Viewpoints	Programs offered	Assessment

Source: Adapted from Anderson (2004).

Elise Boulding (2000) defined a peace culture as "a mosaic of identities, attitudes, values, beliefs, and institutional patterns that lead people to live nurturantly with one another and the earth itself without the aid of structured power differentials, to deal creatively with their differences, and share their resources" (p. 196). In the Hague Appeal for Peace, 1999 meeting, several issues considering peace culture were discussed by approximately 600 delegates from several countries, but many issues remained unsolved, including what should be the nature of peace.

How do we judge that a community has reached a significant level of nonviolent orientation? According to Anderson (2004), if we identify the indicators of peace vis-a-vis violence then we can easily understand and measure the preference for peace and nonviolence in a community. For this purpose, Anderson prepared and classified subjective and objective indicators with reference to violence and harmony and specifically exemplified each subcategory. The reader will notice in Table 7.1 that both violence and harmony have been compared with respect to objectivity and subjectivity in global and cultural contexts. If the number of deaths that occurred due to violence constitutes the objective measure on the one hand, the number of programs to develop and implement harmony provides the objective measure in the opposite category. *For any appreciation of our significant success toward nonviolence during the 21st century, we will need such efforts to establish whether the focus has shifted from violence to nonviolence.* We cannot simply rely on the viewpoints of the community members that violence has increased or decreased, but we will have to substantiate it with objective measures, such as deaths caused by violence, to determine the change in the level of violence.

Is developing a culture of peace easily possible? Fernadez-Dols, de-Mendoza and de-Lucas (2004) did not think so because culture is not stable and changes continually. For example, the knowledge of peace (script) at the time of war is different than without war. Further, a society may be violent but it may not be at war or vice versa. Other issues like class, ethnic and caste differences may jeopardize the notion of equality that is central to the task of creating a culture of peace. Langholtz (1998) argued that any program designed for implementing peace culture would suffer during the 21st century owing to the levels of feasible operations:

- Peace keeping (intervention by a third party such as the UN),
- Peace making (removing tension), and
- Peace building (new structures and offering alternatives).

A good example here would be that of Rwanda. Traditionally, the members of this community solved their disputes with intervention by the elders and in the presence of community members. After the prolonged war between the two groups, Hutu and Tutsi, and the genocide that followed, the social order of the community broke down with no "obedience to authority". On a pilot basis, a new transitional system of justice has been introduced in Rwanda. It is called Inkiko-Gacaca that would involve 250,000 people in 10,000 units and 19 judges. It seems that the spirit of the original justice system would be resurrected with war effects subsiding, and the community moving on toward a better life (Staub, 2004). The South African Truth and Reconciliation Commission (TRC) is another example of the positive steps that would contribute to the healing of a violent and divided society. The TRC was established with the belief that telling the truth by the members of the community would result in healing by bringing the community divided on racial and other lines closer to each other. Specifically, the task of the TRC was:

1. Analyzing the gross violations of human rights between 1 March 1960 and 10 May 1994.
2. Restoring human dignity.
3. Granting amnesty to those telling the truth.

Byrne (2004) believes that the proceedings of the TRC showed positive consequences in bringing communities together through open public discourse and in helping the transition from apartheid to post-apartheid era. Ray and Owens (1988) concluded that the hearings by the TRC on human rights abuses had remarkably significant therapeutic effect but they were also skeptical if the effect would last to make South Africa more harmonious and peaceful in the new millennium.

A great deal of labor has been invested in studying the Israel-Palestine conflict and in developing strategies to find a solution to the problem. Among the many academic endeavors, a study by Albeck, Adwan and Bar-On (2002), in which they brought together a group of nine descendents of Nazi perpetrators in Germany and nine Jewish survivors to meet initially at Ben Gurion University in Israel and share their stories on the holocaust is very relevant (see Chapter 6 for more information). During the several meetings in Israel and elsewhere, the method used to analyze the experiences of the participants consisted of field notes, transcriptions, tape recordings, and evaluations by the independent judges. The concept used in bringing together the German and Jewish groups was based on "Working Through" that became popular among the therapists during World War II. It described how traumatized people survived and were coping following the tragedy. Analyses of the data from this study revealed the emergence of several psychological problems, for example, parents did not share their experiences with their children; the children did not ask about the tragedy; they avoided meeting with the professionals; and so on. The BBC has made a documentary on this study as well.

Efforts in peace building are relatively new as compared to war and, as mentioned earlier, with the predominant orientation of adversarialism, war is a preferred choice than peace. Therefore, it is not surprising that war is "as old as humankind and that serious planning for peace is barely two centuries old" (Schwebel, 2005, p. 52). Echoing the same sentiment, Nigel Young (1996) wrote that the institution of peace is several thousand years younger than the institution of war. In short, in order to develop nonviolence, "peace as an institution" would be needed to counteract the "institution of war" (Oppenheimer, 1995).

Terrorism

A major threat to nonviolence during the 21st century will arise out of terrorism, which is defined as "the process of inducing fear in the general population by acts that undermine an established sense of trust, stability, and confidence in one's world" (Zimbardo, 2001). The key factor in terrorism is fear that derails normal and optimum human life. We all know how the world order has changed after the September 11, 2001 attacks in the USA and the insecurity that has resulted in the minds of people as a consequence of this brutal incident (Prentice & Miller, 2002). It seems that terrorism, if not controlled properly, will result in counterviolence leading to increased loss of lives and denial of justice and freedom.

It is well-known that the discipline of psychology was not ready to deal with the etiology and control of terrorism until the September 11 incident. According to Blumberg (2002), after 2001 there was a significant increase in the number of publications as evident in the citation index that he prepared. The American Psychological Association began publishing books and setting up committees to have a closer look at the issues of psychology of terrorism. In an American Psychological Association publication, *In the Wake of 9/11: The Psychology of Terror*, Pyszcznski, Greenberg and Solomon (2002) proposed their Terror Management Theory (TNT) that provides insights into why terrorists attack and what reaction the public makes. The source of such destruction is anxiety, a concept that has its roots in psychoanalysis. Unfortunately, critics argue that the TNT does not have testable propositions and validity (Stratton, 2002).

Bandura (2004) linked terrorism with moral disengagement. The genesis of violence is rooted in the shaping of moral ideas and respect for life. As inhibitions for moving away from the moral conduct become salient, atrocities increase and the individual tends to morally disengage from the community. This is the perspective of the victim, but most of the terrorists are very morally engaged, not disengaged, within their own group. Upon transformation of their belief, their subjective interpretation matches with the mission of terrorism and they begin to reason that their action will bring terror and helplessness that will in turn fulfill the mission of their group. In other words, they are not morally disengaged (?) within their new group and are labeled as freedom fighters. As we mentioned earlier, Baumeister (1999) pointed out that the issues in identifying evil become highly complicated as per the side you take to develop an argument: the perpetrator tends to underrate his/her crime, but the victim tends to overrate the harm. Who are you siding with? Arafat, the legendary Palestine leader, was called a terrorist and Gandhi a mischief maker, but look at how both, in the twist of history and politics, became "nonviolent" leaders.

Within the context of psycho-historical changes, our interpretation of behavior changes. Therefore, Gergen (2001) is right when he pointed out that much of our interpretation of behavior is based on the construction of reality that we make retrospectively. To this extent, social psychological studies make a poor science as they tend to create a reality after the fact. Thus, for example, if we offer an explanation for southerners being more aggressive than northerners in America (Nisbett, 1993), it will be a post-operational conceptualization. Psychological research focusing on terrorism is also undergoing this critical period. With terrorism on the rise at the beginning of this new millennium, there is a pressing need, both within the practitioners of psychology and the policy makers, including international bodies, for a major contribution from psychologists for seeking solutions to deal with the problems of terrorism.

In a thought-provoking article published recently by Moghaddam (2005), of Georgetown University, he used a metaphor of a staircase that grows narrower as the terrorist embarks in action. According to him, this staircase of terrorism has six floors.

1. *The ground floor*: It's one where most people live without being identified as terrorists. Millions of people face injustice and live in abject poverty, but they somehow compromise with their lives. Those who feel deprived of their position in the group (egoistical deprivation) or of being in a relatively inferior position compared to the other group (fraternal deprivation) and express discontentment.
2. *The first floor*: At this level, two factors significantly contribute in the growth of a terrorist. First are the roadblocks to personal mobility in a group. Moghaddam quoted Plato in this context that a society would collapse if it blocks the growth of talented individuals in the hierarchy. Second, if one's personal efforts are not rewarded, fairly there will be issues of justice—procedural, distributive and interpersonal—as discussed in Chapter 2, and these will fuel discontentment.
3. *The second floor*: This floor consists of those who harbor aggressive tendencies but are unable to express their behavior. As a result they look for scapegoats and, in Freud's view, express displacement of aggression on some other target. For example, dissatisfied with their authoritarian rulers, people in the Middle-East find America a convenient target. Although Egypt receives substantial aid from the USA, I witnessed frequent, massive demonstrations against the USA in the streets of Cairo during 2001 through 2003.
4. *The third floor*: A significant feature at this level is moral disengagement, a concept discussed earlier, but from the point of view of the terrorist organization, it will be conversely labeled as "moral engagement". This is a stage

in which a terrorist lives a parallel life: leads a normal life and yet enjoys the membership of the isolated group by endorsing their radical views and violence.

5. *The fourth floor*: The real recruitment to a terrorist organization begins at this floor. Having arrived on this floor, there is little or no chance for exit, as the recruited individual is now a member of a small cell consisting of a few members of the organization who are assigned specific operations lasting, in most cases, less than 24 hours. The new member receives a lot of attention and credit for displaying the terrorist act.
6. *The fifth floor*: After reaching this apex floor, the inhibitions for loss of life and other brutalities tend to fade away in accomplishing the mission of the organization. Moghaddam contended that two psychological processes characterize this stage. First, outside their own group, everyone is categorized as enemy (social categorization). And second, an effort is made to create psychological distancing from the masses. The new recruit is "brainwashed" to appreciate the myth that an act of terror will sway people to think about changing the social order.

In his analysis of terrorism, Philip Zimbardo (2004) emphasized that any ordinary human being can be transformed into a terrorist. Looking at the background of the terrorists, it is obvious that many decent and intelligent young people were persuaded to end their lives through suicidal bombings. Out of 95 suicide bombings by Palestinians against Israelis, most youngsters participating in this heinous crime were students belonging to normal families. Such findings contradict the notion that terrorists come from poor, isolated and disorganized families. In fact, Zimbardo (2002) posits that normal people show symptoms of madness owing to "reasoning with insufficient data" and the situational forces that encourage them to take refuge to violence.

The problem of terrorism is very complex as it involves historical, political and cultural issues that are way beyond the scope of current levels of psychology. And so are the issues of nonviolence. In the rest of this chapter, classical psychological researches that are helpful in understanding and preventing violence and also in promoting peace and nonviolence are discussed.

Insights from classic researches in psychology

In Chapter 5, the personality characteristics of some nonviolent individuals were illustrated. It was also contended that owing to failure to identify such characteristics in some enduring form, it is not easy to describe nonviolent individuals. Conversely, focusing on individual characteristics has its disadvantages. Zimbardo (2004) argued that psychologists tend to overrate the effect of personality features. According to him, except for the personality variable, namely, authoritarianism that had predictive value, no other personality disposition was found to bear any relationship to violence. After analyzing the personality characteristics of 19 murderers in a California prison, Zimbardo reported that only half of them showed problems with impulse control and were extraverted; the remaining murderers were "Shy Sudden Murderers" with mild manners and no prior history of violence. Summarizing the findings of his work and that of his colleagues, he remarked that it was virtually impossible to predict from prior knowledge of their personalities the identity of a killer.

Will personality psychologists agree to what Zimbardo and his colleagues concluded through their researches? Probably, the answer will be "No". Chapters 4 and 5 report a number of personality characteristics of nonviolent individuals, but they were extreme cases. In our day-to-day lives, violence is an exception, not a way of life. Therefore, studying nonviolent individuals in terms of their personality dispositions is something that is not likely to yield any significant finding(s), for we are expected to behave nonviolently in our routine lives. Given that aggression has survival value, as evolutionary psychologists claim, as are emotions of hate and jealousy; it is not surprising to find that Zimbardo's incarcerated killers were no different from normal human beings. The impact of a situation in committing a crime cannot be denied, but at the same time, to say that personality features are redundant in research, will be unfair as well. Some people show greater proneness to violence than others.

From the laboratory research that we cited in Chapter 2 and elsewhere in this book, it is obvious that personality does indeed play an important role in controlling aggression. In his argument, Zimbardo not only cited his own work but also that of Stanley Milgram (see Chapter 2) to show how overpowering is the effect of situational variables in triggering violence. Without denying his contentions, it is argued here that not everyone succumbs to the situation identically. Even in Milgram's experiments, a small number of subjects refused to deliver shocks and stood firm in their conviction of not harming the "learner". Our laboratory research confirmed that believers in nonviolence in India also refused to deliver shocks to the erring learner. Research based on the scores on the NVT also bears testimony to, as illustrated in Chapters 1 and 2, increase in nonviolence scores with age (Matsumoto, 1993), self-actualization (Kool, 1994), attributions of self-blame (Baumgardner, 1990), dogmatism (Hammock & Hanson, 1990), and authoritarianism (Sen, 1993).

In dealing with aggression and nonviolence, it will be unfair to draw parallels in the research orientation on these two topics. For example, in his studies on aggression, a noted psychologist, Russell Geen (1998), posits that aggression stemming out of brain pathology should be only considered as a predisposing variable in aggression research. Upon drawing a parallel between the two concepts, we find that (un)fortunately there is no pathology of nonviolence unless one considers a castrated human being or those with poor levels of testosterone and ACTH as nonviolent. On the other hand, it is reasonable to consider absence of self-interest, compassion and forgiving as pathological because they are not normative behavior when expressed in plenty. So, pathology of the biological system does not seem to be a fair and uniform criterion for judging violence and nonviolence. While pathology of aggression provides an objective, reliable and valid parameter for deciphering the antecedental condition of aggression, there is no such bottom line established for nonviolent behavior.

In the context of a situation, interpreting nonviolent behavior is, therefore, elusive as compared to the study of aggression.

There is another way for comparing violence and nonviolence. Whereas law punishes those who are aggressive, it does nothing to reward nonviolent forms of behavior that are standard ways of living in society. Hence, there is an established benchmark for aggression, but not for nonviolence.

Will there be a debate on pathology of nonviolence during the 21st century? There was, there is, and there will be a debate on the use of nonviolence as a method to solve disputes. As long as Fellman's (1998) Rambo and the Dalai Lama represent the adversarialism and mutualism of our society, nonviolence will always be on trial. So, let's now examine the pathology of nonviolence.

As parameters of nonviolence, is too much of compassion, forgiving and sacrifice harmful for normal living? Given the structure and functions of our modern society, the answer is in the affirmative. Remember the example we quoted from Batson's work earlier (Chapter 5) that if we all continue to do laundry work for each other, no one would be served. We need to conserve something, at a minimum in the form of self-interest, for our survival. I met many parents in Egypt and India who sacrificed everything to educate and help their children, but many among them also suffered when this support was not reciprocated by their own offspring. Gandhi's wife, Kasturba, and his children were also unhappy with Gandhi because he did not keep a bank balance for his family and had given up his successful legal practice. And of course, we all know the leader of all nonviolent leaders, Henry David Thoreau, who endured retaliation against his nonviolent protests. He was banned from his county and struggled for his survival.

Are there any limits to compassion, sacrifice and tolerance? Idealists would say that they are fathomless, but the realists would speak otherwise. Great thinkers like Max Weber argued that some self-interest is needed for our survival and that an idealistic view of nonviolence is only for the saints. According to Steger (2003), "Christian leaders who refused to abandon their political objectives eventually were forced to abandon their nonviolent principles" (p. 39).

In Chapter 2, we raised issues concerning the dilemma faced by the nonviolent individuals in their preference for justice or compassion in awarding sentence to a culprit. You cannot have both: pardon him for the killing and at the same time do justice to the aggrieved family. Pope John Paul pardoned his assassin, but not President Reagan. Thus, nonviolence involves splitting of thought processes that is called schizophrenia in abnormal psychology; but in coping with such difficult conditions, and in seeking positive solutions, such schizophrenia of nonviolent individuals deserves a better nomenclature, the spiritual schizophrenia (Kool, 1993). After all, the fanatic nonviolent leader is addressed with similar negative labels until they begin to appear god-like.

Let's return to the point of evaluating the significance of the situational context in the study of nonviolence. From the examples cited above, no one would disagree that situational context is important, but its interpretation will be best understood when personality dispositions limit or expand the outcome of behavior. After all, trust, compassion, forgiveness and tolerance are personal dispositions that are judged in a context. Take for example the case of empathy that binds the individual self to the social self (see Chapter 4). If a rapist develops empathy, it is dangerous because it feeds his lust, but in a positive context, it serves humanity and stands to be a reliable predictor of nonviolence (Baumeister, 1999; Mayton & coworkers, 2002). Thus, a study of nonviolent behavior in a situational context is better but it would be best understood in interaction with personal dispositions.

In at least one way, focus on an individual's disposition will be harmful for the study of nonviolent behavior. Social psychologists have long argued that we tend to judge others in terms of their personal dispositions, but, for a similar scenario, we tend to blame the situation for our problems. This bias is referred to as the "fundamental attribution error" (FAE). So, when I see my neighbor unemployed, I interpret that he is lazy (personal disposition), but when I myself become unemployed, I blame the job market conditions (situation). When a blonde trips, we blame her for wearing spiky shoes (her preference/disposition), but when I trip, I blame the smoothness of the floor (situation). The cognitive processes that fuel such biases in dealing with issues of violence and nonviolence have serious implications. For one thing, they create two worlds: us and them (Box 7.6). In addition, this dichotomy between "us" and "them" is sustained by continued attributions of this nature and lead to the formation of various types of prejudices. According to Zimbardo (2004),

> I believe that dispositional orientations are more likely to correlate with affluence, since the rich want to take full credit for their success, while situations arise more from the lower classes who want to explain away—onto external circumstances—the dysfunctional life styles of those around them. (p. 5)

BOX 7.6 US VERSUS THEM: CHANGING RULES OF WAR

In a well-designed research study, Mann (1993), in collaboration with Gartner, gave a fictitious story of the invasion of Nigeria by the USA, England and Soviet Union to his students. In 1/3 of the transcripts, the invader was the USA, UK and Soviet Union, respectively. The second independent variable was the tactic used by them: highly violent or moderately violent. According to Mann: "Subjects rated tactics by the Soviet invaders (M = 5.77) as significantly more inappropriate than identical tactics by the U.S. (M = 5.10) or England (M = 5.01). There was no significant difference between the ratings of the U.S. and British invaders. One way to explain this pattern is that it is consistent with a Realistic Conflict Theory of intergroup bias. This theory suggests that subjects will be biased against groups with which their group has a competitive relationship, e.g., as the U.S. did with the Soviet Union …" (p. 99).

It is our considered opinion that focusing too much on personal disposition, as correctly pointed out by Zimbardo, would be counterproductive, albeit there will always be formulations based on FAE distorting our cognitive processes and ability to judge violence and nonviolence objectively. This is one important lesson that psychology has to offer to practitioners and policy makers involved in conflict resolution and controlling violence. Zimbardo further pointed out that FAE should be taken seriously in individualistic cultures, as individuals in such culture tend to take all the credit for their achievements. *The issues concerning nonviolence during the 21st century will involve a debate between the personal and the situational orientation, for the race for materialism is accelerating and collective cultures are diminishing.*

The foregoing discussion provided the pros and cons of situational effects. Now I will mention a few psychological studies that highlight the impact of situation in promoting or reducing aggression and nonviolence.

In an article published in *Peace and Conflict: Journal of Peace Psychology*, Thomas Pettigrew (2003) referred to three macro level suggestions based on researches that apply to conflict resolution and nonviolence:

1. Osgood's Graduated and Reciprocated Initiatives in Tension (GRIT)—reference in Chapters 1 and 6.
2. Myths concerning war—discussed in this chapter—the Seville Statement on Violence, and
3. Empathy—presented in Chapters 4 and 5.

The popular work of Sherif and coworkers (1961) was presented in detail in Chapter 6. Following a lead from their work, Pettigrew and Meertens (1995) remarked that, when competition for economic resources begins, direct hostilities also emerge, as we find in many communities in Europe; Asians versus blacks in Los Angeles during the LA riots, West Indians versus British in London, Dutch versus Turks and Surinamese in Holland, or practically in any part of India where people of different languages, religion and other ethnic backgrounds compete for meager resources. Emerging out of such studies is the realistic group conflict theory in social psychology that proposes development of prejudices owing to actual competition for meager resources.

At the micro-level, several studies have focused on the individual. A few significant research findings are cited below:

Zimbardo's Prison Experiment

Perhaps the best illustration of the effect of the situation is Zimbardo's (1975) classic study in which he asked the participating subjects to act as guards or prisoners. This randomly assigned role, according to Zimbardo, was about tapping the net effect of societal learning, as subjects worked in their eight-hour duty as guards or prisoners. The roles that set them apart were power (guards) or powerlessness (prisoners) (for details of the experiment, the reader is referred to the website: www.prisonexp.org). The experiment, though slated for two weeks, was abandoned within six days because of the pathological behavior displayed by the subjects such as humiliation, treating prisoners as inferior, dehumanizing them and overzealously following the orders, and so on. Zimbardo wondered if within six days of the experiment, he could "walk, talk and act" as if he was incharge of the prison, imagine what would be happening to those subjects who were discharging their duties in the eight-hour shift of the study. Not surprisingly, madrasas in Pakistan and other Muslim countries, that teach fundamentalism of the Muslim religion, are being blamed for encouraging violence against non-Muslims and the Talibans are taking full advantage of such establishments.

As mentioned earlier in Chapter 1, in his famous work, *The moral equivalent of war*, William James had also highlighted the significance of the roles of members of the society, for example, those in helping professions like teachers, and nurses, in promoting nonviolence; otherwise, he believed that caring and helping in society would take a rear seat to make room for violence at the front.

The perils of obedience

In Chapter 2, we cited the work of Milgram and how his subjects complied with instructions for giving electric shocks to the "learner". A normal human being does not punish others by delivering electric shocks. Even among psychiatric patients it would not be a normal activity. For Zimbardo (2004), there is only one explanation for this behavior: the situation created through the setup of the experiment, for example, the status of Yale University, its laboratory where the experiment was conducted; the professor engaged in behavior; working for the academic pursuit; and merely following the instructions of the experimenter. Of course, the situational effects could not be designed any better to elicit aggression at such extraordinary levels from the subjects.

Why did the ordinary people do things in Milgram's experiment that they would normally not do in their daily lives? According to Zimbardo (ibid.), among several reasons in support of how the situational influence mechanism worked, here are a few examples:

1. Imposing a contractual obligation in Milgram's experiment that the level of shock would be raised each time—not lowered or kept at the same level.
2. Assigning a meaningful role to the subject—a teacher or student.
3. Providing a rationale: The subjects were given justification for the procedure used.
4. Manipulating semantics: "We are helping them" instead of "We are hurting them".
5. Starting the experiment with insignificant shock of 15 volts and luring them into the evil act of shock delivery.

It is a fact that the experiment of Milgram was conducted in several countries and it yielded, by and large, similar results. However, as we mentioned earlier, the nonviolent disposition in our study was a factor in attenuating the effect of Milgram's situational effect. Also, a few subjects in Milgram's study disobeyed and refused to deliver the shocks. Were they unsung heroes? According to Zimbardo, any individual who has the capacity to resist the situational pressures is a hero. In his own words,

> the situationst approach redefines heroism. When the majority of ordinary people can be overcome by such pressures toward compliance and conformity, the minority who resist should be considered heroic. Acknowledging the special nature of this resistance means we should learn from their example by studying how they have been able to rise above such compelling pressures. (p. 20)

The uninvolved bystander

When other people are present, psychological research shows that the likelihood of receiving help is lower when more people are present than when only one or two are present (Latane & Darley, 1970). Popularly known as the bystander effect, it is a significant concept for the psychology of nonviolence. In his book, *The Roots of Evil*, Staub (1989) pointed out that genocide and other brutalities continued when other nations did not intervene in international conflicts. In his later work, Staub (1999) distinguished between two types of bystanders: internal and external. The internal bystanders are those who are members of the group where violence is perpetrated. They learn to devalue the victims and remain passive. They also distance themselves from the victim to reduce their guilt and do not empathize with the sufferer. The external bystander is one who is not a member of the group but maintains some connection, for example, another country that continues its cultural and trade relations with the barbaric regime.

Boulding's concept of integrative power emerges out of the active involvement of people, not by their passivity. When people act collectively, they are empowered, which helps to bring change in the social order (Box 7.7). As mentioned earlier, many Germans could not passively watch the massacre of Jews and rescued them by risking their own lives (Lifton & Markusen, 1990; Oliner & Oliner, 1988). At the international level, when nations remained silent bystanders, the brutalities in Rwanda, Bosnia and other countries continued for a long time.

BOX 7.7 INACTION IN THE FACE OF VIOLENCE: WHAT GANDHI HAS TO OFFER

No doubt the nonviolent way is always the best, but where that does not come naturally the violent way is both necessary and honorable. Inaction there is rank cowardice and unmanly. (Gandhi writing in *Young India*, December 1931; Source: Iyer, 1983)

Baumeister (1999) stated that when bystanders do not intervene, it implies affirmation and the aggressor construes it as justification for his act. Hitler and his henchmen were very systematic and clever in their misdeeds, for they would watch the reactions of other communities before stepping up their orgy of violence.

Deindividuation and its effects

In another classic work, when Zimbardo (1970) concealed the appearance of his subjects, they tended to raise the level of shocks to their victims. When identity is hidden, individuals show strange behavior, including increased violence. During Halloween, when children disguise themselves in masks and fanciful costumes, the level of their aggression increases (Fraser, 1974). When military personnel wear their uniform, they tend to look alike. Such conditions increase the level of their anonymity and so does their level of aggression. Psychologists argue that, as the level of self-awareness changes, the level of aggression also changes (Carver, 1974).

A very sensitive point that Baumeister (1999) has presented in the context of deindividuation is: "One effect of being part of a group is that people lose awareness of themselves as individuals and cease to evaluate their own actions thoughtfully. Because self-awareness and self-scrutiny constitute a central, integral aspect of self-control, the normal restraints and inhibitions tend to be reduced when people blend into a group ..." (p. 325).

BOX 7.8 JAPANESE "KENSHOGODA": OVERPOWERING THE EFFECTS OF DEINDIVIDUATION

Why worry about the loss of your identity? Following Buddhism, the Japanese have been practising *kenshogoda*, which means seeing and realizing one's nature. It is equivalent to satori, or enlightment. Kensho is not just focusing on oneself, but realizing who others are. A state of interdependence in which we are with others can develop kensho, but it also allows us to keep ourselves in the state of self-realization, self-reflection and self-discovery.

While citing the applications of psychological researches above, I presented a few representative studies. As this book is not a compendium on nonviolence, it only offers insights into the psychology of nonviolence. There is a dearth of books on this subject and the application of material ranges from the very clearly scientific and tangible to the somewhat speculative and pseudoempirical. We are sure that the reader would find, at a minimum, some of the important studies on nonviolence serving as a base for their academic and other professional pursuits.

Need for an interdisciplinary approach

One of the main problems for psychology during the previous century was its inability to make an impact on public policy issues. For whatever reasons, the policy makers did not pay much attention to psychology and its applications (Groebel & Hinde, 1989). Whereas other social scientists are members of several leading national and international committees, the number of psychologists are far and few.

One lesson for psychologists is that they need to join hands with their fellow professionals from other disciplines. The need for such an approach for studies in peace and nonviolence cannot be overstated. For example, if we need to understand terrorism and help in a prevention program, psychology alone will not be enough. Terrorism is a problem that has its roots predominantly in history, politics and economic conditions, and yet the problem is very psychological in nature, for it involves fear. Analyzing the psychological nature of genocide, Staub (1999) wrote: "Individual psychology, group psychology, culture, social institutions, the social conditions in a country, the political system, and the system of international relations all have roles in both causation and prevention" (p. 304).

Robert Putnam, of the Kennedy School of Government, Harvard University, has a message for psychologists (as reported by Benson, 2002). According to Putnam, Americans have become less community-minded over the past 25 years, but this apathy resurrects with some local or national tragedy. Citing the example of the days of Pearl Harbor that ignited community action among Americans, Putman remarked that the social capital of America would need prompting; otherwise social bonds would be weakened. For promoting nonviolent behavior both at the individual and at the community levels, we will undoubtedly need both social bonding and community-mindedness.

Structural violence and adversarialism

A noted sociologist, Galtung (1966) distinguished between direct violence and structural violence. Direct violence deals with observable violence for establishing and defending the system. It may involve killing, torturing, beating and so on, and the perpetrators can be traced. Structural violence mainly deals with decreasing the privileges. It is difficult to identify because it is not direct. Examples of structural violence are: inequality, social marginality and poverty.

The caste system in India, the power of business groups, and privileges of the rich do not appear to inflict harm directly, but they do in fact stand in our way of seeking procedural, distributive and interpersonal justice. For Galtung (1998), structural violence is the source of denying people their basic human needs and mobility in the social order.

Montiel (2003), a professor of psychology in Philippines, argued that, taken together, colonial occupation, authoritarian regimes, poverty and cultural heterogeneity contributed to violence in the Asian countries and the issues for establishing peace and nonviolence are very different in this part of world as compared to that of the west. The nature of psychological analyses will therefore vary, giving way to the situational pressures that foster or hinder violence and nonviolence. For example, poverty is a relative phenomenon and is assessed in terms of consumption and comparison with others (Pilisuk, 1998). Thus, the parameters of structural violence would have different baselines in the east and the west.

Rather than defining the nature of peace psychology, Montiel (2003) suggested a plan for developing peace psychology in Asia as under:

1. Reexamine the meaning of peace
2. Study nonviolent transformations
3. Study trauma
4. Focus on economic democratization
5. Examine social identity and marginalization
6. Examine cultural factors in peace keeping, and
7. Set up conditions for intergroup fairness

Obviously, any program for promoting nonviolence and peace would involve issues far above the realm of psychology and it is therefore contended that the growth of psychology of nonviolence will depend to a large extent on how this field relates tangibly with other sister disciplines. In addition, psychologists should also look to decide the balance between theory and practice. The controversy regarding the levels of training has already affected the scene of professional psychology (Box 7.9).

BOX 7.9 THE SCIENTIST-PRACTITIONER MODEL: GANDHI WAS RIGHT AGAIN

Called Boulder Model, a model for training the clinical psychologists was developed in 1947 by a committee led by Shakow. It was rooted in the prevalent medical model that explained organic diseases and recommended that psychologists should be placed in psychiatric centers for their training. It has been debated since then and seeking a reasonable balance between the role of theory and practice in the training of professional psychologists has become a major bone of contention among the American psychologists.

How do we solve the above problem? For this purpose, Stricker quoted Gandhi when he was asked what he thought about the western civilization. Gandhi replied that someone should test it. Similarly, comprehensively testing scientist-practitioner models would tell us about the success of a therapy.

Stricker (2000) in *American Psychologist*.

Some practical considerations

Creating a culture of peace or a nonviolent society appears to be a great exercise and good talk, but it is another thing to walk the talk. The practitioners of nonviolence will testify the difficult nature of their task. Here are a few remarks that any policy maker will like to take into consideration while building peaceful communities and using nonviolence as a tool for the resolution of conflict:

a. Nonviolence has historically been viewed as the power of the weak and poor.
b. There will always be doubts about the success of nonviolence. The history of nonviolence around the globe testifies how followers of great nonviolent leaders abandoned their mentors and adopted violent means to serve their end. For example, Subhas Chandra Bose, a very popular leader in India, defected from Gandhi's camp and joined hands with Germany and Japan to wage a war against the Allied forces during World War II. See also the reference to Nelson Mandela in this book.
c. Nonviolence requires solutions other than harming the adversary. For this purpose, a lot of time is needed to offer alternatives to aggression and for building trust and harmony. Do we have enough patience to bear with the process?
d. Besides time, nonviolence puts a drain on our cognitive resources. The cost to our behavior is enormous as we engage in deliberations and move slowly toward reconciliation.
e. Whether we take a small step, like using words, not weapons to solve a dispute (Schwebel, 1999), or a big leap, like establishing a culture of peace, psychologists have to focus on factors that promote harmonious behavior, rather than disharmony and conflict, as suggested by the Director General of the UNESCO, Fedrico Mayor (1995).
f. As our focus should be the future generation, psychologists must design appropriate curricula for promoting nonviolent behavior. According to Nelson and Christie (1995) a curriculum should include the following:

    - Competencies in peace keeping, for example, impulse control.
    - Conflict resolution for peace making.
    - Sustainable development and positive peace for peace building.

Staub (2003), in his collection of 47 lifetime articles, stated that there are three ways to promote good:

1. Teach children to become practical,
2. Promote bystander intervention, and
3. Enhance well-being.

SUMMARY

We began this chapter with a four-tiered approach that depicts the applied nature of a discipline: basic research issues in nonviolence and their applications, applicability and applied nature. Further, we distinguished between the ways the issues of nonviolence will seek the benefits of psychological science.

In judging the role of psychology for issues of nonviolence during the 21st century, topics such as culture of peace, terrorism, and myths concerning violence were discussed. Further, insights from classic experiments in psychology that have bearing on nonviolence were presented. In particular, limits to dispositional characteristics were analyzed in detail in the context of Zimbardo's recent analysis. The chapter ended with a plea to go interdisciplinary to expand and apply the contributions of the psychology of nonviolence.

SUGGESTED READINGS

Boulding, K. (1993). Nonviolence in the 21st century. In V. K. Kool (Ed.), *Nonviolence: Social and psychological issues*. Lanham, MD: The University Press of America.

Christie, D. J., Wagner, R. V., & Winter, D. D. (Eds.). (2001). *Peace, conflict and violence: Peace psychology in the 21st century*. Upper Saddle River, NJ: Prentice Hall.

Miller, A. (Ed.). (2004). *The social psychology of good and evil: Understanding our capacity for kindness and cruelty*. New York: Guilford.

References

Abrams, D., Hogg, M. A., & Marques, J. M. (2005). *The social Psychology of inclusion and exclusion.* New York: Psychology Press.

Ackerman, P., & DuVall, J. (2000). *A force more powerful: A century of nonviolent conflict.* New York: St. Martin Press.

Ackerman, P., & Kruegler, C. (1993). *Strategic nonviolent conflict: The dynamics of people power in the 20th century.* Westport, CT: Praeger.

Adams, D. (2000). Toward a global movement for a culture of peace. *Peace and Conflict: Journal of Peace Psychology, 6,* 259–266.

Adorno, T., Frenkel-Brunswik, E., Levenson, D., & Sanford, R. N. (1950). *The authoritarian personality.* New York: Harper.

Albeck, J. H., Adwan, S., & Bar-On, D. (2002). Dialogue groups: TRT's guidelines for working through intractable conflicts by personal storytelling. *Peace and Conflict: Journal of Peace Psychology, 8,* 301–322.

Allan, A., & Allan, M. M. (2000). The South African Truth and Reconciliation Commission as a therapeutic tool. *Behavioral Science and the Law, 18,* 459–477.

Allport, G. W. (1954). *The nature of prejudice.* Reading, MA: Addison-Wesley.

Allport, G. W. (1968). The historical background of social psychology. In G. W. Lindzey & E. A. Aronson (Eds.), *The handbook of social psychology* (Vol. 1). Reading, MA: Addison-Wesley.

Anderson, C. A. (1989). Temperature and aggression: The ubiquitous effects of heat on the occurrence of human violence. *Psychological Bulletin, 106,* 74–96.

Anderson, C. A. (1997). Effects of violent movies and trait irritability on hostile feelings and aggressive thoughts. *Aggressive Behavior, 23,* 161–178.

Anderson, C. A., & Anderson, K. B. (1998). Temperature and aggression: Paradox, controversy, and a (fairly) clear picture. In R. Geen & E. Donnerstein (Eds.), *Human Aggression: Theories, research and implications for policy.* San Diego, CA: Academic Press.

Anderson, C. A., & Bushman, B. J. (2002). Human aggression. *Annual Review of Psychology, 53,* 27–51.

Anderson, R. (2004). A definition of peace. *Peace and Conflict: Journal of Peace Psychology, 10,* 101–116.

Ardrey, R. (1976). *The hunting hypothesis.* New York: Atheneum.

Arndt, J., Greenberg, J., Schimel, J., Pyszczynski, T., & Soloman, S. (2002). To belong or not belong that is the question: Terror management and identification with gender and ethnicity. *Journal of Personality and Social Psychology, 83,* 26–43.

Aronson, E., & Osherow, N. (1980). Cooperation, prosocial behavior and academic performance: Experiments in the desegregated classroom. *Applied Social Psychology Annual, 1,* 163–196.

Aronson, E., & Patnoe, S. (1997). *The jigsaw classroom: Building cooperation in the classroom.* New York: Addison-Wesley.

Asthana, H. S. (1990). TAT responses of some nonviolent individuals. In V. K. Kool (Ed.), *Perspectives on nonviolence.* New York: Springer-Verlag.

Auerbach, Y. (2005). Conflict resolution, forgiveness and reconciliation in material and identity conflicts. *Humboldt Journal of Social Relations, 29,* 41–80.

Avruch, K., Black, P. W., & Scimecca, J. A. (1991). *Conflict resolution: Cross cultural perspective.* Westport: Greenwood Press.

Azar, F., & Mullet, E. (2002). Willingness to forgive: A study of Muslim and Christian Lebanese. *Peace and Conflict: Journal of Peace Psychology*, *8*, 17–30.

Bales, R. F. (1968). Interaction process analysis. In D. L. Sills (Ed.), *International Encyclopedia of the Social Sciences.* New York: Macmillan, Free Press & Collier.

Bandura, A. (1965). Influence of model's reinforcement contingencies on the acquisition of imitative responses. *Journal of Personality and Social Psychology*, *1*, 589–595.

Bandura, A. (1977). *Social learning theory.* Englewood-Cliffs: Prentice Hall.

Bandura, A. (1990). Selective activation and disengagement of moral control. *Journal of Social Issues*, *46*(1), 27–46.

Bandura, A. (1997). *Self-efficacy: The exercise of control.* New York: Freeman.

Bandura, A. (1999). Moral disengagement in the perpetration of inhumanities. *Personality and Social Psychology Review*, *3*, 193–209.

Bandura, A. (2004). The role of selective moral disengement in terrorism and counterterrorism. In F. M. Moghaddam & A. J. Marsella (Eds.), *Understating terrorism: Psychological roots, causes and consequences.* Washington, DC: American Psychological Association.

Bandura, A., Barbaranelli, C., Caprara, G. V., & Pastorelli, C. (1996). Mechanism of moral disengagement in the exercise of moral agency. *Journal of Personality and Social Psychology*, *71*, 364–374.

Bandura, A., Ross, D., & Ross, S. A. (1963). Imitation of film-mediated aggressive models. *Journal of Abnormal and Social Psychology*, *66*, 3–11.

Barak, G. (2003). *Violence and nonviolence: Pathways to understanding.* Thousand Oaks, CA: Sage.

Baron, J., & Miller, J. G. (2000). Limiting the scope of moral obligation to help: A cross-cultural investigation. *Journal of Cross-Cultural Psychology*, *31*, 703–725.

Baron, R. A. (1984). Reducing organizational conflict: An incompatible response approach. *Journal of Applied Psychology*, *69*, 272–279.

Baron, R. A. (1989). Personality and organizational conflict: The Type A behavior pattern and self-monitoring. *Organizational Behavior and Human Decision Proceses*, *44*, 281–297.

Baron, R. A. (1990). Conflict in organizations. In K. R. Murphy & F. E. Saal (Eds.), *Psychology in organizations.* Hillsdate, NJ: Lawrence Erlbaum.

Baron, R. A. (1997). Positive effects of conflicts: Insights from social cognition. In C. K. W. De Dreu & E. Vande Vlient (Eds.), *Using Conflicts in organization.* London: Sage.

Baron, R. A., & Richardson, D. (1994). *Human aggression.* New York: Plenum.

Bar-Tal, D. (1997). Formation and change of ethnic and national stereotypes: An integrative model. *International Journal of Intercultural Relations*, *21*, 491–523.

Batson, D. (1990). How social an animal? The human capacity for caring. *American Psychologist*, *45*, 336–346.

Batson, D. (1991). *The altruism question.* Hillsdale, NJ: Lawrence Erlbaum.

Batson, D. (2002). Addressing the altruism question experimentally. In S. G. Post & L. G. Underwood (Eds.), *Altruism and altruistic love: Science, philosophy, and religion in dialogue.* London: Oxford University Press.

Baumeister, R. F. (1999). *Evil: Inside human violence and cruelty.* New York: Freeman.

Baumeister, R. F., & Boden, J. M. (1998). Aggression and self: High self-esteem, low self-esteem and ego threat. In R. G. Geen & E. Donnerstein (Eds.), *Human aggression: Theories, research, and implication for social policy.* New York: Academic Press.

Baumeister, R. F., Bratskvsky, E., Mauraven, M., & Tice, D. M. (1998). Ego depletion: Is the achieved self a limited resource? *Journal of Personality and Social Psychology*, *74*, 1252–1265.

Baumeister, R. F., & Heatherton, T. F. (1996). Self-regulation failure: An overview. *Psychological Inquiry*, *7*, 1–15.

Baumeister, R. F., & Vohs, K. D. (2004). Self-regulation and self-control: Four roots of evil. In A. Miller (Ed.), *The social psychology of good and evil: Understanding our capacity for kindness and cruelty.* New York: Guilford.

Baumgardner, S. R. (1990). Attributions of cause, responsibility and blame among violent and nonviolent individuals. In V. K. Kool (Ed.), *Perspectives on nonviolence.* New York: Springer-Verlag.

Bayer, L. (1988). Creative problem solving: A comparison of performance under different instructions. *Journal of Creative Behavior, 22,* 55–61.

Bazerman, M., Curhan, J., Moore, D., & Valley, K. (2000). Negotiation. In J. Spence, J. Darley, & D. Foss (Eds.), *Annual Review of Psychology, 51,* 279–315.

Beck, A. (1999). *Prisoners of hate: The cognitive basis of anger, hostility and violence.* New York: Harper Collins.

Becker, S. W., & Eagly, A. H. (2004). The heroism of women and men. *American Psychologist, 59*(3), 163–178.

Beersma, B., & De Dreu, C. K. W. (2002). Integrative and distributive negotiation in small group: Effects of task structure, decision rule and social motive. *Organizational Behavior and Human Decision Processes, 87,* 227–252.

Benbenishty, R., Zeira, A., & Astor, R. (2000). *Principals and teachers rights of school violence in Israel-Wave II: Fall 1999.* Jerusalem, Israel: Israeli Ministry of Education.

Benjamin, L. T. (1985). On defining aggression: An exercise for class discussion. *Teaching of Psychology, 12*(1), 41.

Benson, E. (2002, November). Investing in social capital. *American Psychological Association Monitor,* 26–27.

Benson, E. (2003, March). Goo, gaa, grr? *American Psychological Association Monitor,* 30.

Bereby-Meyer, Y., Moran, S., & Unger-Aviram, E. (2004). When performance goals deter performance: Transfer of skills in integrative negotiations. *Organizational Behaviour and Human Decision Processes, 93,* 142–154.

Berkowitz, L. (1962). *Aggression: A social psychological analysis.* New York: Mcgraw-Hill.

Berkowitz, L. (1993). *Aggression: Its causes, control and consequences.* New York: McGraw-Hill.

Berkowitz, L., & LePage, A. (1967). Weapons as aggression-eliciting stimuli. *Journal of Personality and Social Psychology, 7,* 202–207.

Beroldi, G. (1994). Critique of the Seville Statement or violence. *American Psychology, 49,* 847–848.

Betancourt, H. (2004). Attribution-emotion processes in White's realistic empathy approach to conflict and negotiation. *Peace and Conflict: Journal of Peace Psychologist, 10,* 369–380.

Bettencourt, B. A., Brewer, M. B., Croak, M. R., & Miller, N. (1992). Cooperation and the reduction of intergroup bias: The roles of reward structure and social orientation. *Journal of Experimental Social Psychology, 28,* 301–319.

Blair, R. J. R., & Charney, D. S. (2003). Emotion regulation. In M. Mattson (Ed.), *Neurobiology of aggression: Understanding and preventing violence.* Totowa, NJ: Humana Press.

Blake, R., & Mouton, J. (1962). The intergroup dynamics of win-lose conflict and problem solving collaboration in union-management relations. In M. Sherif (Ed.), *Intergroup relations and leadership* (pp. 94–140). New York: Wiley.

Blass, T. (2000). *Obedience to authority: Current perspectives on the Milgram paradigm.* Mahwah, NJ: Lawrence Erlbaum Associates.

Blight, J. G., & Lang, J. M. (2004). Lesson number one: "Empathize with your enemy". *Peace and Conflict: Journal of Peace Psychology, 10,* 349–368.

Blumberg, H. H. (2002). Understanding and dealing with terrorism: A classification of some contribution from behavioral and social sciences. *Peace and Conflict: Journal of Peace Psychology, 8*(1), 3–16.

Bohart, A. C., & Stipek, D. J. (Eds.). (2001). *Constructive and destructive behavior: Implications for family, school and society.* Washington, DC: American Psychological Association.

Bonanno, G. A. (2004). Loss, trauma and human resilience: Have we underestimated the human capacity to thieve after extremely aversive events? *American Psychologist, 59,* 20–28.

Bondurant, J. V. (1965). *Conquest of nonviolence: The Gandhian philosophy of conflict.* Berkeley: University of California Press.

Bono, G. (2005). Commonplace forgiveness: From healthy relationships to healthy society. *Humboldt Journal of Social Relations, 29,* 85–110.

Bonta, B. D. (1993). *Peaceful peoples: An annotated bibliography.* Metuchen, NJ: Scarecrow Press.

Bonta, B. D. (1997). Cooperation and competition in peaceful societies. *Psychological Bulletin, 121*(2), 299–320.

Bonta, B. D. (2001, September). *Cultures of the peaceful societies.* Paper presented at the Conference on Assessing Cultures of Peace, Clark University, Worcester, MA.

Boulding, E. (2000). A new chance for human peaceableness? *Peace and Conflict: Journal of Peace Psychology, 6,* 193–215.

Boulding, K. E. (1990). Inaugural address. In V. K. Kool (Ed.), *Perspectives on nonviolence.* New York: Springer-Verlag.

Boulding, K. E. (1993). Nonviolence in the 21st century. In V. K. Kool (Ed.), *Nonviolence: Social and psychological issues.* Lanham, MD: The University Press of America.

Boyden, J. (2003). The moral development of child soldiers: What do adults have to fear. *Peace and Conflict: Journal of Peace Psychology, 4,* 343–362.

Bredemeir, B. J. (1983). Athletic aggression: A moral concern. In J. H. Goldstein (Ed.), *Sport violence.* New York: Springer-Verlag.

Bredemeir, B. J. (1994). Children's moral reasoning and their assertive, aggressive and submissive tendencies in sport and daily life. *Journal of Sport and Exercise Psychology, 16,* 1–14.

Briggs, J. L. (1994). "Why don't you kill your baby brother?" The dynamics of peace in Canadian Inuit camps. In L. E. Sponsel & T. Gregor (Eds.), *The anthropology of peace and nonviolence.* Boulder, CO: Lynne Reinner.

Bronfenbrenner, U. (1961). The mirror image in Soviet-American relations. *Journal of Social Issues, 17,* 45–56.

Brown, R. J., & Wade, G. (1987). Superordinate goals and intergroup behavior: The effect of role ambiguity and status on intergroup attitudes and task performance. *European Journal of Social Psychology, 17,* 131–142.

Browning, C. R. (1992). *Ordinary men: Reserve police battalion 101 and the final solution in Poland.* New York: Harper Collins.

Bullock, H. E., Wyke, K. F., & Williams, W. R. (2001). Media images of the poor. *Journal of Social Issues, 57,* 229–246.

Burlingame-Lee, L. (2004). Forgiveness, emotion and evolution in making peace. *Peace and Conflict: Journal of Peace Psychology, 10,* 181–183.

Bushman, B. J., & Anderson, C. A. (1998). Methodology in the study of aggression: Integrating experimental and nonexperimental findings. In R. G. Geen & E. Donnerstein (Eds.), *Human aggression: Theories, research and implications for social policy.* New York: Academic Press.

Bushman, B. J., Baumeister, R. F., & Stack, A. D. (1999). Catharsis, aggression and persuasive influence: Self-fulfilling or self-defeating prophecies. *Journal of Personality and Social Psychology, 76,* 367–376.

Buss, A. (1961). *The psychology of aggression.* New York: Wiley.

Buss, A. H., & Durkee, A. (1957). An inventory for assessing different kinds of hostility. *Journal of Consulting Psychology, 21*(4), 343–349.

Buss, A. H., & Perry, M. (1992). The aggression questionnaire. *Journal of Personality and Social Psychology, 63,* 452–459.

Buss, A. H., & Warren, W. L. (2000). Aggression Questionnaire, Los Angeles, CA: Western Psychological Services.

Buss, D. M. (2004). *Evolutionary psychology: The new science of mind.* New York: Basic Books.

Buss, D. M., Haselton, M. G., et al. (1998). Adaptation, exaptation and spandrels. *American Psychologist, 53*, 533–548.

Buyer, L. (1988). Creative problem solving: A comparison of performance under different instructions. *Journal of Creative Behavior, 22*, 55–61.

Byrne, C. C. (2004). Benefit or burden: Victim's reflection on TRC participation. *Peace and Conflict: Journal of Peace Psychology, 10*, 237–256.

Capozza, D., Voci, A., & Licciardallo, O. (2000). Individualism, collectivism and social identity theory. In: D. Capozza & R. Brown (Eds.), *Social identity processes: Trends in theory and research.* London: Sage.

Caprara, G. V., et al. (1984). The eliciting value of aggressive slides reconsidered in a personological perspective: The weapons effect and irritability. *European Journal of Social Psychology, 14*, 313–322.

Carlson, M., Marcus, S., Newhall, A., & Miller, N. (1989). Evidence of a general construct of aggression. *Personality and Social Psychology Bulletin, 15*, 377–389.

Carr, A. (2004). *Positive psychology: The science of happiness and human strengths.* Hove & New York: Brunner-Routledge.

Carver, C. S. (1974). Facilitation of physical aggression through objective self-awareness. *Journal of Experimental Social Psychology, 10*, 365–370.

Carver, C. S., Ganellen, R. J., Froming, W. J., & Chambers, W. (1983). Modeling: An analysis in terms of category accessibility. *Journal of Experimental Social Psychology, 19*, 403–421.

Carver, C. S., & Scheier, M. F. (1981). *Attention and self regulation: A control theory approach to human behavior.* New York: Springer-Verlag.

Cattell, R. B. (1965). *The scientific analysis of personality.* Baltimore: Penguin.

Charney, I. S. (Ed.). (1999). *Encyclopaedia of genocide.* Santa Barbara, CA: ABC-Clio.

Christie, D. J., Wagner, R. V., & Winter, D. D. (Eds.). (2001). *Peace conflict and violence: Peace psychology in the 21st century.* Upper Saddle River, NJ: Prentice Hall.

Christie, R. (1970). Scale construction. In R. Christie & F. L. Geis (Eds.), *Studies in Machiavellianism.* New York: Academic Press.

Cicchetti, D., Rappaport, J., Sandler, L., & Weissberg, R. P. (Eds.). (2000). *The promotion of wellness in children and adolescents.* Washington, DC: Child Welfare League of American Press.

Cohrs, J. C., & Moschner, B. (2002). Antiwar knowledge and generalized political attitudes as determinants of attitude toward the Kosovo war. *Peace and Conflict: Journal of Peace Psychology, 8*, 139–155.

Colby, A., et al. (1983). A longitudinal study of moral judgment. *Monographs for the Society for Research in Child Development, 201.*

Coleman, P. (2004). Paradigmatic framing of protracted intractable conflict: Toward the development of a meta framework—II. *Peace and Conflict: Journal of Peace Psychology, 10*(3), 197–235.

Coleman, P. T. (1997). Redefining Ripeness: A social psychological perspective. *Peace and Conflict: Journal of Peace Psychology*, 3, 81–103.

Coleman, P. T. (2000). Intractable conflict. In M. Deutsch & P. T. Coleman (Eds.), *The handbook of conflict resolution: Theory and practice* (pp. 428–450). San Francisco: Jossey-Bass.

Coleman, P. T. (2003). Characteristics of protracted, intractable conflict: Toward the development of a metaframe-I. *Peace and Conflict: Journal of Peace Psychology, 9*, 1–37.

Cooney, C. (1995). *Relationship between moral exclusion and nonviolence.* Unpublished report. Utica, NY: State University of New York, Institute of Technology.

Cooney, R., & Michalowski, H. (1987). *The power of people: Active nonviolence in the United States.* Philadelphia: New Society Publisher.

Costa, P. T., & McCrae, R. R. (1992). *NEO-PI-R. Professional manual.* Odessa, FL: Psychological Assessment Resources.

Cox, R. H. (1998). *Sport psychology: Concepts and applications.* New York: McGraw-Hill.

Csikszentmihalyi, M. (1990). *Flow: The psychology of optimal experience.* New York: Harper.

Csikszentmihalyi, M. (1997). *Finding flow.* New York: Basic Books.

Daly, M., & Wilson, M. (2000). Not quite right. *American Psychologist, 55*, 679–680.

Davidson, J., & Versluys, M. (2000). Conflict resolution training within a school setting. *Australian Educational & Developmental Psychologist, 17*, 117–134.

Davis, M. H. (2004). Empathy: Negotiating the border between the self and other. In L. Z. Leach & C. Z. Tiedens (Eds.), *The social life of emotions.* New York: Cambridge University Press.

Dawes, R. M. (1980). Social dilemmas. *Annual Review of Psychology, 31*, 109–193.

DeAngelis, T. (1993, August). *American Psychological Association Monitor*, 16.

De Dreu, C. K. W. (2003). Time pressure and closing of the mind in negotiation. *Organizational Behavior and Human Decision Processes, 91*, 280–295.

De Dreu, C. K. W., & Carnevale, P. J. (2003). Motivational bases for information processing and strategic choice in conflict and negotiation. *Advances in Experimental Social Psychology, 35*, 235–291.

De Dreu, C. K. W., & McCuster, C. (1997). Gain-loss frames and cooperation in two-person social dilemmas: A transformational analysis. *Journal of Personality and Social Psychology, 72*, 1093–1106.

De Dreu, C. K. W., & van Knippenberg, D. (2005). The possessive self as a barrier to conflict resolution: Effects of mere ownership, process accountability, and self concept clarity on competitive cognitions and behavior. *Journal of Personality and Social Psychology, 89*, 345–357.

De Dreu, C. K. W., Weingart, L., & Kwon, S. (2000). Influence of social motives on integrative negotiation: A meta analytic review and test of two theories. *Journal of Personality and Social Psychology, 78*, 889–905.

De Rivera, J. (2004). A template for assessing cultures of peace. *Peace and Conflict: Journal of Peace Psychology, 10*, 125–146.

de Waal, F. B. M. (1996). *Good natured: The origins of right and wrong in human and other animals.* Cambridge, MA: Harvard University Press.

de Waal, F. B. M., & Van Roosmalen, A. (1979). Reconciliation and consolidation among chimpanzees. *Behavioral Ecology and Sociobiology, 5*, 55–66.

Dellinger, D. (1975). *More power than we know: The people's movement toward democracy.* Garden City, NY: Ancher Press.

Denton, R. K. (1968). *The Semai: A nonviolent people of Malay.* New York: Holt, Rinehart & Winston.

DePasquale, J. P., Geller, E. S., Clarke, S. W., & Littleton, L. C. (2001). Measuring road rage: Development of the propensity for angry driving scale. *Journal of Safety Research, 32*, 1–16.

Deutsch, M. (1949). A theory of cooperation and competition. *Human Relation, 2*, 129–152.

Deutsch, M. (1951). Interracial housing. In A. Rose (Ed.), *Readings in prejudice and discrimination.* New York: Knopf.

Deutsch, M. (1962). Cooperation and trust: Some theoretical notes. In M. Jones (Ed.), *Nebraska Symposium on Motivation* (pp. 275–319). Lincoln: University of Nebraska Press.

Deutsch, M. (1983). The prevention of world war III: A psychological perspective. *Political Psychology, 4*, 3–31.

Deutsch, M. (1985). *Distributive justice: A social psychological perspective.* New Haven, CT: Yale University Press.

Deutsch, M. (1990). Psychological roots of moral exclusion. *Journal of Social Issues, 46*, 21–25.

Deutsch, M. (1992). *On negotiating the non-negotiable.* Paper presented at the meeting of the American Psychological Association, Washington, DC.

Deutsch, M. (1993, June). Constructive conflict resolution for world today. Lifetime Award Address, Annual Meeting of the International Association of Conflict Management, Heugelhoef, Belgium.

Deutsch, M. (2003). Cooperation and conflict: A personal perspective on the history of the social psychological study of conflict resolution. In M. A. West, D. J. Tsojvold, & K. G. Smith (Eds.), *International handbook of organizational teamwork and cooperative working.* San Fransisco: Wiley.

Deutsch, M. (2005). Commentary on morality, decision making and collateral casualities. *Peace and Conflict: Journal of Peace Psychology, 1*(1), 63–66.

Deutsch, M., & Coleman, P. T. (2000). *Handbook of conflict resolution.* San Francisco: Jossey-Bass.

Deutsch, M., & Collins, M. E. (1951). *Interracial housing: A psychological evaluation of a social experiment.* Minneapolis, MN: University of Minnesota Press.

Diener, E. F. (1976). Effects of prior destructive behavior, anonymity, and group presence on deindividuation and aggression. *Journal of Social and Personality Psychology, 33*, 497–507.

Dittman, M. (2005). Anger on the road. *APA Monitor*, 26–27.

Dodge, K. A., Murphy, R. R., & Buchsbaum, K. (1984). The assessment of intention-cue detection skills in children: Implications for developmental psychopathology. *Child Development, 55*, 163–173.

Dollard, J., Doob, L., Miller, N., Mowrer, O. H., & Sears, R. R. (1939). *Frustration and aggression.* New Haven, CT: Yale University Press.

Dovidio, J. E., Fen Vergest, M., Stewart, T. L., Gaertner, S. K., et al. (2004). Perspective and Prejudice: Antecedents and mediating mechanisms. *Personality and Social Psychology Bulletin, 30*, 1537–1549.

Dovidio, J. F., Kawakami, K., & Gaertner, S. L. (2002). Implicit and explicit prejudice and interracial interaction. *Journal of Personality and Social Psychology, 82*, 62–68.

Dovidio, J. F., et al. (1993, October). *Androgyny, sex roles and helping.* Paper presented of the meeting of Society of Experimental Social Psychology, Santa Barbara, CA.

Droba, D. D. (1931). A scale of military-pacifism. *Journal of Educational Psychology, 22*, 96–111.

Druckman, D. (2001). Nationalism and war: A social psychological perspective. In D. J. Christie, R. V. Wagner, & D. D. Winter (Eds.), *Peace, conflict and violence: Peace psychology for the 21st century* (pp. 49–65). Upper Saddle River, NJ: Prentice Hall.

Duntley, J. D., & Buss, D. (2004). The evolution of evil. In A. Miller (Ed.), *The social psychology of good and evil: Understanding our capacity for kindness and cruelty.* New York: Guilford.

Einstein, A., & Freud, S. (1933). *Why war?* Paris: Institute of Intellectual Cooperation, League of Nations.

Elechi, O. O. (1999). Victims under restorative justice systems: The Afikpo Nigeria model. *International Review of Criminology, 6*, 359–375.

Ellemers, N. E., Spears, R., & Doosje, B. (2002). Self and social identity. *Annual Review of Psychology, 53*, 161–186.

Elliott, G. C. (1980) Componenets of pacifism. *Journal of Conflict Resolution, 24*, 27–54.

Erikson, E. (1958). *Young Luther.* New York: Norton.

Erikson, E. (1965). Problems of identity, hatred and nonviolence. *American Journal of Psychiatry, 122*, 241–253.

Erikson, E. (1968). *Identity, youth and crisis.* New York: Norton. (Also reprinted in A. P. Hare and H. H. Blumberg, Eds., 1968, *Nonviolent direct action.* Washington, DC: Corpus Book).

Erikson, E. (1969). *Gandhi's Truth.* New York: Norton.

Eron, L. D., Gentry, J. H., & Schlegel, P. (1996). *Reason to hope: A psychosocial perspective on violence.* Washington, DC: American Psychological Association.

Etzioni, A. (1967). Mixed scanning: A "Third" approach to decision making. *Public Administration Review, 27*, 385–392.

Evans, G. W., Palsane, M. N., & Carriere, S. (1987). Type A behavior and occupational stress: A cross-cultural study of blue collar workers. *Journal of Personality and Social Psychology, 52*, 1002–1007.

Exline, J. J., Baumeister, R. F., Bushman, B. J., Campbell, W. K., & Finkel, E. J. (2004). Too proud to let go: Narcissistic entitlement as a barrier to forgiveness. *Journal of Personality and Social Psychology, 87*, 894–912.

Eysenck, H. J. (1965). *The fact and fiction in psychology.* San Diego: Edits Publishers.

Farnham, B. (2004). War and reconciliation: Reason and emotion in conflict resolution. *Political Psychology, 25*, 313–316.

Farrell, A. D., Mayer, A. L., Sullivan, T. N., & Kung, E. M. (2003). Evaluation of the responding in peaceful and positive ways (RIPP): Seventh grade violence prevention curriculum. *Journal of Child and Family Studies, 12*, 101–120.

Feeney, M., & Davidson, J. (1996). Bridging the gap between the practical and the theoretical: An evaluation of a conflict resolution model. *Peace and Conflict: Journal of Peace Psychology, 2*, 255–269.

Fellman, G. (1998). *Rambo and the Dalai Lama: The compulsion to win and its threat to human survival.* Albany: State University of New York Press.

Fernandez, C. F., & Lapidus, L. B. (1998). Nuclear weapons attitudes in relation to dogmatism, mental representation of parents, and image of a foreign enemy. *Peace and Conflict: Journal of Peace Psychology, 54*, 59–68.

Fernadez-Dols, J. F., de-Mendoza, A. H., & de-Lucas, I. J. (2004). Culture of peace: An alternate definition and its measurement. *Peace and Conflict: Journal of Peace Psychology, 10*, 117–124.

Feshbach, S. (2001). The prerequisites of peace. *Peace and Conflict: Journal of Peace Psychology, 7*, 357–359.

Fisher, R., & Ury, W. (1981). *Getting to yes: Negotiating agreement without giving in.* Boston: Houghton Miffin.

Fisher, R., Ury, W., & Patton, B. (1991). *Getting to say yes: Negotiating agreement without giving in.* New York: Penguin Books.

Fisher, R. J. (1994). Generic principles for resolving intergroup conflict. *Journal of Social Issues, 50*, 47–66.

Flanagan, O. (1991). *Varieties of moral personality.* Cambridge: Harvard University Press.

Folger, R., & Baron, R. (1996). Violence and hostility at work: A model of reactions to perceived injustice. In C. R. VandenBos & E. Q. Bulatao (Eds.), *Violence on the job.* Washington, DC: American Psychological Association.

Follett, M. (1940). Constructive conflict. In H. Metcalf & L. Urwick (Eds.), *Dynamic Administration: The collected papers of Mary Parker Follett* (pp. 30–49). New York: Harper.

Frantz, C. M., & Bennigson, C. (2005). Better late than early: The influence of timing on apology effectiveness. *Journal of Experimental Social Psychology, 41*, 201–207.

Fraser, S. C. (1974). *Deindividuation: Effects of anonymity on aggression in children.* Unpublished report. Los Angeles: University of Southern California.

Fredrickson, B. (2001). The role of positive emotion in positive psychology: The broad and built theory of positive emotions. *American Psychologist, 56*, 218–226.

Fredrickson, B. (2002). Positive emotions. In C. R. Snyder & S. Lopez (Eds.), *Handbook of positive psychology.* New York: Guilford Press.

Freud, S. (1920). *A general introduction to psychoanalysis.* New York: Boni & Liverght.

Friedman, T. L. (2002, April 17). George W. Sadat. *The New York Times.* Retrieved from http://www.nytimes.com

Fromm, E. (1959). *Sigmund Freud's mission.* New York: Harper.

Gable, S., & Haidt, J. (2005). What (and why) is positive psychology. *Review of General Psychology, 2*, 103–110.

Gaertner, S. L., Dovidio, J. F., Anastasio, P. A., Bachman, B. A., & Rust, M. C. (1993). The common ingroup identity model: Recategorization and the reduction of intergroup bias. In W. Stroebe & M. Hewstone (Eds.), *European Review of Social Psychology* (Vols. 4, 26). London: Wiley.

Gaertner, S. L., Dovidio, J. F., Banker, B. S., Houlette, M., Johnson, K. M., & McGlynn, E. A. (2000). Reducing intergroup conflict: From superordinate goals to decategorization, recategorization and mutual differentiation. *Group Dynamics: Theory, Research and Practice, 4*, 98–114.

Galtung, J. (1966). Rank and social integration. A multidisciplinary approach. In J. Berger, M. Zelitsch, & B. Anderson (Eds.), *Sociological theories in progress.* Boston, MA: Houghton Mifflin.

Galtung, J. (1969). Violence, peace and peace research. *Journal of Peace Research, 6*, 167–191.

Galtung, J. (1996). *Peace by peaceful means: Peace and conflict, development and civilization.* London: Sage.

Galtung, J. (1998). On the genesis of peaceless worlds: Insane nations and insane states. *Peace and Conflict: Journal of Peace Psychology, 4*(1), 1–13.

Gandhi, A. (2004). Nonviolence as a comprehensive philosophy. *Peace and Conflict: Journal of Peace Psychology, 10*, 87–90.

Garmezy, N. (1981). Personality development. In A. J. Robin, et al. (Eds.), *Further explorations in personality.* New York: Wiley.

Geen, R. G. (1990). *Human aggression.* Pacific Grove, CA: Brooks/Cole.

Geen, R. G. (1998). Processes and personal variables in affective aggression. In R. G. Geen & E. Donnerstein (Eds.), *Human aggression: Theories, research and implications for social policy.* New York: Academic Press.

Geen, R. G., & Donnerstein, E. (Eds.). (1998). *Human aggression.* New York: Academic Press.

Gergen, K. J. (2001). Psychological science in postmodern context. *American Psychologist, 56*, 803–813.

Gerstein, L. H., & Moeschberger, S. L. (2003). Building cultures of peace: An urgent task for counseling professionals. *Journal of Counseling and Development, 81*, 115–119.

Gilligan, C. (1982). *In a different voice.* Cambridge: Harvard University Press.

Girard, K., & Koch, S. J (1996). *Conflict resolution in schools: A manual for educators*, San Francisco: Jossey-Boss.

Goldberg, L. R. (1990). An alternate "description of personality". The big-five factor structure. *Journal of Personality and Social Psychology, 59*, 1216–1229.

Goldstein, J. (1986). *Aggression and crimes of violence.* New York: Oxford University Press.

Goldstein, J., & Pawel, M. (1996). Doing justice to nonviolence. *Contemporary Psychology, 4*, 131–132.

Golec, A. (2002). Cognitive skills as predictor of altitudes toward political conflict: A study of Polish politicians. *Political Psychology, 4*, 731–759.

Golec, A., & Frederico, C. M. (2004). Understanding responses to political conflict: Interactive effects of the need for closure and salient conflict schemas. *Journal of Personality and Social Psychology, 87*, 750–762.

Goleman, R. (1998). *Working with emotional intelligence.* New York: Bantom.

Gottfredson, M. R., & Hirschi, T. (1990). *A general theory of crime.* Stanford, CA: Stanford University Press.

Gould, S. J. (1991). Exaptation: A crucial tool for evolutionary psychology. *Journal of Social Issues, 47* , 43–65.

Groebel, J., & Hinde, R. (Eds.). (1989). *Aggression and war.* New York: Cambridge University Press.

Grussendorf, J., McAlister, A. L., Sandstrom, P., Udd, L., & Morrison, T. (2002). Resisting moral disengagement in support for war: Use of peace test scale among student groups in 21 nations. *Peace and Conflict: Journal of Peace Psychology, 8*, 73–83.

Hagberg, J. (1984). *Real power.* Minneapolis, MN: Winston Press.

Hammock, G., & Hanson, D. (1990). Nonviolence attribution of intentionality and dogmatism. In V. K. Kool (Ed.), *Perspectives on nonviolence.* New York: Springer-Verlag.

Harak, G. S. (Ed.). (2000). *Nonviolence for the Third millennium: Its legacy and future.* Macon, GA: Mercer University Press.

Hare, A. P. (1968). Introduction to theories of nonviolence. In A. P. Hare & H. H. Blumberg (Eds.), *Nonviolent direct action: American cases and social psychological analyses.* Washington, DC: Corpus Books.

Harre, R., & Lamb, R. (1983). *The encyclopaedia dictionary of psychology.* Oxford, England: Basil Blackwell.

Hasan, Q., & Khan, S. R. (1983). Dimensions of Gandhian (nonviolent) personality. *Journal of Psychological Researches, 2*, 100–116.

Hastings, T. H. (2002). *Meek ain't meek: Nonviolent power and people of color.* Lanham, MD: University Press of America.

Heaven, P. C., Rayab, D., & Bester, C. L. (1984). Psychometric properties of Elliott's measure of pacifism: Cross-cultural comparisons. *Journal of Cross Cultural Psychology, 15*, 227–232.

Heider, F. (1958). *The psychology of interpersonal relations.* New York: Wiley.

Helson, H. (1964). *Adaptation level theory.* New York: Harper & Row.

Herman, T. (1990). Seven forms of nonviolence for peace research: A conceptual framework. In V. K. Kool (Ed.), *Perspectives on nonviolence.* New York: Springer-Verlag.

Herman, T. (1993). Exercises in nonviolent action. In V. K. Kool (Ed.), *Nonviolence: Social and psychological issues.* Lanham, MD: University Press of America.

Herr, C. (1992). Psychological variables discriminating differential response to nuclear arnament (Doctoral dissertation, Columbia University, New York).

Hoffman, E. A. (2005). Dispute resolution in a worker cooperative: Formal procedures and procedural justice. *Law and Society Review, 39*, 51–82.

Hofstede, G. (1983). Dimension of national cultures in fifty countries and their regions. In J. Deregowski, S. Dzuirawiec, & R. Annis (Eds.), *Explorations in cross-cultural psychology.* Lisse: Swets and Zeitinger.

Hokvoort, I. (1996). Children's conception of peace and war: A longitudinal study. *Peace and Conflict: Journal of Peace Psychology, 2*, 1–15.

Holt, J. L., & Devore, C. J. (2005). Culture, gender, organizational role and styles of conflict resolution: A meta analysis. *International Journal of Intercultural Relations, 29*, 165–196.

Homans, G. C. (1961). *Social behavior: Its elementary forms.* New York: Harcourt.

Hora, T. (1983). *Forgiveness.* Orange, CA: PAGL Press.

Horney, K. (1937). *The neurotic personality of our time* . New York: Norton.

Howard, R. W. (1990). Mohan K. Gandhi: Nonviolence, principles, and the chamber pots. In V. K. Kool (Ed.), *Perspectives on nonviolence.* New York: Springer-Verlag.

Huesmann, L. R. (1998). The role of information processing and cognitive schema in the acquisition and maintenance of habitual aggressive behavior. In R. G. Green & E. Donnerstein (Eds.), *Human aggression: Theories, research and implications for policy.* New York: Academic Press.

Huesmann, L. R., & Guerra, N. G. (1997). Children's normative beliefs about aggression and aggressive behavior. *Journal of Personality and Social Psychology, 72*, 408–419.

Hull, C. L. (1943). *Principles of behavior.* New York: Appleton-Century-Crofts.

Hunt, M. (1993). *The story of psychology.* New York: Doubleday.

Hunter, J. A., Stringer, M., & Watson, R. P. (1991). Intergroup violence in intergroup attributions. *British Journal of Social Psychology, 30*, 261–266.

Islam, M. R., & Hewstone, M. (1993). Dimensions of contact as predictors of intergroup anxiety, perceived out group variability and out group attitude: An integrative model. *Personality and Social Psychology Bulletin, 19*, 700–710.

Iyer, R. (1983). *Moral and political thought of Mahatma Gandhi.* New York: Concord Grove Press.
Jacobs, M. S. (1989). *American psychology in the quest for nuclear peace.* New York: Praeger.
James, L., & Nahl, D. (2000). *Road rage and aggressive driving* Steering clear of highway warfare. Amherst, NY: Promethesus.
James, W. (1910/1995). The moral equivalent of war. *Peace and Conflict: Journal of Peace Psychology, 1*, 17–26.
Jervis, R. (1985). Perceiving and coping with threat: Psychological perspectives. In R. Jervis, R. N. Lebow, & J. Stein (Eds.), *Psychology and Deterrence.* Baltimore: Johns Hopkins University Press.
Johnson, D. W., & Johnson, R. T. (1989). *Cooperation and competition: Theory and research.* Edina, MN: Interaction Book Company.
Johnson, D. W., & Johnson, R. T. (1995). *Teaching students to be peacemakers.* Edina, MN: Interaction Book Company.
Johnson, D. W., & Johnson, R. T. (2000). Civil discourse in action: The controversy in psychology. *Peace and Conflict: Journal of Peace Psychology, 6*, 191–317.
Johnson, D. W., & Johnson, R. T. (2003). Field study of integrative negotiations. *Peace and Conflict: Journal of Peace Psychology, 9*, 39–68.
Johnson, D. W., Johnson, R. T., & Dudley, B. (1992). Effect of peer mediation training on elementary school students. *Mediation Quarterly, 10*, 89–99.
Johnson, P., et al. (1998). *Nonviolence: Constructing a multidimensional attitude measure.* Paper presented at the Annual Meeting of the American Psychological Association, San Francisco.
Johnson, R. A. (1993). *Negotiation Basics: Concepts, skills and exercises.* Newbury Park, CA: Sage.
Jordon, P. J., & Troth, A. C. (2002). Emotional intelligence and conflicts resolution: Implications for human resource development. *Advances in Developing Human Resources, 4*, 62–79.
Josephson, W. L. (1987). Television violence and children's aggression: Testing the priming, social script, and disinhibiting predictions. *Journal of Personality and Social Psychology, 53*, 882–890.
Kahneman, D. (1973). *Attention and effort.* Englewood-Cliffs, NJ: Prentice Hall.
Kahneman, D. (2003). A perspective on judgment and choice: Mapping bounded rationality. *American Psychologist, 58*, 697–720.
Kahneman, D., Fredrickson, D. L., Schreiber, C. A., & Redelmeir, D. A. (1993). When more pain is preferred to less: Adding a better end. *Psychological Sciences, 4*, 401–405.
Kahneman, D., & Tversky, A. (1979). Prospect theory: An analysis of decisions under risk. *Econometrica, 47*, 263–291.
Kahneman, D., & Tversky, A. (Eds.). (2000). *Choices, values and frames.* New York: Cambridge University Press.
Katz, N. (1990). Action research in nonviolent movement. In V. K. Kool (Ed.), *Perspectives on nonviolence.* New York: Springer-Verlag.
Kelly, H. H., & Thibaut, J. W. (1978). *Interpersonal relations: A theory of interdependence.* New York: Wiley.
Kelman, H. C. (1990). Applying a human needs perspective to the practice of conflict resolution: The Israeli Palestinian case. In J. Burton (Ed.), *Conflict: human needs theory.* New York: St. Martin's.
Kelman, H. C. (1995). Contributions to an unofficial conflict resolution effort to the Israeli-Palestinian breakthrough. *Negotiation Journal, 11*, 19–27.
Kelman, H. C. (1999). The interdependence of Israeli and Palestinian national identities: The role of the other in existential conflicts. *Journal of Social Issues, 55*, 581–600.
Kelman, H. C. (2004). In appreciation of Ralph White—Valued friend and colleague for the past 50 years. *Peace and Conflict: Journal of Peace Psychology, 4*, 341–348.
Kelman, H. C. (2005). Building trust among enemies: The control challenge for international conflict resolution. *International Journal of Intercultural Relations, 29*, 639–650.
Keniston, A. H. (1990). Dimensions of moral development among nonviolent individuals. In V. K. Kool (Ed.), *Perspectives on nonviolence.* New York: Springer-Verlag.

Kenrick, D. T., Neuberg, S. L., & Cialdini, R. B. (2005). *Social psychology: Unraveling the mystery.* New York: Pearson.

Kersting, K. (2004, February & October). Lessons in resilience & custom-tailored resilience APA Monitor, 30–34.

Kimble, A. (1994). A frame of reference to psychology. *American Psychologist, 49*, 510–519.

Kimmel, P. R. (1994). Cultural perspectives on international negotiation. *Journal of Social Issues, 50*(1), 179–196.

Kimmel, P. R. (2000). Culture and conflict. In M. Deutsch & P. T. Coleman (Eds.), *The Handbook of Conflict Resolution.* San Francisco: Jossey-Bass.

Kitayama, S., Markus, H. R., Matsumoto, H., & Noraskkunkit, V. (1997). Individual and collective processes in the construction of self: Self enhancement in the United States and Self-criticism in Japan. *Journal of Personality and Social Psychology, 72*, 1245–1267.

Klot, J. (1998). The Graca Machel/UN study on the impact of armed conflict on children. *Peace and Conflict: Journal of Peace Psychology, 4*, 319–320.

Kobasa, S. C. (1979). Stressful life events, personality and health: An inquiry into hardiness. *Journal of Personality and Social Psychology, 37*, 1–11.

Kobasa, S. C. (1982). The hardy personality: Toward a social psychology of stress and health. In G. S. Sanders & J. Suls (Eds.), *Social Psychology and Illness.* Mahwah, NJ: Lawrence Erlbaum Associates.

Kohlberg, L. (1976). Moral stages and moralization: The cognitive-development approach. In T. Lockina (Ed.), *Moral development and behavior.* New York: Holt, Rinehart, and Winston.

Konen, K., Mayton, D. M., Delva, Z., Sonnen, M., et al. (1999). Paper presented at the Annual meeting of the American Psychological Association, San Francisco.

Kool, V. K. (1988). *Patterns of nonviolence: A cross cultural study of Polish, Indian and American samples.* Paper presented at the International Cross-Cultural Psychology Convention, University of New Castle, New Castle, Australia.

Kool, V. K. (Ed.). (1990). *Perspectives on nonviolence.* New York: Springer-Verlag.

Kool, V. K. (1992, May). *Correlates of nonviolence.* Paper presented at the Symposium on Nonviolence, SUNYIT, Utica, NY.

Kool, V. K. (1992, August). Main speaker at the symposium on the social psychology of nonviolence. American Psychological Association Convention, Washington, DC.

Kool, V. K. (Ed.). (1993). *Nonviolence: Social and psychological issues.* Lanham, MD: University Press of America.

Kool, V. K. (1994, August). *The measurement of nonviolence as multi-dimensional concept.* Paper presented at the Peace Psychology Division, American Psychological Association, Los Angeles.

Kool, V. K., & Agrawal, R. (2006). *Applied social psychology: A global perspective.* New Delhi: Atlantic.

Kool, V. K., Diaz, J., Brown, J., & Hama, H. (2002). Psychological research, nonviolence and cultural orientation: An empirical analysis. *Regional Peace Studies Consortium Annual Journal*, 55–74.

Kool, V. K., & Keyes, C. M. L. (1990). Explorations in the nonviolent personality. In V. K. Kool (Ed.), *Perspectives on nonviolence.* New York: Springer-Verlag.

Kool, V. K., & Ray, J. J. (Ed.). (1983). *Authoritarianism across cultures.* Bombay: Himalaya Publishing House.

Kool, V. K., & Sen, M. (1984). The nonviolence test. In D. M. Pestonjee (Ed.), *Second handbook of psychological and sociological instruments* (pp. 48–54). Ahmedabad: Indian Institute of Management.

Kool, V. K. & Sen, M. (2005, June). *Research based on the nonviolence test by Kool and Sen.* Paper presented at the German Peace Psychology Conference, University of Erlangen, Germany.

Kosslyn, S. M., Caciappo, J. T., & Davidson, R. J., et al. (2002). Bridging psychology and biology: The analysis of individuals in groups. *American Psychologist, 57*, 341–351.

Kotre, H. (1984). *Outliving the self: Generativity and the interpretation of lives.* Baltimore, MD: Johns Hopkins University Press.

Krahe, B. (2001). *The social psychology of aggression.* London: Taylor and Francis.

Kriesberg, L. (1991). Introduction: Timing conditions, strategies and errors. In L. Kriesberg & S. J. Thorson (Eds.), *Timing the de-escalation of international conflicts* (pp. 1–24). Syracuse, NY: Syracuse University Press.

Kruglanski, A. W., Bar-Tal, D., & Klar, Y. (1993). A social cognitive theory of conflict. In K. S. Larson (Ed.), *Conflict and social psychology* (pp. 45–56). London: Sage.

Krugman, P. (2002, October 15). Still living dangerously. *The New York Times.* Retrieved from http://ww.nytimes.com

Kulaksi, A., Soglu, A., & Dilmac, B. (2003). Imparting education in human values to primary education students and testing it by implementing a moral maturity scale. *Studia Psychologica, 45*, 43–50.

Kuppner, S., & McIntyre, T. M. (Ed.). (2003). *The psychological impact of war trauma on civilians: An international perspective* . Westport, CT: Praeger.

Langholtz, H. J. (1998). The psychology of peacekeeping: Genesis, ethos and applications. *Peace and Conflict: Journal of Peace Psychology, 4*, 217–236.

Latane, B., & Darley, J. M. (1970). *The unresponsive bystander: Why doesn't he help?* New York: Appleton Century Croft.

Lawson, R. B., & Shen, Z. (1998). *Organizational psychology.* New York: Oxford University Press.

Leach, L. Z., & Tiedens, C. W. (Ed.). (2004). *The social life of emotions.* New York: Cambridge University Press.

Leary, T. (1957). *Interpersonal diagnosis of personality.* New York: Ronald Press.

Lerner, M. J. (1970). *The belief in a just world: A fundamental delusion.* New York: Plenum.

Levy, J. (1992). An introduction to prospect theory. *Political Psychology, 13*, 171–186.

Levy, S. G. (1995). Attitudes toward the conduct of war. *Peace and Conflict: Journal of Peace Psychology, 1*, 179–197.

Lewin, K., Lippitt, R., & White, R. (1939). Patterns of aggressive behavior in experimentally created social climates. *Journal of Social Psychology, 10*, 271–299.

Lifton, R. J., & Markusen, E. (1990). *The genocidel mentality: Nazi holocaust and Nazi threat.* New York: Basic Books.

Lindner, E. G. (2001). Humiliation and the human condition: Mapping a minefield. *Human Rights Review, 2*, 46–63.

Linn, R. (2001). Conscience at war: On the relationship between moral psychology and moral resistance. *Peace and Conflict: Journal of Peace Psychology, 7*, 337–355.

Linskold, S. (1978). Trust development, the GRIT proposal and the effects of conciliatory acts on conflict and cooperation. *Psychological Bulletin, 85*, 772–793.

Lipsky, D. B., & Seeber, R. L. (1998). *The appropriate resolution of corporate disputes: A report on the growing use of ADR by US corporations* . Ithaca, NY: Institute of Conflict Resolution.

Little, D. (1995). Introduction. In D. R. Smock (Ed.), *Perspectives on pacifism: Christian, Jewish and Muslim views on nonviolence and international conflicts.* Washington, DC: United States Institute of Peace Press.

Littlefield, L., Love, A., Peck, C., & Wertheim, E. H. (1993). A model for resolving conflict: Some theoretical, empirical and practical implications. *Australian Psychologist, 28*, 80–85.

Long, W. J., & Brecke, P. (2003). *Reason and emotion in conflict resolution.* Cambridge: MIT Press.

Lore, R. K., & Schultz, L. A. (1993). Control of human aggression. *American Psychologist, 48*, 16–23.

Lorenz, K. (1974). *On aggression.* New York: Hartcourt, Bruce, & World.

Louis, W. R., Taylor, D. M., & Neil, T. (2004). Cost-benefit analyses for your group and yourself: The rationality of decision making in conflict. *International Journal of Conflict Management, 15*, 110–143.

Lumsden, P. R., & Wolpe, R. (1996). Evolution of conflict solving workshop: An introduction to social psychological approaches to conflict resolutin. *Peace and Conflict: Journal of Peace Psychology*, *2*(1), 37–67.

Luthans, F. (1995). *Organizational behaviour*. New York: McGraw Hill.

Lykes, M. B. (1999). Doing psychology at the periphery: Constructing just alternatives to war and peace. *Peace and Conflict: Journal of Peace Psychology*, *1*, 27–36.

Lynd, S. (1966). *Nonviolence in America: A documentary history*. New York: Bobbs-Merrill Company.

Mackie, D. M., Silver, L. A., & Smith, E. R. (2004). Intergroup emotions: Emotion as an intergroup phenomenon. In L. Z. Leach & E. Z. Tiedens (Eds.), *The social life of emotions*. New York: Cambridge University Press.

MacNair, R. M. (2003). *The psychology of peace*. Westport, CT: Praeger.

Macrae, C. N., Milne, A. B., & Bodenhausen, G. V. (1994). Stereotypes energy saving devices: A peek into the cognitive toolbox. *Journal of Personality and Social Psychology*, *66* , 165–173.

Malley, J., Beck, M., & Adorno, D. (2001). Building an ecology for nonviolence in schools. *International Journal of Reality Therapy*, *21*, 22–26.

Mann, J. (1993). A social psychology of rules of war: A research strategy for studying civilian-based defense. In V. K. Kool (Ed.), *Nonviolence: Social and Psychological Issues*. Lanham, MD: University Press of America.

Maoz, I. (2000). Multiple conflicts and competing agenda: A framework for conceptualizing structured encounters between groups in conflicts—the case of a coexistence project of Jews and Palestinians in Israel. *Peace and Conflict: Journal of Peace Psychology*, *6*, 135–156.

Marcia, J. (1994). Ego identity and object relations. In J. M. Mashling & R. F. Bornstein (Eds.), *Empirical perspectives in object relations theory*. Washington, DC: American Psychological Association.

Marcus, R. F., & Kramer, C. (2001). Reactive and proactive aggression: Attachment and social competence predictors. *The Journal of Genetic Psychology*, *102*, 260–275.

Maslow, A. H. (1954). *Motivation and personality*. New York: Harper.

Masten, A. S. (2001). Ordinary magic: Resilience processes in development. *American Psychologist*, *56*, 227–238.

Masten, A. S., Hubbard, J. J., Gest, S. D., Tellegen, A., Garmezy, N., & Ramirez, M. (1999). Competence in the context of adversity: Pathways to resilience and maladaptation from childhood to late adolescence. *Development and Psychopaethology*, *11*, 143–169.

Matsumoto, M. (1993). *The Nonviolent Personality of Student Nurses: A pilot study*. Juntendo College report, Urayasush, Japan.

Mattaini, M. A. (2001). Constructing cultures of nonviolence: The peace power strategy. *Education and Treatment of Children*, *24*, 430–447.

Mauraven, M., & Baumeister, R. F. (2000). Self regulation and depletion of limited resources: Does self-control resemble a muscle? *Psychological Bulletin*, *126*, 247–259.

May, R. (1972). *Power and innocence*. New York: Norton.

Mayer, J. D. (2005). A tale of two visions: Can a new view of personality help integrate psychology? *American Psychologist*, *69*, 294–307.

Mayor, F. (1995). How psychology can contribute to a culture of peace? *Peace and Conflict: Journal of Peace Psychology*, *1*, 3–10.

Mayton, D. (2001). Nonviolence within cultures of peace: A means and ends. *Peace and Conflict: Journal of Peace Psychology*, *7*, 143–155.

Mayton, D. M., Diessner, R., & Granby, C. (1996). Nonviolence and human values: Empirical support for theoretical relations. *Peace Conflict: Journal of Peace Psychology*, *2*, 245–253.

Mayton, D. M., Nogle, K. S., Mack, J. L., et al. (1998, August). *Teenage Nonviolence Test: A new measure of nonviolence*. Paper presented at the annual meeting of the American Psychological Association, San Francisco.

Mayton, D. M., Peters, D. J., & Owens, R. W. (1999). Values, militarism, and nonviolent predispositions. *Peace and Conflict: Journal of Peace Psychology, 5*, 69–77.

Mayton, D. M., Susnjic, S., Palmer, B. J., Peters, D. J., Gierth, R., & Caswell, R. N. (2002). The measurement of nonviolence. *Peace and Conflict: Journal of Peace Psychology, 8*, 343–354.

McAdams, D. P. (1988, April). The Henry A. Murray lecturers on personality. University of Michigan, Ann Arbor.

McAdams, D. P., & de St. Aubin, E. (1998). *Generativity and adult development.* Washington, DC: American Psychological Association.

McAdams, D. P., Ruetzel, K., & Foley, J. M. (1986). Complexity generativity at midlife: Relations among social motive, ego development and adults' plans for the future. *Journal of Personality and Social Psychology, 50*, 800–807.

McAlister, A. L. (2001). Moral engagement: Measurement and modification. *Journal of Peace Research, 38* , 87–99.

McAlister, A. L., Ama, E., Barroso, C., Peters, R. J., & Kelder, S. (2000). Promoting tolerance and moral engagement through peer modeling. *Cultural Diversity and Ethnic Minority Psychology, 6*, 363–373.

McClelland, D. C. (1961). *The achieving society.* New York: D. Nostrand Co. Inc.

McCoullough, M., & Witliet, C. (2002). The psychology of forgiveness. In C. R. Snyder & S. Lopez (Eds.), *Handbook of positive psychology.* New York: Oxford University Press.

McCullough, M., Pargament, K., & Thoresen, C. (2000). *Forgiveness: Theory, research and practice.* New York: Guilford.

McLernon, F., & Cairns, E. (2001). Impact of political violence on images of war and peace in the drawings of primary school children. *Peace and Conflict: Journal of Peace Psychology, 7*(1), 45–57.

Meyer, A., Allison, K. W., Reese, L. E., & Gay, F. W. (2004). Choosing to be violence free in middle school. The student component of the GREAT school and families program. *American Journal of Preventive Medicine, 26*, 20–28.

Meyer, A., Ferrell, A. D., et al. (2000). *Promoting nonviolence in early adolescence: Responding in peaceful and positive ways.* New York: Kluwer.

Milburn, T., & Isaac, P. (1995). Prospect theory: Implications for international mediation. *Peace and Conflict: Journal of Peace Psychology, 1*, 333–342.

Milgram, S. (1974). *Obedience to authority.* New York: Harper.

Miller, A. (2004). *The social psychology of good and evil.* New York: Guilford.

Miller, D. T. (1999). The norm of self-interest. *American Psychologist, 54*, 1053–1060.

Miller, J. G. (1984). Culture and the development of everyday explanation. *Journal of Personality and Social Psychology, 46*, 961–978.

Miller, J. G., Bersoff, D. M., & Harwood, R. L. (1990). Perceptions of social responsibility in India and in the United States: Moral imperatives on personal decisions. *Journal of Personality and Social Psychology, 58*, 33–47.

Miller, N. E. (1944). Experimental studies of conflict. In M. Hunt (Ed.), *Personality and behavior disorders* (Vol. 1). New York: Ronald.

Miller, N. E. (1948). Theory and experiment relating psychoanalytic displacement to stimulus–response generalization. *Journal of Abnormal and Social Psychology, 43*, 155–178.

Moerk, E. L. (2002). Scripting war-entry to make it appear unavoidable. *Peace and Conflict: Journal of Peace Psychology, 8*(3), 229–248.

Moeschberger, S. L., & Ordonz, A. (2003). Working towards building cultures of peace: A primer for students and new professionals. *International Journal for the Advancement of Counseling, 25*, 317–323.

Moghaddam, F. M. (2005). The staircase of terrorism: A psychological expression. *American Psychologist, 60*, 161–169.

Montagu, A. (1976). *The nature of human aggression.* New York: Oxford Press.

Montagu, A. (1978). *Learning nonaggression: The experience of nonliterate societies.* Oxford, England: Oxford University Press.

Montiel, C. J. (2003). Peace psychology in Asia. *Peace and Conflict: Journal of Peace Psychology, 9,* 195–218.

Moran, S., & Ritov, I. (2002). Initial perceptions in negotiations: Evaluation and response to logrolling offers. *Journal of Behavioural Decision Making, 15,* 101–124.

Mork, G. R. (2003). Fundamentals of genocide scholarship. *Peace and Conflict: Journal of Peace Psychology, 9* , 175–176.

Morris, E. (2003). *The fog of war. Eleven lessons from the life of Robert, S. McNamara* [Motion picture]. United States: Sony Pictures Classics.

Muley, E. P., & Cauffman, E. (2001). The inherent limits of predicting school violence. *American Psychologist, 56,* 797–892.

Mullet, E., Houdbive, A., Laumonier, S., & Girard, M. (1998). Forgiving: Factorial structure in a sample of young, middle age and elderly adults. *European Psychologist, 2,* 289–297.

Murphy, K. R. (1992). *Honesty in the workplace.* Belmont, CA: Brooks/Cole.

Murray, B. (2003, October). Rebounding for losses. *American Psychological Association Monitor,* 42–43.

Myers, D. G. (1999/2004). *Social Psychology.* New York: McGraw-Hill.

Myers, D. G. (2000). The funds, friends, and faith of happy people. *American Psychologist, 55,* 56–67.

Nagata, D. (1993). Moral exclusion and nonviolence: The Japanese American Internment. In V. K. Kool (Ed.), *Nonviolence: Social and psychological issues.* Lanham, MD: University Press of America.

Nelson, L. L., & Christie, D. J. (1995). Peace in the psychology curriculum: Moving from assimilation to accomodation. *Peace and Conflict: Journal of Peace Psychology, 1,* 161–178.

Nelson, L. L., & Milburn, T. W. (1999). Relationship between problem-solving competencies and militaristic attitudes: Implications for peace education. *Peace and Conflict: Journal of Peace Psychology, 5* , 149–168.

Nelson, S. A. (1980). Factors influencing young children: use of motives and outcomes as moral criteria. *Child Development, 5,* 823–829.

Ng, J., & Ang, S. (1999). Attributing bias: Challenges, issues and strategies for mediation. *Mediation Quarterly, 16,* 377–387.

Nisbett, R. E. (1993). Violence and US regional culture. *American Psychologist, 48,* 441–449.

Observer Dispatch (2006, October 2). Amish.

Ohbuchi, K., & Takada, N. (2001). Escalation of conflict and forgiveness: A social psychological model of forgiveness. *Tohoku Psychologica Folia, 60,* 61–71.

Oliner, S. P., & Oliner, P. M. (1988). *The altruistic personality: Rescuers of Jews in Nazi Europe.* New York: Free Press.

Oliner, S. P., & Oliner, P. M. (1995). *Toward a caring society: Ideas into action.* Westport, CT: Praeger.

Opotow, S. (1990). Moral Exclusion and Injustice: An Introduction. *Journal of Social Issues, 46,* 1–20.

Opotow, S. (2001). Social injustice. In D. J. Christice, R. V. Waguer, & D. Winter (Eds.), *Peace, conflict and violence: Peace psychology for the 21st century* (pp. 102–109). Upper Saddle River, NJ: Prentice Hall.

Oppenheimer, L. (1995). Peace, but what about social constraints? *Peace and Conflict: Journal of Peace Psychology, 4,* 383–397.

Osgood, C. H. (1962). *An alternate to war or surrender.* Urbana, IL: University of Illinois Press.

Osgood, C. H. (1980). The GRIT strategy. *Bulletin of the Atomic Scientists, 36,* 58–60.

Osgood, C. H., Suci, G. J., & Tannenbaum, P. H. (1957). *The measurement of meaning*. Urbana, IL: The University of Illinois Press.

Oskamp, S. (1990). The editor's page. *Journal of Social Issues*, 46.

Oskamp, S. (2000). Multiple paths to reducing prejudice and discrimination. In S. Orkamp (Ed.), *Reducing prejudice and discrimination*. Thousand Oaks, CA: Sage.

Oskamp, S., & Schultz, P. (1998). *Applied social psychology*. Upper Saddle River, NY: Prentice Hall.

Ozer, E. J., Best, J. R., Lipsey, T. L., & Weiss, D. S. (2003). Predictions of post traumatic stress disorder and symptoms in adults: A meta analysis. *Psychological Bulletin*, *129*, 52–71.

Pandey, N., & Naidu, R. K. (1992). Anasakti and health: A study of non-attachment. *Psychology and Developing Societies*, *4*, 89–104.

Parakrama, A. (2001, April). *Social cleaning: Resistance and loss within a bereaved culture*. Working paper presented at the Carnegie Council on Foreign Relations, New York.

Pelton, L. H. (1974). *The psychology of nonviolence*. New York: Pergamon.

Pervin, L. A., & John, O. P. (2001). *Personality: Theory and Research*. New York: Wiley.

Pettigrew, T. F. (2003). People under threat: American, Arabs and Israelis. *Peace and Conflict: Journal of Peace Psychology*, *9*, 69–90.

Pettigrew, T. F., & Meertens, R. W. (1995). Subtle and blatant prejudice in Western Europe. *European Journal of Social Psychology*, *25*, 57–75.

Piaget, J. (1932). *The moral judgment of the child*. New York: Free Press.

Pilisuk, M. (1998). The hidden structure of counterparty violence. *Peace and Conflict: Journal of Peace Psychology*, *4*, 197–216.

Platt, J. (1973). Social traps. *American Psychologist*, *28*, 641–651.

Plous, S. (1993). The nuclear arms race: Prisoner's dilemma or perceptual dilemma? *Journal of Peace Research*, *30*, 163–179.

Pondy, L. R. (1967). Organizational conflict: Concepts and models. *Administrative Science Quaterly*, *12*, 296–320.

Poulin, F., & Boivin, M. (2002). Proactive and reactive aggression and boys' friendship quality in mainstream. *Journal of Emotional and Behavioral Disorders*, *7*(3), 168–180.

Prentice, D. T., & Miller, D. (2002). The emergence of homegrown stereotypes. *American Psychologist*, *57*, 352–359.

Presbey, G. M. (2006). Evaluating the legacy of nonviolence in South Africa. *Peace and Change*, *31*(2), 141–174.

Pruitt, D., & Olczak, P. (1995). Beyond hope: Approaches to resolving seemingly intractable conflict. In B. B. Bunker & J. Z. Rubin (Eds.), *Conflict cooperation and justice: Essays inspired by the work of Morton Deutsch*. New York: Sage.

Pruitt, D. G. (2000). Alternate dispute resolution. In A. E. Kazdin (Ed.), *Encyclopedia of Psychology*. New York: Oxford University Press.

Pruitt, D. G., & Carnevele, P. J. (1993). *Negotiation in social conflict*. Pacific Grove, CA: Brooks/Cole.

Pruitt, D. G., & Rubin, J. Z. (1986). *Social conflict*. New York: Random House.

Purdon, C. (1999). Thought suppression and psychopathology. *Behavior Research and Therapy*, *37*, 1029–1054.

Pyszczynski, T., Greenberg, J., & Solomon, J. (2002). *In the wake of 9/11: The psychology of terror*. Washington, DC: American Psychological Association.

Rafferty, A. (2002). Sentencing in Crown courts in England and Wales. *Criminal Behavior and Mental Health*, *12*, S54–S58.

Rahim, M. A. (1992). *Management conflict in organizations*. Westport, CT: Praeger.

Rappaport, L. (1990). Power, personality and the dialectics, of nonviolence. In V. K. Kool (Ed.), *Perspectives on nonviolence*. New York: Springer-Verlag.

Ratner, R. K., & Miller, D. (2001). The norm of social action and its effect on social action. *Journal of Personality and Social Psychology*, *81*, 5–16.

Ray, C., & Owens, I. (1988). South African Truth and Reconciliation—Commission. *Peace and Conflict: Journal of Peace Psychology*, *4* , 257–270.

Rest, J. (1979). *Development in judging moral issues.* Minneapolis, MN: University of Minnesota Press.

Reykowski, J. (2002). Psychological meaning of democracy and resolving the social coordination problems. *Polish Psychological Bulletin*, *4*, 19–30.

Richardson, D., Vandenberg, R. J., & Humphries, S. (1986). The effect of power to harm in retaliative aggression among males and females. *Journal of Research in Personality*, *20*, 402–419.

Richins, M. (1997). Measuring emotions in consumption experience. *Journal of Consumer Research*, *24*, 127–146.

Ritchins, M. (1999). Consumer emotion test. In B. Wo, R. G. Netemyer, & M. F. Mobley (Eds.), *Handbook of marketing scales: Multi item measures for marketing and consumer behavior research.* Newbury Park, CA: Sage.

Roach, K. (2000). Changing punishment at the turn of the century: Restorative justice on the rise. *Canadian Journal of Criminology*, *42*, 249–280.

Robarchek, C. A. (1979). Conflict, emotion and abreaction: Resolving of conflict among the Semai Senoi. *Ethos*, *7*, 104–123.

Roblyer, D. A. (2005). Beyond precision: Morality, decision making and collateral casualities. *Peace and Conflict: Journal of Peace Psychology*, *11*, 17–40.

Rogers, C. (1961). *On becoming a person* . Boston, MA: Houghton Mifflin.

Roper, R., & Shewan, D. (2002). Compliance and eyewitness testimony: Do eyewitness comply with misleading "expert pressure" during investigative interviewing? *Legal and Crminological Psychology*, *7*, 155–163.

Rothman, A. J., & Hardin, C. D. (1997). Differential use of the availability heuristic in social judgment. *Journal of Personality and Social Psychology Bulletin*, *23*, 123–138.

Rouhana, N. N., & Kelman, H. C. (1994). Promoting joint thinking in international conflicts: An Israeli-Palestinian continuing workshop. *Journal of Social Issues*, *50*, 157–178.

Rubin, J. Z., Pruitt, D. G., & Kim, S. H. (1994). *Social Conflict* (2nd ed). New York: McGraw-Hill.

Rushdie, S. (2002, May 30). The most dangerous place in the world. *The New York Times.* Retrieved from www: http://www.nytimes.com

Russell, G. W. (1993). *The social psychology of sport.* New York: Springer-Verlag.

Ryan, M. F. (1990). *Conflict management training: Effectiveness in the resolution of dyadic conflict.* Unpublished Master's Thesis, La Trobe University, Bundora, Victoria, Australia.

Sanderson, C. A., & Darley, J. M. (2002). I am moral but you are deterred: Differential attributions about why people obey the law. *Journal of Applied Social Psychology*, *32*, 375–405.

Saul, H. (1993, December). Dying swans? *Scientific American*, 25–27.

Schank, R., & Abelson, R. (1977). *Scripts, plans, goals, and understanding.* Hillsdale, NJ: Lawrence Erlbaum.

Schwebel, M. (1998). Introduction: Peace by peaceful means? *Peace and Conflict: Journal of Peace Psychology*, *4*, 89–91.

Schwebel, M. (1999). Looking forward/looking backward: Prevention of violent conflict. *Peace and Conflict: Journal of Peace Psychology*, *5*, 297–302.

Schwebel, M. (2001). Promoting the culture of peace in children. *Peace and Conflict: Journal of Peace Psychology*, *7*, 1–3.

Schwebel, M. (2005). Can wars be just? *Peace and Conflict: Journal of Peace Psychology*, *11*, 47–53.

Schweitzer, M. E., & Gomberg, L. E. (2001). The impact of alcohol on negotiation behavior: Experimental evidence. *Journal of Applied Social Psychology*, *31*, 2095–2126.

Scott, J. P., & Ginsburg, B. E. (1994). The Seville Statement revisited. *American Psychologist, 49*, 849–850.

Seijts, G. H., & Latham, G. P. (2000). The effects of goal setting and group size on performance in a social dilemma. *Canadian Journal of Behavioral Science, 32*, 104–116.

Seligman, M. (1998). *Learned optimism. How to change your mind and your life.* New York: Pocket Books.

Seligman, M. (2002). *Authentic happiness. Using the new positive psychology to realize your potential for lasting fulfillment.* New York: Free Press.

Seligman, M., & Csikszentmihalyi, M. (2000). Positive psychology: An introduction (special issue). *American Psychologist*, 55, 5–14.

Sen, M. (1981). *Reduction of aggression in violent and nonviolent individuals.* Unpublished doctoral dissertation, University of Bombay, Bombay, India.

Sen, M. (1993). An empirical study of nonviolence in India. In V. K. Kool (Ed.), *Nonviolence: Social and psychological issues.* New York: Springer-Verlag.

Seville Statement on violence, The (1994). *American Psychologist, 49*, 845–846.

Sharp, G. (1973). *The politics of nonviolent action.* Boston, MA: Porter Sargent.

Sharp, G. (1979). *Gandhi as a political strategist.* Boston, MA: Porter Sargent.

Sharp, G. (2005). *Waging nonviolent struggle: 20th century practice and 21st century potential.* Boston, MA: Porter Sargent.

Sheldon, K. M., & King, L. (2001). Why positive psychology is necessary? *American Psychologist, 56*, 216–217.

Shepela, S. T., Cook, T., Horlitz, E., Leal, R., et al. (1999). Courageous resistance: A special case of altruism. *Theory and Psychology, 14*, 455–473.

Sherif, M. (1966). *Group conflict and cooperation.* London: Routledge and Kegan Paul.

Sherif, M., Harvey, O. H., White, B. J., Hood, W. B., & Sherif, C. W. (1961). *Intergroup conflict and cooperation: The Robbers Cave experiment.* Norman: University of Oklahoma.

Shoda, Y., Mischel, W., & Peake, P. K. (1990). Predicting adolescent cognitive and self-regulating competencies from preschool delay of gratification: Identifying diagnostic conditions. *Developmental Psychology, 26*, 978–986.

Sinclair, L., & Kunda, Z. (1999). Reaction to a black professional: Motivated inhibition and activation of conflicting stereotypes. *Journal of Personality and Social Psychology, 77*, 885–904.

Skinner, B. F. (1948). *Walden two.* New York: Macmillan.

Skinner, B. F. (1953). *Beyond freedom and dignity.* New York: Alfred Knopf.

Skinner, B. F. (1987). Whatever happened to psychology as the science of behavior? *American Psychologist, 4*, 780–786.

Smith, B. M. (1986). Kurt Lewin memorial address: War, peace and psychology. *Journal of Social Issues, 42*, 23–38.

Soeters, J. L. (1996). Culture & conflict: An application of Hofstede's Theory to the conflict in former Yugoslavia. *Peace and Conflict: Journal of Peace Psychology, 2*, 233–244.

Stagner, R. (1942). Some factors related toward war. *Journal of Social Psychology, 16*, 131–142.

Stanovich, K. E., & West, R. F. (2000). Individual differences in reasoning: Implications for the rationality debate. *Behavioral and Brain Sciences, 23*, 645–665.

Staub, E. (1989). *The roots of evil: The origin of genocide and other group violence.* New York: Cambridge University Press.

Staub, E. (1990). Moral exclusion, personal goal theory and extreme destructiveness. *Journal of Social Issues, 46*(1), 47–64.

Staub, E. (1999). The origins and prevention of genocide, mass killing and other collective violence. *Peace and Conflict: Journal of Peace Psychology, 5*, 303–336.

Staub, E. (2003). *The psychology of good and evil: Why children, adults and groups harm others.* Cambridge, England: Cambridge University Press.

Staub, E. (2004). Understanding and responding to group violence: Genocide mass killing, and terrorism. In F. M. Moghaddam & A. J. Marshella (Eds.), *Understanding terrorism: Psychological roots, consequences and interventions.* Washington, DC: American Psychological Association.

Steger, M. B. (2003). *Judging nonviolence: The dispute between realists and idealists.* London: Routledge.

Stephens, D. E., & Bredemeir, B. J. (1996). Moral atmosphere and judgments about aggression in girls' soccer: Relationships among moral and motivational variables. *Journal of Sport and Exercise Psychology, 18,* 158–173.

Sternberg, R. J. (1986). A triangular theory of love. *Psychological Review, 93,* 119–135.

Sternberg, R. J. (2000). *Handbook of intelligence.* Cambridge: Cambridge University Press.

Storr, A. (1968). *Human aggression.* New York: Atheneum.

Stratton, L. (2002, September). New book explains theory behind terrorism. *APA Monitor,* 38. Also see www.apa.org/monitor/sept02

Stricker, G. (2000). The scientist practitioner model: Gandhi was right again. *American Psychologist, 55,* 254.

Suleiman, R. (2002). Minority self categorization: The case of Palestinians in Israel. *Peace and Conflict: Journal of Peace Psychology, 8,* 31–46.

Summers, C., & Morin, S. (1995). Politics and ethics in post-cold war demilitarization: Empirical evidence for decision trap and value tradeoffs. *Peace and Conflict: Journal of Peace Psychology, 1,* 343–364.

Suskind, L. E., Babbitt, E. F., & Segal, P. N. (1993). When ADR becomes the law: A review of federal practice. *Negotiation Journal, 9,* 59–75.

Tajfel, H. (1969). Cognitive aspects of Prejudice. *Journal of Social Issues, 25,* 79–97.

Tajfel, H., Billig, M. G., Bundy, R. F., & Flament, C. (1971). Social categorization and intergroup behaviour. *European Journal of Social Psychology, 68,* 199–214.

Taylor, S. P. (1967). Aggressive behavior and physiological arousal as function of provocation and the tendency to inhibit aggression. *Journal of Personality, 35,* 297–310.

Tewari, A. K. (2000). Anasakti and mental health. *Indian Psychological Review, 45*(3), 156–160.

Thompson, C. E., Murray, S. L., Harris, D., & Annan, J. R. (2003). Healing inside and out: Promoting social justice and peace in a racially divided US community. *International Journal for the Advancement of Counseling, 25,* 215–223.

Tiger Temple in Thailand. Webmaster@tigertemple.com

Time (2006, October 9). Letters to the Editor.

Tobin, R. J., & Eagles, M. (1992). US and Canadian attitudes toward International Interactions: A cross national test of the double standard hypothesis. *Basic and Applied Social Psychology, 13,* 447–459.

Toch, H. (1969). *Violent men.* Glenside, PA: Aldine Press.

Toch, H. (1975). *Living in Prison.* New York: Free Press.

Tolman, C. E. (1942). *Drives toward war.* New York: Appleton Century Croft.

True, M. (1995). *An energy field more intense than war: The nonviolent tradition and American literature.* Syracuse, NY: Syracuse University Press.

Tversky, A., & Kahneman, D. (1982). Evidential impact of base rates In D. Kahneman, P. Solvic, & A. Tversky (Eds.), *Judgment under uncertainty: Heuristic and biases.* New York: Cambridge University Press.

Tversky, A., & Kahneman, D. (1992). Advances in prospect theory: Cumulative representation for uncertainty. *Journal of Risk and Uncertainty, 5,* 297–323.

Twenge, J. M., & Baumeister, R. F. (2005). Social exclusion increases aggression and self-defeating behavior while reducing intelligent thought and prosocial behavior. In D. Abrams, M. Hogg, & J. M. Marques (Eds.), *The social psychology of inclusion and exclusion.* New York: Psychology Press.

Ulijn, J., Rutkowski, A. F., Kumar, R., & Zhu, Y. (2005). Patterns of feelings in face-to-face negotiation: A Sino-Dutch Pilot study. *Cross Cultural Management, 12*, 103–118.

Verbeek, P., & de Waal, F. B. M. (2001). Peace making among preschool children. *Peace and Conflict: Journal of Peace Psychology, 7*, 5–28.

Vohs, K. D., & Heatherton, T. F. (2000). Self-regulatory failure: A resource-depletion approach. *Psychological Science, 11*, 249–252.

Walzer, M. (1988). *The company of critics: Social criticism and political commitment in the twentieth century.* New York: Basic Books.

Weatherford, J. (2004). *Genghis Khan and the making of the modern world.* New York: Crown Publisher.

Wegner, D. M. (1994). Ironic processes of mental control. *Psychological Review, 101*, 34–52.

Wertheim, E. H., Love, A., Littlefield, L., & Peck, C. (1992). *I win, you win: How to have fewer conflicts, better solutions and more satisfying relationships.* Melbourne, Australia: Penguin.

Wessells, M. G. (1993). Psychological obstacles to peace. In V. K. Kool (Ed.), *Nonviolence: Social and psychological issues.* Lanham, MD: University Press of America.

Wessells, M. G. (1998a). Children, armed conflict, and peace. *Peace and Conflict: Journal of Peace Psychology, 35* , 635–646.

Wessells, M. G. (1998b). The changing nature of armed conflict and its implications for children: The Graca Machel/UN study. *Peace and Conflict: Journal of Peace Psychology, 4*, 321–334.

Wessells, M. G. (2001). Linking theory and practice in conflicts resolution: Foundation and challenges. *Peace and Conflict: Journal of Peace Psychology, 7*, 289–292.

Wessells, M. G., & Monteiro, C. (2001). Psychosocial interventions and post-war reconstruction in Angola: Interweaving western and traditional approaches. In D. J. Christie, R. V. Wagner, & D. D. Winter (Eds.), *Peace, conflict and violence: Peace psychology for the 21st century*, 262–275. Upper Saddle River, NJ: Prentice Hall.

White, R. K. (1977). Misperception in the Arab-Israeli conflict. *Journal of Social Issues, 33*, 190–221.

White, R. K. (1984). *Fearful warriors: A psychological profile of US-Soviet relations.* New York: Free Press.

Wildchut, T., Pinter, B., Vevea, J. L., Insko, C. A., & Schopter, J. (2003). Beyond the group mind: A quantitative review of group discontinuity effect. *Psychological Bulletin, 129*, 698–722.

Wilson, E. O. (1975). *Sociobiology: A new synthesis.* Cambridge, MA: Belknap.

Wilson, R. J., Huculek, B., & McWhinnie, A. (2002). Restorative justice innovations in Canada. *Behavioral Science and the Law, 20*, 363–380.

Wilson, T. D., & Schooler, J. (1991). Thinking too much: Introspection can reduce the quality of preferences and decisions. *Journal of Personality and Social Psychology, 60*, 181–192.

Witvliet, C., Ludwig, T., & Vander Laan, K. (2001). Granting forgiveness or harboring grudges: Implication for emotions, physiology and health. *Psychological Science, 121*, 117–123.

Worchel, S. (2005). Culture's role in conflict and conflict management: Some suggestions, many questions. *International Journal of Intercultural Relations, 29*, 739–757.

Young, N. (1996). Review of peace reference works. *Peace and Conflict: Journal of Peace Psychology, 2*, 291–293.

Zartman, I. W. (Ed.). (2000). *Traditional cures for modern conflict: African conflict "Medicine".* Boulder, CO: Lynne Rienner.

Zartman, I. W., & Aurik, J. (1991). Power strategies in de-escalation. In L. Kriesberg & S. J. Thorson (Eds.), *Timing the de-escalation of international conflicts.* Syracuse, NY: Syracuse University Press.

Zillman, D. (1988). Cognitive-excitation interdependencies in aggressive behavior. *Aggressive Behavior, 14*, 51–64.

Zillman, D. (1993). Mental control of angry aggression. In D. M. Wegner & J. W. Pennebaker (Eds.), *Handbook of Mental Control.* Englewood Cliffs, NJ: Prentice Hall.

Zillman, D. (1994). The escalation of anger and angry aggression. In M. Potegal & J. F. Knutson (Eds.), *The dynamics of aggression: Biological and social processes.* Hillsdale, NJ: Lawrence Erlbaum.

Zimbardo, P. (1975). www.prisonexp.org

Zimbardo, P. (2001, December 22). *The psychology of terrorism.* San Francisco Chronicle. http://www.sfchron.com

Zimbardo, P. (2002, August). Why and how normal people go mad. Presidential lecture, American Psychological Association convention, Chicago (Report by J. Daw in American Psychological Association monitor, 2002 November, pp. 20–21).

Zimbardo, P. G. (1970). The human choice: Individuation, reason, and order versus deindividuation, impulse and chaos. In W. J. Arnold & D. Levine (Eds.), 1969 *Nebraska Symposium on Motivation.* Lincoln: University of Nebraska Press.

Zimbardo, P. G. (2004). A situation perspective on the psychology of evil: Understanding how good people are transformed into perpetrators. In A. Miller (Ed.), *The social psychology of good and evil: Understanding our capacity for kindness and cruelty.* New York: Guilford.

Author Index

Subject Index